Cowboy Life on the Llano Estacado

Cowboy Life on

he Llano Estacado

by V. H. Whitlock (Ol' Waddy)

University of Oklahoma Press
Norman

The paper on which this book is printed bears the watermark of the University of Oklahoma Press and has an effective life of at least three hundred years.

F
596
W564

International Standard Book Number: 0-8061-0874-6

Library of Congress Catalog Card Number: 69-16724

Copyright 1970 by the University of Oklahoma Press, Publishing Division of the University. Composed and printed at Norman, Oklahoma, U.S.A., by the University of Oklahoma Press. First edition.

THIS BOOK is dedicated to my little pioneer mother, who braved a lonely life and the hardships of early days on the bleak Llano Estacado, and calmly sleeps today in a little cemetery in a land that was changed from a wilderness to an empire overnight—the Cherokee Strip of the Indian Territory.

Also to my uncles—George, Bob, John, and Mark Causey—who helped tame and settle the Staked Plains. They are buried in Roswell, New Mexico; Safford, Arizona; Inglewood, California; and Alva, Oklahoma, respectively.

Included in this dedication are the rugged riders of the open range who helped guide the footsteps of a fatherless and wayward boy safely around pitfalls in his boyhood days on the range. Almost all those old buckaroos are quietly waiting to attend the Last Great Roundup when it is thrown together.

Preface

MUCH of the information in Part I of this book has been compiled from letters written to my mother by her brother, George Causey, during the late 1870's and early 1880's, when he was on the buffalo range.

Some of these tales were told to me by Uncle George and his hunting partner, George (Old Jeff) Jefferson, during my childhood—and as I grew older—at the Causey ranch on the Llano Estacado. I was fed stories of buffalo hunting, Indian fighting, mustanging, and life on the frontier in the wild-and-woolly towns, along with sourdough biscuits, fresh beef, son-of-a-gun stew, frijole beans, and black coffee.

Later, while staying in a lonely camp with Old Jeff at the 7HR Ranch, and while helping care for my uncle from the time he was injured by a falling horse until his death, I heard these stories rehashed time and again. With forethought, I jotted many of them down.

Many of the incidents recounted in this book have been included, in different form, in articles published in *The Western*

Horseman, True West, and other magazines, and in newspapers such as *The Enterprise* and *The Journal* of Beaumont, Texas, and the *Daily News-Sun* of Hobbs, New Mexico. J. Frank Dobie in his book *The Mustang* and J. Evetts Haley in his book *George W. Littlefield: Texan* have quoted from my unfinished manuscript.

Three persons mentioned in this book—Little Red, Sutty (not to be confused with "Suttie" Formwalt), and Britches—are true characters who have been given fictitious names for obvious reasons. Nicknames such as Bill, Bud, Bob, Jim, Shorty, Slim and Fatty replaced given names of many men in those days, and some cattlemen were even known by their brands. The Negro LFD cowpuncher I mention frequently was known only as Old Negro Ad. All place names are true. Ol' Waddy (meaning old cowhand) is the pen name I used for many years.

I am indebted to Raymond F. Waters of Hobbs, New Mexico, for editing the manuscript and furnishing some of the photographs.

V. H. WHITLOCK (OL' WADDY)

San Fernando, California

Introduction:
Llano Estacado — The Staked Plains

"WE traveled mile after mile after mile toward the distant horizon, but never reached it." Casual visitors and long-time residents alike thus describe the wide treeless plateau of western Texas and eastern New Mexico known as the Llano Estacado, or Staked Plains. A person can stand at one spot in this region, and with a sweeping glance see a very large portion of the earth's crust. It is somewhat like looking out over an ocean, the sense of vastness and emptiness is so intense. It is said that the Llano Estacado is the most level stretch of land of its size in the world.

Opinions differ about the meaning of the word "staked" in this context, and about how the area got its name. The most common and probably the most likely explanation is that it was named for the stakelike boles of yucca plants that grow there. The yucca, a member of the lily family, has a cluster of narrow needle-pointed leaves about fifteen inches long. In the spring of the year, long slender stems grow up from the center of the cluster and bloom at the top. After the bloom drops off, the stem dies, and a "stake" stands upright several feet high. The stake finally rots at the base and is blown over by the wind, but another sprouts up the next year.

Some people claim the plains used to be bounded on both sides by steep escarpments, or palisades, and that Llano Estacado can be translated "palisaded plains." Others say that early explorers staked their trails with heaps of buffalo skulls and bones so that they could backtrack their way out if they became lost. Still others believe that early visitors found the plateau "staked" by the stumps of a forest that had been destroyed by fire. Buffalo hunters and some of the first settlers used only the first word, Llano—pronounced in Spanish "lyah-noh" or "yah-noh," and sometimes corrupted to "yar-nah."

When the buffalo hunters arrived in the 1870's, the feeling of emptiness and loneliness about the region was heightened by the knowledge that there were few humans, other than lurking Indians, closer than one hundred miles. There was nothing to break the great expanse of rolling prairie from horizon to horizon except grass waving in the wind, yucca plants, catclaw bushes, and other small vegetation. Great herds of buffaloes drifted over the landscape, gathered around salt licks, and rolled in the buffalo wallows to rid themselves of vermin and their winter coat of hair.

The Llano held unexpected and often fatal dangers, particularly for those who traveled alone. Animal and rodent holes pocked the terrain, and small animals and snakes scurried and crawled over the ground. If a horse stepped into one of those holes, it would very likely throw its rider, killing him instantly or injuring him so severely that he might lie there alone, dying a slow, painful death, for days.

To the untrained and inexperienced, there was always the danger of becoming lost, for there were no landmarks. On cloudless days, experienced plainsmen could determine directions from the position of the sun, or from shadows. When the skies were overcast, the traveler who lacked the guiding instinct of an Indian or a homing pigeon might determine his course from the way grass and other vegetation leaned—away from the southwest, the direction the wind usually blew.

Experienced men had no trouble traveling at night if the sky was clear. They knew that two stars in the Big Dipper always pointed to the North Star. But when the stars were hidden by clouds, a journey at night without a compass was dangerous. One way to continue on the right course would be to remember from which direction the wind was blowing when darkness settled over the plains. But sometimes the wind shifted, and the rider who changed with it would find himself traveling in circles.

In the early morning hours, mirages were common. In the dry and clear atmosphere, the phenomena sometimes resembled lakes of cool water, and inexperienced and thirsty travelers were often fooled by these. A tenderfoot could wander for days on the Llano, and, unless he knew how to live off the land, might die of starvation.

The weather could also be a formidable enemy. A man caught far from shelter could die in a short time if a blizzard should come sweeping down out of the north. In the early spring, sandstorms that lasted for several days came howling out of the southwest.

American explorers who visited the high plateau many years before white buffalo hunters came reported back to civilization that the area was desolate, with few water holes and no wood for fuel. They recommended that that part of the United States be left to the Plains Indians and their bison.

The first white man to visit the Llano Estacado is said to have been the Spanish explorer Francisco Vásquez de Coronado. In 1541, he brought from Mexico an army of 250 cavalrymen, 200 foot soldiers, and several hundred Indians, who acted as guides, grooms, and servants. He had a pack train of 1,000 horses and mules to transport camp supplies, and herds of cattle, sheep, goats, and pigs for food. He crossed the High Plains at two places in a wandering search for the fabled Seven Cities of Cíbola. Instead of finding cities whose streets were paved with gold and whose inhabitants wore precious gems, he found hostile savages and vast herds of hump-back cattle grazing on oceans of waving prairie grass. Had he abandoned his quest for gold and gems and colonized the area, with its abundant natural resources, his expedition might have been a success instead of a dismal failure. Unaware that buffalo meat was good food for his soldiers and buffalograss good fodder for his stock, Coronado feared starvation in a land of plenty. He returned to his headquarters at Tiguex on the Río Grande in New Mexico, leaving the plains to the Indians for another 300 years.

The Apaches and Comanches who confronted the Spaniards when they invaded the high plateau were some of the fiercest and most warlike tribes in North America, perhaps in the entire world. Since food, clothing, and shelter were all supplied them by the buffalo, they had acquired much skill and cunning in stalking and killing the animal with bow and arrow. They were roving buffalo hunters who had no permanent settlements and whose existence depended upon their ability to follow the great herds wherever they wandered.

Before the Spaniards came, there had been no horses in the area. The Indians traveled by "travois," a primitive vehicle made by tying two poles together with a net to hold a load near the rear end. The people walked between the poles and pulled the load.

Descendants of horses which were abandoned or which escaped from the herd that Coronado brought with his men to the plains in 1541 multiplied rapidly on the Llano Estacado and were captured by the Indians. From the Spanish missionaries and early settlers south and west of the Staked Plains, the Indians learned the art of horsemanship. Horses gave them a tremendous advantage, not only in buffalo hunting, but also in wars against invaders.

Later explorers and settlers who came in from the East in greater numbers found that the Indians of the Llano Estacado, like all of the Plains Indians, were skilled riders. When the warriors were not hunting buffaloes, they raided and stole horses from one another and anyone else unfortunate enough to fall prey to their savage attacks. Despite their ferocity and determination to defend their land from encroaching civilization, however, the Indians' days were numbered on the Llano Estacado, as elsewhere. Although pleas were made to the Texas government to stop the wanton slaughter of the buffaloes, the carnage was allowed to continue until the hump-back shaggies were almost exterminated.

In 1868, U.S. soldiers under General Philip H. Sheridan put many Comanche, Kiowa, and Apache Indians on a reservation at Fort Sill in Oklahoma. But bands of those Indians would occasionally leave the reservation and make "vacation" hunting trips to their old home range on the Llano, and while there, make depredations upon and deal misery to any white settlers they found. White buffalo hunters, who killed the shaggy creatures only for whatever profit they might obtain by selling hides, meat, and tongues, were natural enemies of the Indians and were sometimes targets of their raids.

In 1874, the last of the Comanche and Kiowa Indians on the plains of Texas and New Mexico were rounded up by the U.S. Army under the command of General Ranald S. Mackenzie in a surprise attack upon a large encampment on the Palo Duro and Tule canyons in the Texas Panhandle. They were herded back to a life of confinement on a reservation in the Indian Territory, a life they despised.

With the Indian menace removed, the Llano Estacado became more accessible to white settlers. First ranchers, then nesters, moved in to find out what life in this wide, desolate country had to offer.

Contents

Illustrations

The John Causey ranch house
The George Causey ranch house
Ol' Waddy and his bride
Mr. and Mrs. J. D. Earnest
The High Lonesome ranch house

PART ONE
George Causey — A Brief History

1.

Following the Buffalo Herds

DURING the late 1860's, a young man named T. L. (George) Causey drove mule teams for the government, hauling supplies to the army outposts in western Kansas and to the "last chance" trading stations that furnished provisions to the wagon trains headed for the Pacific Coast.

As the railroads were built westward, establishing end-of-the-line towns at Abilene, Ellsworth, Hays City, and other points, Causey saw an end to his means of livelihood approaching. With a frontiersman and former army scout named George (Old Jeff) Jefferson, he organized a buffalo-hunting outfit, and they hunted along the Smoky Hill River, using Hays City for a trading point.

When the Santa Fe Railroad established a "rail-end" town near Fort Dodge, Kansas, and named it Dodge City, hide buyers and traders opened shop there. The hunters moved to that vicinity then, finding buffaloes plentiful and the new town a profitable trading post.

Only a few years had passed since the end of the Civil War, and the beef bonanza was in full swing. Wild herds of longhorn steers driven by wilder trail drivers came up from Texas to the shipping pens at Dodge City. Men from below the Mason-Dixon line and former Union soldiers often fought the Civil War over in the saloons and streets of that notorious old town.

Bad men from far and near fought gun battles with famous lawmen. The losers were buried with their boots on in shallow graves on what was known as "Boot Hill."

When buffaloes became too scarce on the north side of the Arkansas River for hunting to be profitable, Causey and others crossed to the south side to a region reserved by treaty as a hunting ground for the Indians. The white men knew they were on dangerous ground and hunted at their own risk.

The Indians on that part of the Great Plains—roving tribes who depended upon buffalo for meat, clothing, and tipis—resented the white hunters who invaded their reserve and killed off their only means of subsistence. They were aware that if their game was exterminated, they would be at the mercy of the white man, whose reservations they knew of and dreaded.

An article in a *New York Sun*, dated May 8, 1875, which Causey kept for many years in his old rawhide trunk, cited the rapid rate at which the hump-backed shaggies were being destroyed: "In 1874, 2,160,000 pounds of buffalo meat was shipped over the Kansas Pacific Railway and its connections. In the same year the following was shipped over the Topeka and Santa Fe Railroad: Hides 1,314,000; meat 631,000 pounds; and bones 6,934,000 pounds."

Causey moved across the Cimarron River into the No Man's Land of the Indian Territory, then on south into the Panhandle of Texas, still using Dodge City as a trading point. At Buffalo Springs he heard that a trading post had been opened in the Adobe Walls ruins on the Canadian River where he could dispose of his hides and buy supplies without making the trek to Dodge City.

Constantly on the alert for Indian attacks, the hunters moved farther south into the forbidden area. They heard that a camp near them had been raided, the white hunters killed and scalped, and their wagon burned. They knew that the Adobe Walls trading post itself was in danger, for it had guns, ammunition, and provisions.

Five men operated the post, but they were seldom alone, because hunting outfits or freighters bringing supplies from Dodge City and hauling back loads of hides were usually camped there. Causey and his hunters, who were working a few miles from the post, for several days had heard distant gunfire but thought nothing of it because other hunting outfits were in the vicinity.

A few days later, however, when they moved their wagons in to the trading post, they found that a large band of Indians had been making repeated assaults for several days. Among the hunters already camped there were Billy Dixon and Bat Masterson.

The post was in horrible condition, with dead horses, mules, and oxen lying around and inside the stockade. The store section of the adobe building was a mess. Bullets from Indian guns had torn through wooden portions of the walls, hitting and bursting cans of food, the contents of which ran out over the shelves and floor. The weather was hot, and flies were bad.

The Indians evidently had expected little resistance when they made their first attack at daybreak several days before. Had they found everyone asleep, they could have massacred the white men. But some of the hunters had been awake and had had time to close the gates to the stockade and spread the alarm. The Indians had then faced large-caliber rifles in the hands of men who knew how to use them. It was learned afterward that a medicine man had told his braves his medicine was strong enough to prevent the hunters' guns from firing.

The men at the post drew straws to see who would go for help, and the youngest man got the short straw. Taking nothing with him but two derringer pistols, a bowie knife, and a small sack of jerked buffalo meat, he slipped outside the stockade at night, ran along the bed of the Canadian River, and sneaked through the Indian encampment. Those left behind had no way of knowing whether he got through the Indian lines until they saw the cavalry coming to the rescue, with flag waving and bugle blowing.

The battle put a stop to buffalo hunting for a time on that

part of the plains. The Adobe Walls post was abandoned, and traders, hide buyers, and hunters went back to Dodge City.

Again Causey moved north of the Arkansas River and hunted for several months, but the shaggy animals were getting so scarce he began looking for something else to do. Discovery of gold in the Black Hills of South Dakota by a military expedition headed by General Custer touched off a gold rush to that region. Many people in Dodge City headed for the Black Hills, a part of the country continually disturbed by wars with the Sioux Indians. A few years before the discovery of gold, a war with Red Cloud had been settled by the Laramie Treaty, which reserved for the Sioux all the land between the Missouri River and the Big Horn Mountains.

Causey thought of trying his luck prospecting for gold, and made preparations for the trip. Before his outfit had left Dodge City, however, reports came in that Sioux chiefs Red Cloud, Sitting Bull, and Spotted Tail were on the warpath against the flood of prospectors and other whites invading the territory in violation of the treaty, and the hunters decided not to go.

Trail drivers from the south told Causey of a rumor that buffaloes were plentiful on the Llano Estacado and under the breaks to the east of the plains. Furthermore, General Sherman's investigation of Indian raids on settlers of northwest Texas had resulted in the arrest and trial of chiefs Santank, Satanta and Big Tree before civil authorities at Jacksboro, Texas, in an effort to stop roving bands of marauding Indians from obstructing the westward advance of civilization to the High Plains.

Texas trail drivers coming up the Dodge City Trail added that General Mackenzie had rounded up the main body of Comanche and Kiowa Indians in the Texas Panhandle, and returned them to their reservation in the Indian Territory.

Causey was pleased with this news and joined other hide hunters in a trip to West Texas. They crossed the Cimarron and North Canadian rivers and went by way of Camp Supply around the east side of the hunting grounds of the hostile Indians. Causey and Jefferson took on a partner named Karr when they left Dodge

City. Their outfit was said to be the best equipped and most efficient on the buffalo range.

They hunted along the Canadian and Washita rivers, using Camp Supply as a trading point. After a while they moved on south to Sweetwater Creek under the protection of the U.S. Army at old Fort Elliot. Causey became quite friendly with a man named Springer, who operated a small trading post on the old military road between Fort Elliot and Camp Supply, and did considerable trading with the old man. A mushroom town sprang up near Fort Elliot. First known as Sweetwater, it was later renamed Old Mobeetie.

The hunters did well in the Sweetwater area, but the buffalo herds were constantly on the move. Men followed animals south across the North, South, and Prairie Dog Town forks of Red River to the Pease River. Traders and hide buyers moved south with the hunters and opened up shop at old Fort Griffin, Texas, on the Clear Fork of the Brazos River.

Fort Griffin became the trading point for a large area—not only for buffalo hunters, but also for trail drivers taking herds of longhorn cattle from South Texas up the Western, or Dodge City, Trail by way of Griffin, Doan's Crossing on Red River, and Camp Supply, then on to the shipping pens at Dodge City. Fort Griffin soon rivaled Dodge City as a rip-roaring town.

The Causey outfit gradually moved on south to the Salt Fork and Double Mountain Fork of the Brazos River, where they found plenty of the hump-back shaggies on which to train their Sharps rifles. At one time while camped there, Causey had about four thousand hides stretched, dried, and stacked, ready to haul to market. He sold many hides at Fort Griffin, but he occasionally put his bull teams into service and hauled large loads to the railroad at Fort Worth, Texas, where he received a better price.

In early 1877, the Causey outfit mounted the cap rock and went west across the Llano Estacado to establish a permanent camp at a spring on Yellow House Draw, a tributary of the Double Mountain Fork of the Brazos River.

The location received its name—Casas Amarillas (Yellow

7

Houses)—from a flattop yellow bluff about a hundred feet high with caves in its side. When seen from a distance, it resembled flat houses with windows.

The bluff was a landmark for west-bound travelers across that part of the Llano Estacado in the early days. But it couldn't be seen by travelers headed east until they rode up on its brink, where a vast panorama of wide-open spaces unfolded suddenly before their eyes.

The spring of good water at the yellow bluff made it a welcome stopping place for thirsty visitors, from the early explorers to roving bands of Indians, Mexican mustangers from the Pecos River country in New Mexico, and others.

The caves in the side of the bluff were good places to hole up for protection from fierce northers and blizzards. One cave had a hole that went clear through the top of the bluff and served as a chimney. The chimney was said to have been used by Indians for making smoke signals.

When George Causey settled there, he dammed up the spring to conserve the water supply and built a sod house, which may have been the first permanent living quarters on that part of the Llano Estacado. It became widely known as "Causey's Sod House Camp on the Yellow Houses."

2.

Sod House Camp on the Yellow Houses

THE Causey hunting outfit found all the buffaloes they could kill around the Yellow Houses. During the winter of 1878–79, they shot about 7,800 of the shaggy animals and delivered their hides to the buyers at Fort Griffin. They hunted there until the buffaloes were almost exterminated.

George Causey did most of the killing with a .45–90-caliber buffalo gun that was so heavy he had to use a rest stick to hold it up. Old Jeff Jefferson carried Causey's cartridges, and the skinners followed, removing the hides and leaving the carcasses for the wolves.

The hunters saved their rifle shells, molded bullets from bar lead, and, adding powder and primers, reloaded the cartridges. The hides were hauled to camp, stretched out on the ground with the flesh side up, pegged down, and allowed to dry.

Once during a slack period, George Causey and Old Jeff went on a scouting trip across the sands south of the Yellow Houses to see what the water conditions were and whether there were any buffaloes in that part of the plains.

9

They rode good horses, and each led a pack mule carrying blankets, water, and provisions. Knowing they were going into dangerous regions, the hunters were heavily armed, and both men carried powerful field glasses with which they could distinguish objects at great distances across the level prairie.

Jeff, once an Indian captive, was as well versed in tracking and training as any Indian, and as they traveled south, he watched closely for signs of an east-west Indian trail. Army officers and Texas Rangers had told the hunters that they thought such a trail existed between the widely separated water holes believed to be in that area. Old Jeff remembered that during his captivity he had heard mention of a route across the South Plains, referred to in Spanish as *La Pista de Vida Agua* (The Trail of Living Water).

During the second day of their journey, after traveling about fifty miles south from their camp, the hunters found an east-west trail covered with horse tracks. They followed it about twenty miles west and found a small spring at the head of Sulphur Draw, across the state line in New Mexico, about five miles northwest of the present town of Bronco, Texas. Ashes of campfires, bones recently picked clean of meat, and fresh horse tracks led them to believe Indians had recently camped there. Later, the hunters learned that the nearest water to that spring along the trail toward the east was at Rich Lake, a distance of about sixty-five miles.

They followed the trail on west about ten miles and came to an alkali lake, with a spring of good water on its west side. Signs around it showed that it also was a campground. While the hunters were there, two Indians driving horses appeared on the hill to the east. They stopped and looked the situation over; then one of them rode down near the hunters' camp and in sign language, which Jeff understood, told the white men that they were friendly and only wanted water for themselves and their horses.

"All right," Jeff answered in sign language, "but don't start any trouble."

On west along the trail about twelve miles, they came upon four more alkali lakes, one of which was fed by a spring of good water, with Indian signs around it. Those lakes were later named Four Lakes and became the headquarters ranch of the Littlefield (LFD) Cattle Company.

Following the trail on west about fifteen miles, they suddenly, without warning, rode up to the edge of the Cap Rock escarpment of the west breaks of the plains and saw, across the Mescalero sand hills and the Pecos River Valley, the Capitán Mountains more than one hundred miles away.

They followed the winding trail down the steep bluff to a small stream of pure water flowing from the side of the 500-foot-high cliff. The stream wandered along a gully through scrub mesquite bushes, and finally spread out and disappeared into the flat toward some sand hills. Rocks around the spring displayed Indian sign writings. This location was widely known in later years as Mescalero Spring and was the LFD Horse Camp.

The hunters saw large herds of antelopes, bunches of mustang horses, and many buffaloes around the lakes, but decided the place was too far from a trading post. Having found the unmarked Indian cross-country trail and the water holes along its route, and having checked the hunting conditions, they returned to the Yellow Houses feeling that their scouting expedition had been a success.

Recollecting incidents involving Indians while he was at the Sod House Camp, Causey in later years said: "The Indians, who knew the country and where all the water holes were, could easily escape from anyone who pursued them across the bald prairies where there were no landmarks to guide the pursuers.

"A good example was the time a detachment of U.S. Cavalry followed a band of marauding redskins into that waterless desert west of Tahoka Lake southeast of my camp after raiding the settlers on the east side of the plains. The cavalrymen soon became lost and chased imaginary lakes of cool water. Some of them killed their horses and drank the blood to quench their thirst. A few straggled into our camp to tell the tale.

"A couple of years later, a company of Texas Rangers, led by a captain named Arrington, followed a bunch of Indian horse thieves over the same route that was followed by the U.S. Cavalry. Arrington, remembering the fate of the cavalrymen and knowing nothing about the water holes west of Tahoka Lake, was afraid to follow the Indians on west. He turned north and came to our camp.

"When Arrington told me why he was out on the plains and said he would like to find the trail that was traveled by the Indians from the west, I told him about the trail we had found on our trip into that part of the country. He was so interested in my story that he decided to leave his wagon at our camp and make a scouting trip into that section of the Llano Estacado.

"Us buffalo hunters helped the Rangers make some pack-saddles out of buffalo hides so that they could carry kegs of water on several pack mules we loaned them for the trip. I also gave them jerked buffalo meat and sketched a map of the trail and the watering places we found.

"After a big blizzard about two weeks later, one of the Rangers, leading a pack mule, came to our camp to get more grub. He told us the other Rangers were holed up in a cave in Yellow House bluff with nothing to eat and were almost frozen.

"We fed the Ranger and put him to bed, because we didn't think he would be able to make the return trip. Jeff and I hitched a team to a wagon and drove through the snow to the cave a few miles southwest of our place and brought the snowbound Rangers back to our camp. They stayed with us until the weather cleared and they were able to return to their home station.

"While at our camp, Arrington told me his party hid out in the sand hills around the single alkali lake I told them about, which they had named Ranger Lake, watching for Indians until they were almost out of grub. They had started on the fifty-mile return trip to our camp and were about halfway back when the storm caught them. It was lucky that they reached the cave."

When Causey realized that buffaloes were becoming too scarce on the plains to be hunted only for their hides, he started saving some of the meat—the hump, tenderloin, tongue, and best parts of the young animals. The hunters removed the meat from the bone, salted it, and hung it on lines of rope, wire, or rawhide to dry. After being "jerked," as that process was called, the meat could be handled like cordwood and would keep indefinitely.

When they had a sufficient quantity, they loaded it into wagons, hauled it to Las Vegas, New Mexico, and sold it to railroad construction gangs building the Santa Fe Railroad into that state. Later, when the Texas-Pacific Railroad was built through Texas, there was a good market for buffalo bones at the towns along that line. The bones were sold at the railroad and shipped out to be used for fertilizer. The hunters put their bull teams into service hauling bones from old killing grounds on the Llano Estacado to market at Colorado City, Texas. On the return trip, the haulers delivered supplies to settlers along the route.

One man always stayed in camp to look after things while the others were away on trips with hides to Fort Griffin, meat to Las Vegas, or bones to Colorado City. Old Jeff was the one who usually remained behind. While in camp alone, Jeff had Indian callers on two occasions. Once, they kept him hiding out in the gullies around camp for two days, until they finally became tired of playing hide-and-seek with him and left. The other time, they came at night and stole all his horses except one he had staked near camp.

Jeff tracked the horse thieves for two days, until, late in the afternoon of the second day, he came in sight of them. He watched them camp for the night, then, cunning and stealthy as the savages he was following, he staked his horse and crawled on his belly to the edge of the little gully where they were gathered around a small fire.

When he returned to camp, he had not only his own horses, but two others that had belonged to the Indians.

"During the six years I lived at the Sod House Camp, we had all kinds of visitors," George Causey recalled, "but there were long spells when we never saw anyone. Charles Goodnight had chased the buffaloes out of Palo Duro Canyon north of us and moved his herd of cattle, branded JA connected, in there to start the first big cattle ranch on the Staked Plains.

"About a year later, other ranchers moved in herds north of the Goodnight outfit. They were Bates and Beals, with their LX brand; R. L. McNulty, who started a ranch near Adobe Walls, where he ran his Turkey Track cattle; and George W. Littlefield and his nephew, Phelps White, with their LIT cattle.

"I had become acquainted with Littlefield and White several years before when they were trailing herds from South Texas to Dodge City. Two towns had also sprung up in the Texas Panhandle—Old Mobeetie and Tascosa.

"Sometimes, cowhands from those northern cow outfits came as far south as the Yellow Houses looking for cattle that had drifted south during the winter blizzards.

"Other visitors were Texas Rangers, buffalo hunters, mustangers from the Pecos River country, and U.S. cavalrymen. Some visitors we knew were on the dodge from the law, and others we believed to be of doubtful character. If we traded horses with a man who warned us not to take the animal in a certain direction, for instance, we could pretty well guess that the horse was stolen. But we treated them all alike. Our camp was so far from civilization outlaws had little fear of being bothered by law-enforcement officers."

Old Jeff's older brother, John Jefferson, who had features, complexion, and characteristics of an Indian, was known as "Squaw Johnnie." An occasional visitor at the Sod House Camp, Johnnie was as wily and cunning as any of the Comanches he and Jeff had lived with so long. He also had a reputation of being a little wild.

"Late one evening," Causey recalled, "Squaw Johnnie and two pals came to our camp driving about fifteen horses. They spent the night with us, and the next morning headed on west toward the Pecos River.

"About noon, several U.S. cavalrymen showed up, hot on their trail. They ate dinner with us and headed on west. Two days later, the cavalrymen came walking into our camp and told us someone had sneaked into camp in the darkness, surprised and overcome the sentry, and taken their mounts."

Other visitors included several groups of eastern people who came out from Fort Griffin to see frontier life in the raw. The hunters took them out and let them shoot buffaloes and try skinning them. They showed them how to remove the tongues, humps, and meat that was fit to eat from the carcass.

In camp the visitors spent the evening around a smoking buffalo-chip fire watching the hunters cook them a feed of buffalo meat, frijole beans, and sourdough biscuits. They swapped yarns far into the night, the guests telling the hunters what was happening back east and the hunters spinning them some windies about life on the frontier. Some of the visitors turned out to be writers who later published stories of the visit in eastern newspapers.

Causey had trouble with Mexicans who came over from New Mexico and killed buffaloes with spears or lances. When the white hunters had a "stand" on a herd of buffaloes, they could kill the entire herd without moving if nothing frightened the animals. Occasionally, however, the lancers would appear, charge and stampede the herd, and run alongside the fleeing animals on fast horses spearing them until they fell. The angry white hunters would then start shooting at the Mexicans' horses instead of the shaggies.

Causey settled the argument by making an agreement with the lancers: They could follow him along and take all the flesh they wanted from the animals he killed. This gave them plenty of meat to convert into jerky, pack on their burros, and take home.

George Causey always had a warm spot in his heart for an old friend and hunting partner named Jim White, who once saved his life and his good name. On a return trip to the plains from Fort Griffin, Causey camped one night on the Clear Fork of the Brazos River. When some strangers rode up and asked if they could spend the night with him, he told them they were welcome.

Just after supper, he was surprised by the sudden appearance of the local vigilante committee, who rode into camp, "threw down" on the campers, and took all their guns. The visitors were horse thieves, and the vigilantes, who were planning a "necktie party," thought Causey was one of them. Luckily, White, who knew some of the vigilantes, came along before the party got under way, recognized Causey, convinced the lynchers that he wasn't a horse thief, and saved him from swinging from the limb of a post oak tree by the Brazos River.

Causey killed his last herd of buffaloes—the last of those animals on the Llano Estacado except for the ones in captivity—in 1882 at Cedar Lake, near the present town of Seminole, the county seat of Gaines County, Texas.

He killed them in the winter when the weather was cold enough to preserve the meat. He removed the heads, feet and intestines, and, leaving the hides on the carcasses, hauled them to Midland, Texas, to the Texas-Pacific Railroad, and sold the hides and meat together. He had hunted buffaloes for about thirteen years. Because hunters were criticized severely while the slaughter was going on, he would never divulge how many he had killed. Men who hunted with him, however, estimated the number at more than 40,000.

"Causey killed more buffaloes in one winter on the Yellow Houses," Old Jeff used to say, "than Buffalo Bill Cody killed in his entire lifetime. But Causey didn't have Ned Buntline for a publicity agent."

3.

The Buffalo Hunter Turns Rancher

AFTER the buffaloes were exterminated, Causey and Old Jeff turned to ranching. They decided to walk down mustangs and start their own herd of horses. Working together—each man riding one horse and leading another carrying bedroll, grub, and drinking water—they rode out to hunt up a bunch of the wild horses.

The herd ran away on first sighting the horsemen, but the men doggedly followed, riding along at a slow gait that never changed. When they came in sight of the herd again, the horses ran, but not as far as before. Each time the men caught up, the horses ran a shorter distance than the time before.

When night came, the men camped, and at daybreak they stalked the same herd, never changing their appearance or the manner in which they traveled. The horses soon became so accustomed to the riders that instead of running when the men caught up with them, they would merely trot on out of sight.

By the third day, the men could ride up very close to the horses before they moved on; and by the fifth day, the riders were

17

keeping up with the drags in the herd. A day or so later, they were driving the horses at will, and by the tenth day, they were able to corral the entire bunch, except for a few of the leaders. Once they had corralled the mustangs, they kept them from running by tying a forefoot to a hind foot with a short length of rope or chain around the ankle until the animals became quite tame.

Running with the wild bunches were some branded, domesticated animals that had probably been stolen from the settlers on the east side of the plains by marauding Indians. Occasionally the men captured a horse or mule bearing the U.S. Army brand. They found that an old mule could be wilder than any mustang when it got in with a wild herd.

Causey and his partner bred their mustangs to good stallions obtained in East Texas, and gradually produced a good grade of stock.

In 1879 the Texas Legislature appropriated 3,000,000 acres of land in the Panhandle to finance the building of a new state capitol building in Austin. In 1881 a special session of the legislature awarded the contract for construction of the capitol to the Capitol Syndicate Company. The 3,000,000 acres payment became the XIT Ranch, named for the brand the company put on its cattle.

The southernmost part of this land was the Yellow House region. Finding himself in an area about to be fenced in, Causey started looking for a place to move. He decided on Ranger Lake in the northeastern part of what it now Lea County, New Mexico, where there were several springs. Selling his water rights and improvements on the Yellow Houses to Jim Newman (who grazed his DZ cattle there until the XIT Syndicate crowded him out), Causey moved his cattle into New Mexico.

Since it was a wet year and the surface lakes were full of water, Causey had time to improve the spring at Ranger Lake, and the one at the head of Sulphur Draw to the east near the Texas line, before a drought dried up the lakes. He dug out and enlarged the area around the shallow spring on Sulphur Draw to create a larger storage capacity, then drew water for the stock in rawhide buckets tied to a rope that passed over a wheel. He used burros to pull the rope and draw the water. This watering place was later named OHO for the brand on the cattle that ranged there. It was known among the Indians as Living Water.

Causey built a dam around the spring at Ranger Lake, increasing its water-storage capacity also. Since the early range land was controlled by those who claimed the water rights at the natural springs, Causey's two watering places gave him a large grazing area for his stock.

Causey and Jeff by that time had more than a hundred mustangs and their descendants. They had about fifty head of cattle, many of which had been unbranded "mavericks" they found. Others had strayed away from trail herds and settlers to the east, wandered out on the plains, and never been claimed. In addition, there were several buffaloes, captured as calves and raised around camp. With the saddle horses, mule and bull teams, and a few burros, it became a problem to water so many animals at the small springs.

It was then that Causey discovered water just beneath the surface of the ground. He dug the first shallow wells on the Llano Estacado, erected a windmill, and found that he had access to an almost unlimited supply of water.

When Phelps White, manager of the Littlefield Cattle Company, learned of this discovery, he bought Causey's water rights and improvements at Ranger Lake, planning to dig more wells and move his herd of LFD cattle from Bosque Grande, on the Pecos River, to the Staked Plains. Before Causey turned his watering places over to White, however, he found himself another location about thirty-five miles south of Ranger Lake, near the future site of Knowles, New Mexico.

He hauled water from Monument Spring at the west side of the plains to use while digging his new well. This spring got its name from a "marker" set up by the Indians. Built of *caliche* rocks, the marker could be seen for a great distance across the level prairie and guided travelers to the water hole. Buffalo hunters built a fort there from rocks in the Indian marker to protect themselves from the savages. The old fort still stands at the Hat Ranch headquarters twelve miles southwest of Hobbs, New Mexico.

Causey brought a windmill and lumber for its tower from Midland and erected it over his new well. He threw up a wall of sod in a circle for a surface tank and fenced it. Pipes from the tank extended to troughs equipped with float valves to control the flow of water.

He planted Bermuda grass on the tank bank and brought weeping willows, cottonwoods, and poplar trees from Midland and set them out around the tank. These tall poplar trees, which could be seen for many miles across the prairie, made the ranch a landmark in later years.

He built a story-and-a-half house, sheds, corrals, a bunk-house, and a small store building, using *caliche* rocks picked up on the plains and put together with mud mortar. The house, with some additions, is still standing and in good condition. It is located between the present towns of Lovington and Hobbs, New Mexico.

He moved his stock to the new ranch and ran his herd of cattle, branded JHB connected, and his range mares, branded with a round-top open A, on the open range.

In the mid-1880's, my father died and my mother accepted an invitation from George Causey, who was her brother, to move with her children, my older brother and me, to the Llano Estacado to make our home with him. That rock house on the bleak and lonely Staked Plains, one hundred miles from the post office and twelve miles from the nearest neighbor, is the first home I remember. I grew up on Uncle George's ranch, and his tragic death marked the end of my childhood.

PART TWO

Growing Up on the Staked Plains

4.

The Ranch House, the Bunkhouse, and the Store

THE white *caliche* rock ranch house we lived in on the Llano Estacado had five rooms—two on the ground floor of the main part of the building, the largest of which was the living room; two upstairs; and a large lean-to kitchen attached to the rear of the main building. There was an outside entrance to the living room and one to the kitchen. Each of the rooms in the main part of the house had one window. The kitchen had two.

The outside door to the living room had a latch. Attached to it was a leather string that ran through a hole and hung outside. When I was beginning to walk, I could just reach the string by standing on tiptoe. The door was never locked.

The living room had very little furniture, and what there was, was mostly homemade. There were several chairs with bottoms of rawhide, tanned with the hair left on, and a homemade center table holding a large Bible, autograph and photograph albums, and a few well-worn books. Suspended from the ceiling over the table was a large coal-oil lamp with a colored shade from which glass pendants dangled, rattling when the shade was touched.

On one side of the room was an organ, with my father's picture hanging on the wall above it. Opposite was a large fireplace with a hearthstone in front and a mantel above from which my stockings were hung on Christmas Eve. A pair of steer horns adorned the wall above the mantel. The window in the living room had colored curtains held back with strips of cloth tied in bowknots.

To one side of the fireplace, hanging from a pair of antelope horns, was a belt full of cartridges and a six-shooter in a scabbard. Nearby, suspended from a peg in the wall, was a leather case containing a pair of powerful field glasses. Several .38- and .44-caliber rifles and two .45–90 buffalo guns stood in one corner beside a rest stick.

The other downstairs room was Uncle George's bedroom. His homemade bed was covered with a tarpaulin, some quilts, some army and Navaho blankets, and a tanned buffalo robe. A table held some ledgers and a coal-oil lamp. Two chairs stood beside the table. Over in one corner was a rawhide trunk, dilapidated from having been hauled around over the Great Plains for many years. All around the room were Indian relics Uncle George had collected over the years. A complete cartridge reloading outfit for the old .45–90 buffalo guns was stored in a box with a lid.

A shelf holding a shaving mug, hone, and a large hollow-ground razor jutted out from the wall below a small mirror. A razor strop Mother used on me when I became unruly hung from a peg beside the shelf. Hanging on other pegs around the wall were articles of clothing—a riding slicker, a pair of chaps with wide flaps and silver conchos, and a money belt that was usually empty.

A steep stairway led from the living room to the two upper rooms under the bare rafters of the roof. Mother's room had a dresser made from a large dry-goods box with a curtain around the front and a mirror on the wall above it. A curtain across one corner of the room was her closet. A checkered quilt with squares of many colors covered the bed. In one corner of the room was a large round-top trunk.

I slept in the other upstairs room, which was also used for a storage room and filled with all kinds of odds and ends. My bed, covered with a tarpaulin, blankets, and a buffalo robe, stood in front of the window so that I could look outside while lying in bed. In the winter when the blizzards howled, I often couldn't get warm. Mother would put more things over me, saying, "Just anything for weight." Sometimes snow would sift in around the rattling window and settle in a fine layer over my tarpaulin. In the spring, when the March winds blew, sand and dust would cover the bed.

In the summertime when it rained, which was seldom, the roof of the house leaked, and Mother couldn't find a dry spot for my bed. She placed pots and pans on the bed to catch the water as it dripped down. The sound of the water splashing in the pans would lull me to sleep. Sometimes I would have nightmares and kick like a mule, overturning the pots and pans and spilling water all over the bed.

In the lean-to kitchen that also served as a dining room was a large fireplace with a wide hearthstone. Live coals were raked from the fire onto the hearthstone, and Mother set the Dutch ovens and skillets on them to bake sourdough biscuits, roast some beef, or fry beefsteaks. We ate with the cowhands at a long home-made dining table with benches around it. The kitchen was lighted by two coal-oil lanterns hanging from the ceiling over the table. On one side of the fireplace was a table where the sourdough keg sat, close enough for the warmth of the fire to ferment the dough. Dishes, cooking utensils, and provisions were kept on shelves on the other side of the fireplace. Just outside the kitchen door was a long bench with water buckets and tin wash pans where the cowhands washed up before meals.

Along a trail back of the house was a toilet, with a half-moon cut in each side to let in light when the door was closed. I spent a lot of time during my boyhood sitting in there looking at pictures in mail-order catalogues hanging from a nail. I was especially interested in a picture of a magic lantern, and begged Mother to order it for me.

In the early morning hours, objects far out on the prairie often seemed to be inverted and detached from the earth. Uncle George awakened me one morning to come out and see the old Mallet Ranch, which was about twelve miles away, in a mirage. The windmills and houses were upside-down.

Familiar sounds around the ranch were horses nickering, cattle bawling, old bulls bellowing, and burro jacks braying as they came in to water in the heat of the day. At night, a coyote would start yapping and my shepherd dog, named Shep, would begin to bark. In a few moments, the ranch seemed to be surrounded by coyotes. Sometimes we would hear the cry of a loafer (lobo) wolf, and occasionally the scream of a panther. On summer nights, we often heard the zooming roar of bull bats as they dived and skimmed the surface of the water in the water tank looking for insects.

Mockingbirds built their nests in the trees around the water tank in the spring. No one knew where they came from because there were no other trees in that part of the country. Sound carried a great distance in the dry atmosphere of the High Plains, and the first sounds I would hear when I awakened in the morning were Mother grinding Arbuckle's coffee in the coffee mill and the singing of our mockingbirds.

Sometimes, in the early morning, we could hear the cowhands yelling far out on the prairie, and we knew they were on a "circle drive," bringing the cattle in to the watering place for a roundup. After a while we would see the chuck wagon coming in and hear the clucking of the wheels as they moved in and out on the spindles of the heavily loaded wagon. The cook, perched high on bedrolls, drove his team to the windmill and filled his water barrels. Then he pulled off a short distance from the windmill and pitched camp to cook the noonday meal for the cowhands.

Following along behind the wagon was the horse wrangler bringing his remuda of cow ponies to the windmill for water. He helped the cook unharness the chuck wagon mules, which headed straight for the water trough. After the horses had drunk their fill, the wrangler hazed them out on the prairie, where they scattered and grazed. He then walked around over the prairie dragging a tow sack and filling it with cow chips, which the cook used for cooking fuel.

Tanned and grizzled cowhands on loping, sweat-covered horses rode up to the windmill, saddle leather squeaking and spurs jingling. Sliding their horses to a stop, they dismounted and drank water from the barrel out of a gourd dipper. Then they rode back out to where the roundup was being formed. Sometimes to my utter joy, one would reach down, grab me by an arm, and lift me to a seat in front of him, where I proudly held the reins.

From a grandstand seat on the chuck box in the chuck wagon, I was permitted to watch the cowhands form the roundup. After all the cattle were in, the horse wrangler brought the remuda into a corral the cowhands made with their ropes. Drive horses were turned loose, and cutting horses were caught and mounted to work the roundup. I longed for the time when I would be big enough to straddle a horse and ride out with them.

One of my favorite spots was the top of the rock corrals. I perched there, watching the cowboys brand colts and the bronc peelers break the young geldings. I also liked to prowl around the sheds where the cowpunchers kept their saddles, Navaho saddle blankets, ropes, hackamores, quirts, cow whips, rawhide hobbles, branding irons, and other horse jewelry.

Under the sheds were kept the harness, corn, and morrals for the mule team that pulled the chuck and freight wagons. The mules were mean and ornery and couldn't be bridled without the use of a "twister" on the upper lip.

It was under a shed that I learned to plait four, six, and eight strands of leather or rawhide into quirts and cow whips, and tie all kinds of fancy knots in rope and bridle reins. I also learned how to twist hair into long skeins for making hair ropes and saddle girths.

When not in use, the wagons stood near the sheds. Chains, stretchers, and double-trees for hitching up four, six, or eight mules lay on the ground in front of them.

Behind the sheds were several old ox yokes—relics of bygone days when bull teams were used to pull wagons loaded with buffalo hides to the trading posts at Dodge City and Fort Griffin. Later, oxen had been used to haul bleached buffalo bones from the old killing grounds on the Llano Estacado to the Texas-Pacific Railroad at Colorado City.

Although Mother objected, I liked to stay in the bunkhouse at night with the cowhands when they rolled out their beds on the floor. I would hunt up the bootjack for them to pull off their boots with, then watch them play pitch, seven-up, poker, or Canfield solitaire with the worn decks of cards. A pair of horns from a Texas longhorn steer that the hands had scraped and polished hung above the fireplace with two .44-caliber rifles laid across them. Mounted buffalo and antelope horns also decorated the walls.

Hanging on pegs driven between the rocks in the walls were chaps, or "leggins," as they were called then. Some were tanned with the goat hair on the outside, and others had wide flaps decorated with silver conchos. Cowhands on the plains had very little need for chaps, since there was no brush in that part of the country. The ones that hung in our bunkhouse were usually brought in by a "rabbit twister" from down in Coke County, Texas, or some cowboy from the "brush country" in southwest Texas, where they needed them for protection from thorns.

Stetson hats which had been much used for "fanning"—on a bronco when it was "pitching," or to create an artificial draft to get a cow-chip fire to burn when the chips were wet—lined the walls, and riding slickers hung on pegs underneath them.

The cowhands kept their extra supply of clothing and personal gear such as letter-writing material, razor, and other items in what was called a "war bag." This usually remained in the bedroll. Most cowboys had guns which they also kept in their bedrolls, carrying them only on special occasions, usually under their shirts, or stuck inside the waistbands of their trousers.

When the freight wagons made the long trip to the railroad, in addition to supplies for the ranch, they brought back staple articles to sell to cowhands, chuck wagon cooks, and homeseekers passing through the country. These articles were kept in a little one-room store building a short distance from the ranch house. Old Jeff, who lived with us, looked after the store.

The store was a hangout for visiting ranchers, cowhands, line riders, and anyone passing through the country. I spent a lot of time sitting among them listening to tales about the "taming of the Old West," border outlaws, Texas Rangers, Indian fighting, blizzards, sandstorms, trips up the trail with herds of longhorns through the Indian Nation to shipping pens in rip-roaring Kansas "rail-head" towns, stampedes on the trail, fence cutting, the Lincoln County War, and life in the frontier towns.

I listened to discussions of range conditions, calf and colt crops, the price of cow and polo ponies, and whether the best market for beef cattle was at Fort Worth or Kansas City. I also heard talk of the coming of the nesters with their plows and milk cows to settle on 160-acre homesteads in New Mexico or bid on the Texas school land as it was placed on the market. I heard a lot about their reprehensible habit of fencing in the free range and plowing the grass under.

Any person coming our way from the post office brought mail for everyone living in that part of the country, and left it at the store to be called for. Other letters were left there to be taken to the post office and mailed by anyone going to town.

Recipients of our mail probably wondered why the letters from New Mexico were wrinkled and soiled, not knowing they were carried in a cowhand's saddle pockets or wrapped in his slicker tied on behind the cantle of his saddle during the hundred-mile trip to the railroad.

When Uncle George went to Midland for supplies, he usually brought back a bundle of newspapers so we could read about what was happening back in civilization. After everyone in the ranch house and bunkhouse had seen them, Old Jeff stacked them away in the little store so visitors could read them. Even when they were several weeks old, they were news in our area, and everything in them was read—including the advertisements.

29

Mother taught me to read a little, but I enjoyed looking at the papers out in the store, because Old Jeff would read them aloud to me and take pains to explain everything I didn't understand. I owe much of my early education to that old frontiersman.

Many of those newspapers were editions of the *Dallas Morning News*, which, thanks to the late George B. Dealey, covered the Southwest like sunshine covers the state of New Mexico. One issue, published during President Cleveland's second administration and read and explained by my old buddy, Jeff, made an impression on me that has lasted throughout the years. It told of a severe panic and depression that swept the country, of labor troubles, of a general strike against many of the nation's railroads, and of unemployment and suffering throughout the working class.

The paper carried cartoons showing locomotives with "smokeless" smokestacks, cobwebs across the cab windows, and grass growing up through the cowcatcher. In one cartoon, gaunt workmen with barefoot children pleaded for "a full dinner pail."

5.

Old Jeff

GEORGE Jefferson, Old Jeff, had never sprouted wings, but there was nothing so very bad about him. He was the kind of man any red-blooded American boy would enjoy growing up around. That grizzled old plainsman took the place of my dead father in my early days.

Pictures on television of Gabby Hayes with a couple of youngsters sitting beside him listening to stories of the taming of the Old West bring to memory the times I sat beside Old Jeff. I'd listen to his tall tales of his life on the Great Staked Plains when there was no law west of Missouri and no God west of Dodge City.

One of the stories I liked to hear was about the time when he and his older brother, John Jefferson, took the advice, "Go west young man." They ran away from their father's home in central Kansas, with a team and wagon, heading for Cripple Creek.

In western Kansas they were captured by a band of Comanche Indians and held in captivity for nine years, being set free when the U.S. Cavalry rounded up the Indians and took them to a reservation in the Indian Territory. The boys grew as crafty and cunning as any Indian during that time, and almost forgot how to speak their native tongue. Old Jeff told me a lot about living in the wickiups and tipis of the nomadic tribe and being continually on the move.

Sometimes, Jeff and I would go out on the prairie around our ranch and gather Indian artifacts, such as arrowheads and spear points, that were plentiful on the Llano Estacado.

He showed me how and for what reason the Comanche Indians made two kinds of arrows. One was for use in combat against human beings, and the other was for hunting four-legged animals. The different postures of the two kinds of animals placed the ribs in their bodies in different positions, one horizontal, the other vertical. Notches in the ends of the arrow shafts were cut to fit the bow string so that the wide spread of the arrowhead would enter the body between the ribs.

Jeff told how the braves made raids on trading posts and wagon trains to get guns, ammunition, and other supplies. Some of them never returned, but others came back with scalps dangling from their belts. He claimed that Comanches were superb horsemen, proud of their riding ability. He had learned to ride bareback on an Indian pony, holding a buckskin thong tied around the animal's lower jaw.

When Jeff had the croup, stomachache, or other childhood ailments, the old medicine man would brew weeds, grass, or herbs and force him to swallow the concoction. Jeff claimed that one dose would cure him because he didn't wish to take another.

The old fellow told me that Comanche kids would gang up on him and his brother and beat them unmercifully. They had to learn to fight like wildcats in order to survive. His brother, "Squaw Johnnie," was killed about twelve years after his release from captivity while asleep in a tent in Buffalo Jones's camp.

Jeff served as an Army scout for a while after his rescue, before he teamed up with Uncle George to hunt buffaloes. The two men were like brothers, inseparable. They spent the last part of their lives together.

One of Jeff's arms was so crooked that when he tried to straighten it out, it looked like a dog's hind leg. It had been broken by a bullet from the gun of a Dodge City gambler Jeff caught dealing cards from the bottom of the deck.

"The saw-bones who set my arm," Jeff used to say, "must have been a veterinary surgeon and thought he was working on a dog."

Mother thought Jeff was wild, and she didn't like me to be with him so much; but when I got into trouble, I'd always hunt up my old side-kick and tell him all about it. He would sympathize with me and say, "Everything will be all right if you come to me when they get after you. Us menfolks have to stick together, else the womenfolks will be running the country."

Some of my chores around the house were helping Mother wash the dishes, sitting on a bench with a coffee mill between my knees grinding Arbuckle's coffee, carrying in water from the windmill, lugging in cow chips for the fireplace, and packing out ashes. It seemed there were always more ashes to be carried out than chips brought in.

Once, I hunted up Jeff and grumbled about the work I had to do. He squatted down in front of me and said, "You're a lucky boy to be living here on the plains where there isn't much work to doing your chores. When I was a boy up in Kansas, I had to chop the wood and pump the water, besides toting it into the house. All you have to do is carry it in. The wind pumps the water, and the cows cut the wood."

Mother always returned thanks at the table before we began eating. Quite often, strange cowhands would turn their plates up, then gently lay them back down again with a foolish look on their faces when they realized Mother was asking the blessing. She taught me a little prayer to say at the table, and Old Jeff taught another one. Sometimes, I got them mixed up.

One night, when several strangers were at our table, Mother

asked me to return thanks. I was a little bashful and hesitated. She told me to go on like a little man and show the folks how smart I was. I did, but the blessing that came out was the one Old Jeff had taught me, which was, "Bless the meat and damn the skin. Back your ears and all dig in."

Mother jerked me up by the ear, dragged me into Uncle's room, and yanked the razor strop from a nail on the wall. "Who taught you to say that blessing?" she demanded.

I didn't say anything, because I didn't want to get Jeff into trouble.

"Tell me this minute," she stormed, "or I'll pull your pants down and tan your bottom!"

"Jeff did," I murmured.

She stalked into the kitchen and got the old fellow told, but his smiling countenance shed her barrage of words like a Fish Brand slicker sheds water.

During cold winter evenings, cowhands often gathered in the living room of the ranch house to listen to Mother play the organ and sing. Occasionally, some of them joined her in singing old hymns and lyrics they probably hadn't heard since they left home.

She had taught me to recite several little poems. Sometimes the men would each give me a nickel to stand on a box and say them. One she taught me was "Mary Had a Little Lamb."

One night, when Mother asked me to recite the poem about Mary and her lamb, I did so, but thoughtlessly spoke a version Old Jeff had taught me: "Mary had a little lamb. She put it on a shelf. Every time it wagged its tail, it spanked its little self."

This, of course, made my mother hostile. She glared at Old Jeff, who was laughing and clapping his hands, and who showed his appreciation of my recital by tossing me two nickels.

Mother taught me to count, but Jeff told me when I counted to ten, always to continue by saying "jack, queen, king." This angered Mother because she didn't like playing cards and looked askance at anyone who did.

In later years, Jeff taught me that three-of-a-kind beats two pairs and a royal flush is the best hand. He said never to draw to a straight that's open in the middle, always to stand on seventeen when playing blackjack, to bet my alce on a seven-spot at monte, to let it ride if I made "little Joe" as my point when shooting dice, and never to try to bluff a Chinaman in a poker game.

Very often, Jeff and the cowhands would slaughter a beef out on the prairie. I would carry out one of Mother's large dishpans to get the brains, sweetbreads, liver, melt, marrowgut, and some of the kidney fat. From these, Mother made what Jeff called "son-of-a-gun" stew. He advised me to eat plenty of the son-of-a-gun, because "it'll make big muscles and put hair on your chest."

Range cattle far out on the prairie would smell the blood of the beef and come in a long run sniffing the air. They gathered around the offal in large numbers, smelling and bawling as they milled around. Then a bunch of old bulls would cluster around the carcass, bellowing and pawing up the dirt and throwing it over their backs. Finally there was a clashing of horns, and loud thuds caused by impact of skull against skull. The fight sometimes lasted for an hour.

I wanted to know why cattle acted that way when a beef was killed but paid no mind to the carcass of a cow that just lay down and died, or to that of a little dogie that starved to death or was killed by the wolves.

"Just animal instinct," was the only reply Jeff ever gave me.

Sometimes when telling how rustlers stole cattle, he would squat down and scribble different brands in the sand with a pointed stick, then show me how thieves would change them into other brands by using a J branding iron to run over and add something to the original brand. They would also alter the animal's earmark. He told how thieves would kill mother cows for their unbranded calves, and make it appear the cow had died a natural death.

At those times, the old fellow would look me straight in the eye and say, "Boy, if I ever hear that you put your brand on another man's cow or calf, I'll tie you to a fence post, and whup you until you break loose."

6.

Christmas at the Ranch

ON Christmas Eve, 1891, at our ranch, a blue norther was whistling across the level prairie out of an indigo haze along the horizon to the northeast. A vapory mist was falling and, as the temperature dropped, a coat of ice formed over everything. As the morning advanced, the mist turned to sleet. Then about noon, it began to snow. By nightfall, a real blizzard was screaming across the Llano Estacado.

"There's no protection on the plains from those northers but the North Star and some barbed-wire drift fences up north," I often heard the cowhands at the ranch say. "And sometimes the gates in those fences are left open."

Long strings of cattle, with heads down and tails to the storm, had drifted past the ranch all day. The cowhands wondered how far they would have to follow the herds to bring them back after the storm was over.

The saddle horses and mules in the horse pasture came in and were backed up behind the rock corrals and sheds, where they had some protection from the biting wind and blinding snow. The men at the ranch had taken the wagons below the west breaks of the plains about a month before, and brought them back, loaded with dead mesquite roots and scrub cedar. This made excellent fuel for our fireplace, and we were snug as bugs in a rug in the living room of our rock house.

"You'd better be good, if you want Santa to come," Mother had been saying for a month. "He's watching and sees everything you do. If you're bad, he might not bring you anything you asked for."

For the life of me, I couldn't figure out where Old Santa might be hiding around the ranch where he could see me and I couldn't see him. I asked Old Jeff and the cowhands about it, but they gave me the same mysterious look Mother gave me, and shrugged.

Mother told me she would write Santa a letter telling him what I wanted him to bring. I wanted a lot of things and hoped he would bring them all. The list I gave her included a pinto pony and a saddle, a pair of chaps with wide flaps and silver conchos, silver-mounted spurs and bridle bits, a new Stetson hat, a pair of gloves with gauntlets, and a pair of shop-made boots with a lone star stitched on their legs, with plenty of "squeak" in them.

Mother said, "You're old enough to know Santa can't bring all those things in his sled and come down the chimney with them in his pack. Ask him for something smaller that he might be able to bring, or he might not come to see you at all."

I finally cut the request down to the boots, hat, and gloves; some ABC blocks and an ABC book with pictures in it; some oranges and apples, and plenty of horehound, licorice, and striped stick candy; and a magic lantern like the one I had been eagerly saving coupons from Arbuckle's coffee bags to send off for.

When the freight wagons went to the railroad several weeks before, Mother sent the letter containing my requests to be mailed. When the wagons returned, mother took several packages from them and put them away without opening them. From the loaded wagons came such fascinating odors as tobacco, bacon, onions, rope, and the sweet cidery scent of ripe apples.

As darkness settled over the plains that Christmas Eve, I stood at a window and wiped Jack Frost from the pane so that I could see the snow gradually form in drifts around the house. I wondered how Santa Claus could ever find our house in such a storm.

Uncle George lighted a lantern and hung it high up in the windmill tower as he always did during such storms. He said it would serve as a beacon for Santa and anyone else who might be lost in the blizzard, which had come up so "sudden-and-soon" without much warning.

After supper, Mother sat in her rocking chair before the fireplace and read from her big Bible about an angel saying, "Fear not: for, behold, I bring you good tidings of great joy . . . . Ye shall find a babe wrapped in swaddling clothes, lying in a manger . . . . On earth peace, good will toward men."

She then took a book from her trunk and read a poem she said was written by a man named Clement Moore for his children in 1822. It began:

'Twas the night before Christmas, when all through the house,
Not a creature was stirring, not even a mouse.

Then it went on and told about a man catching St. Nick when he came down the chimney with a pack on his back and began putting gifts in the children's stockings hanging from the mantel.

The poem continued:

His eyes—how they twinkled! his dimples, how merry!
His cheeks were like roses, his nose like a cherry!

But the part I liked best was

He had a broad face and a round little belly
That shook when he laughed, like a bowl full of jelly.

When she finished, I stared wide-eyed. "But Mamma," I said, "how come you told me Santa Claus was watching and wouldn't bring me anything if I was bad, when that poem doesn't say anything about him at all. It's all about St. Nick. Does Santa do the watching and St. Nick bring the presents? Or what?"

"That's a long story I'll tell you sometime when you grow older," she replied. "Now don't ask me so many questions. Hang your stockings on the mantel and go to bed, for no one will come as long as you're awake."

I couldn't find a pair of stockings without a hole in them, and Mother had to darn a pair.

"Can Santa slide down this chimney?" I asked as I was hanging them on the mantel. "It's awful small, and I'm afraid he might get burnt and all covered with soot."

"I guess he can make it," she answered.

Mother had been cooking for several days and had all kinds of goodies ready for Christmas, such as cookies and mincemeat, apple, and peach pies, and other pies with meringue over the top that Old Jeff called "calf slobbers."

She had a large Dutch oven full of baked beef with plenty of spuds and good brown gravy, and another oven with a big ham and candied yams in it. The cowhands aimed to kill a calf and concoct a son-of-a-gun stew, but called it off because of the weather.

Mother told me while I was helping her cook that Christmas was a time for festivity, merriment, and the joyful exchange of gifts. She didn't know I had found out over the "grapevine" around the ranch that the cowpunchers had some stuff cached away out in the bunkhouse that made them "cheery, gay, and full of merriment." She also had no inkling of events soon to happen, which would make this a Christmas she would never forget!

As we were getting ready to retire, we heard the crunching of snow and the clucking of wheels. A loaded wagon pulled up close to the house and stopped. We heard footsteps in the snow; then someone was knocking at the door. When Mother opened it, a man stood there shivering. He was a young man, about twenty-five years old, wearing an overcoat and a cap with the flaps pulled down over his ears.

"Our baby is seriously ill," he said wearily. "Will you let me bring it in out of the cold?"

"Of course," Mother answered at once. "Bring the child and its mother in—and any other members of your family."

"There's no one but my wife and baby," he said.

He brought his wife into the room. They were both stiff with cold. She was very young. Draped over her head and around her was a blanket, under which she carried the baby. Mother took the baby and did what she could for it with her limited supply of medicine. I stirred up the fire, and when they had warmed, Mother turned Uncle George's room over to them and fixed them some supper. They ate hungrily.

I went out to the wagon with my uncle and Jeff. They unhitched the mules, took them to the sheds, unharnessed them, and put the harness in out of the weather. Then they watered the mules and put them in the pasture.

It was a fine team of young mules. The new Bain wagon was covered with a new wagon-sheet. From all appearances, the visitors seemed to be in better circumstances financially than most of the families who stopped at our ranch.

The young man told us later that he had already filed upon and improved a homestead somewhere along the Río Hondo west of Roswell, New Mexico. He had then gone back to East Texas to get his wife and baby and their belongings. They were on their way to their new home when the unexpected storm caught them away from shelter.

Mother, Uncle George, and the parents of the infant held a consultation about the baby. Mother said nothing in her small supply of medicine seemed to improve its condition. My uncle, being an old bachelor with no experience with infants, was no help.

They called in Old Jeff, hoping he might know of some Indian remedy that would work. Although he also was an old bachelor, he had himself been treated by Indian medicine men and nursed by Indian women during periods of illness when he was a child. He had also seen many papooses treated and nursed back to health.

He examined the infant closely, observing its inflamed throat, hoarseness, difficult breathing, and high fever. Then he stood looking at the baby a few moments, in deep thought.

"I know of some succulent seed plants the medicine men often brewed for papooses when they were ill," he said, "but I don't have any, and it would be impossible to find any with the ground covered with snow."

The father asked how far it was to medical aid. Uncle George told him the nearest doctor was one hundred miles away.

"Well," the young mother said between sobs, as her husband tried to comfort her, "I guess all we can do is pray."

Later, Mother tucked me in my bed upstairs, listened to me say my "Now I lay me down to sleep," pulled the tarpaulin up over me, and spread the skin of a loafer wolf over my feet. I heard the ever increasing fury of the storm, the bawling of cattle drifting past the ranch, and my dog barking at coyotes out on the prairie. I finally dropped off to sleep and dreamed that a little fat man driving eight reindeer hitched to a sleigh stopped on our roof, got out, and slid down our chimney.

The rattle of pots and pans in our kitchen awakened me, and I peeped out from under the tarp. Day was breaking, and the blizzard was still howling around the house. Snow that had drifted in around the crevices of the window and eaves of the house formed little drifts on the floor.

Because we had company, I knew I couldn't dress in front of the fireplace as I usually did, holding my clothes up in front of the blazing fire to warm them before putting them on. I pulled the tarp back over my head, and lay there wondering if Santa had found us. Finally, I got up and dressed, and with chattering teeth, slipped down the stairway and peeped at my stockings hanging from the mantel. Sure enough, Santy had been there and crammed them full! An orange was visible at the top of one, and a big red apple in the other. A hat and boots just like those I had ordered were on the mantel.

I heard someone crying in the other room. Seeing Mother in the kitchen, I went to her. Her face was drawn and tired, and I could tell that she had been up most of the night.

She stooped down and put her arm around me. "The little baby died last night," she whispered.

I got most of the presents I had asked for, but it was a subdued Christmas for me and everyone else on the ranch. Snow continued to fall throughout Christmas Day. Mother dressed and prepared the baby for burial. I watched Jeff and my uncle make a little coffin from the rough pine boards of an Arbuckle's coffee shipping case.

The following morning, the storm was over and the sun rose from a field of snow. The cowpunchers shoveled out a path from the front door of the house to a little knoll in the horse pasture back of the corrals. They cleared a spot where the snow wasn't so deep, and dug a grave. Everyone at the ranch gathered in the living room for the funeral service. Mother read a chapter from her Bible and sang a hymn, accompanying herself on the organ. Then we kneeled in prayer.

The cowhands carried the little coffin at the head of the funeral procession to the burial site. As it was lowered into the grave with ropes, Mother sang another hymn, standing with her arm around the heartbroken mother.

The parents of the child told Mother that when they became settled in their new home and had enough money to do so, they planned to return with a casket, exhume the body of their child, and take it to their home west of the Pecos River. I have no knowledge, however, of their ever having done so.

It was sorrowful to see the grief-stricken father and mother continue the journey on west, leaving their little one behind buried there on the bleak prairie. Every time I hear that old cowboy song, " 'Neath the Western Skies on the Lone Prairie," I see that father and mother sitting in the spring seat of their wagon as they drove away, looking back at that little grave in our horse pasture.

Mother told me when a baby as young as this one died, its spirit went to heaven and became an angel like those portrayed in her big Bible. Childlike, I often scanned the atmosphere above the grave to see if I could detect the little spirit in its flight. After the snow cleared off, Jeff and I gathered *caliche* rocks from the prairie and laid them over and around the grave to protect it from burrowing animals and rodents and the fierce elements of the Llano Estacado.

7.

A Train Trip to the Indian Nation

ONE day Mother received a letter from her brother, John Causey, inviting us to visit him. He was living on a claim he had won near El Reno when Oklahoma Territory opened for settlement in 1889. She accepted the invitation, and Uncle George took us to Midland to catch the train.

I could hardly wait to board the Texas-Pacific train that evening for my first ride on a "choo-choo," and the moment finally arrived. As I stood on the depot platform holding Mother's hand, looking down the track in the direction from which the train would come, the headlight suddenly swept into view, and my heart beat faster and faster. The whistle blew, and in seconds the engine charged by, bell clanging, and ground to a stop.

A man with a lantern stepped off the train. "All aboard for Fort Worth and the East!" he shouted. We climbed on. The train wasn't crowded, and we found two empty double seats facing each other. When the train started up again, we were heading east.

I sat near the window and looked out at the landscape, which seemed to be moving past us. I wanted to raise the window and see the locomotive, but Mother said she was afraid I might fall out. She finally relented, though, and raised the window for me. Just as I stuck my head out and looked ahead, a cloud of black smoke rolled back over the coaches and I got a cinder in my eye. We had a time getting it out.

The news butch came through the coach yelling "Peanuts, popcorn, chewing gum, candy!"

I begged Mother to buy me something, and knowing a good thing when he saw it, from then on, every time the news butch came through our car, he sat in the seat across the aisle and showed me every item he had for sale.

A man wearing a cap with a metal badge on its front and a coat with shining buttons came through the coach. He was the conductor. "Tickets please," he said to everybody.

After examining and punching our ticket, he shook hands with me. "Did you ever ride on a train before?" he asked.

"Huh-uh," I replied with a violent negative shake of my head.

"Where are you going?" he wanted to know.

"I'm going up there where the Injuns live," I answered.

I apparently made a hit with him, for almost every time he came through, he stopped and said something to me. I took advantage of his friendliness. "What makes the engine run?" I asked him.

"A hot fire in the furnace heats the water in the boiler, which turns into steam," he answered patiently, "and when the engineer opens the throttle, steam flows into the cylinders and moves the pistons which are connected to the engine wheels, and turns them round and round."

I nodded sagely as if I really understood.

The conductor reminded me that when water in a tea-kettle starts to boil, the lid on the kettle begins to move up and down because of the steam.

"The same kind of steam which makes the lid on the kettle move up and down causes the wheels of the locomotive to turn and move the train," he explained.

That conductor had a great capacity for understanding small boys. Another time when he came through, he told me he had a grandson just about my age.

"Where does he live?" I asked.

"In Abilene," he replied.

I asked him if he meant Abilene, Kansas, where the cowhands on our ranch used to drive trailherds of cattle to the shipping pens.

"No," he told me, "Abilene, Texas."

"Is he going to be a railroad conductor when he grows up?" I inquired.

He smiled. "Maybe so, some day," he said, giving me a pat on the head.

Mother and I ate some of the lunch from our basket, and I curled up in the seat and dropped off to sleep. Sometimes the brakeman would open the door of the coach and I could hear the clickity-clack of the wheels passing over the rail joints. The brakeman walked through the coach calling out the names of the stations along the way, "And don't forget your packages," he always added.

Only half-awake, I could barely remember where I was. Then I would realize I was on the train, and press my face against the window with my hands on the pane, to stare intently into the mysterious darkness for a moment before curling up again and going back to sleep.

Sometimes while peering out the window into the darkness as we passed through small towns, I would see green and red lights near the track. I asked Mother what they were. She told me they were lamps on switch stands to light up the rails so that the engineer could see whether they were lined up properly ahead.

"A green light means GO," she said, "and a red light means STOP."

"Our lamps on the ranch burn white coal oil and give white lights," I argued. "Do these lamps burn red and green coal oil to make the lights red and green?"

"I'm glad you didn't ask the conductor that foolish question,"

LLANO ESTACADO

Countless herds of buffalo and nomadic Indian tribes roamed these plains when the Spaniards discovered them in 1541. Francisco Vasquez Coronado, first explorer of New Mexico, named them <u>llano</u> <u>estacado</u>, staked plains, probably because of the yucca stems which dotted the vast expanses. By 1850 the plains gave birth to the cattle industry.

Photograph by the author

This New Mexico historic marker stands on the Staked Plains east of Fort Sumner on U.S. Highway 60.

George (Old Jeff) Jefferson, frontiersman, probably in the 1890's. Old Jeff is buried in a small country cemetery six miles from his childhood home in El Dorado, Kansas.

Thomas L. (George) Causey in 1874, when he and Old Jeff were hunting buffaloes south of the Arkansas River in the Panhandle plains area.

The four Causey brothers and their father in 1900. Seated, *l* tor *r.*:
Mark Causey, G. W. Causey (the father), and T. L. (George)
Causey. Standing, *l.* to *r.*: R. L. (Bob) Causey and John V. Causey.

The headquarters ranch of the Yellow House division of the XIT outfit, sometime before 1908. The bluff in the background, the *Casas Amarillas*, is where George Causey had his Sod House Camp. The arrow in the picture points to the wheel of a 120-foot-high windmill, said to have been the tallest windmill in the United States.

Courtesy of Jim Rawls of the Hobbs Daily News-Sun

The OHO Ranch in 1963. *L. to r.*: Mike Field, of Bronco, Texas; Robert K. (Bobbie) Field, the present owner of the ranch; and R. B. (Casey) Jones, of Plains, Texas. They are examining *caliche* rocks, all that remain of a structure that was built by George Causey.

Monument Spring, as it appears today. Located about twenty-five miles south of Lovington, New Mexico, it is one of the few natural springs on the Llano Estacado. Its name is from a monument of *caliche* rocks the Indians built on a nearby rise as a guide to the oasis.

Courtesy of Jim Rawls of the Hobbs Daily News-Sun

Monument, New Mexico, a small ranching community that also gets its name from the Indian marker.

Nellie (Causey) Whitlock with her two sons, Vivian (Ol' Waddy) and Ralph, in 1891 at El Reno, Oklahoma Territory.

she whispered, looking around to see if anyone had heard me. "These lamps burn the same kind of oil ours do. But you see these lights through red and green glass."

I decided Mother wasn't in the mood to answer questions right then, so I stretched out and went back to sleep.

The sun was shining when I awoke. We were passing through country entirely different from that near our home. The train passed over bridges under which a stream flowed, and the hills were covered with trees. I had never seen so many trees before. We roared through cuts and across fills, and the whistle blew often, as a warning signal, at the many wagon roads crossing the tracks. Occasionally, short toots of the whistle sounded to frighten cattle or horses off the track.

I saw men walking and driving teams in the fields, who, my mother said, were planting cotton and corn, something new to me. People driving near the railroad in wagons and buggies waved as we passed them.

The coach grew more crowded, and I had to give up the seat I had all to myself. I moved in beside Mother and she let me sit by the window. We stopped at a small place Mother said was a section house, where people she called "section hands" lived and worked on the railroad.

A Mexican couple with half a dozen kids boarded the train there and sat in the seats just behind us. The kids raced up and down the aisle, screaming like Comanche Indians. One after another, they went to a container of drinking water with a tin cup in front of it, near the front of the coach. I also wanted a drink, but Mother fished a cup from our lunch basket for me to use, saying, "Don't drink from a public cup. It isn't healthy."

I saw a lot of things in the daylight to ask Mother questions about. Tall posts flashed by with wires strung at their tops which didn't have barbs on them like the wires in the fences at our ranch and this puzzled me. "What are them wires on the tall posts for?" I asked her. "They're so high, cattle and horses can walk right under them."

"They're telegraph wires to send messages over, like the one I sent your Uncle John last night telling him we were coming," she replied.

I thought of a time when Old Jeff made me a kite and sent messages all the way up by running the kite string through holes in small pieces of paper. I asked Mother how a message could travel along wires fastened to posts.

"Let's talk about something else," she said tactfully.

The news butch came through, stopped, and showed me some candy in glass containers and a book with Frank and Jesse James's pictures in it. I got Mother to buy me a glass pistol and a glass locomotive filled with candy. I also managed to talk her into buying me one of the James brothers books to take home to show Uncle George and Old Jeff.

As the butch went on down the aisle hawking his merchandise, Mother exploded. "I wish that man would leave us alone!" she said. "I'm getting to the point where I hate to see him coming. If he stops here any more, I'm going to report him to the conductor. When you see him coming," she ordered me, "play possum and act like you're asleep."

She changed her mind, though. When he came back through our car, she stopped him and bought us each a banana, an orange, and an apple. She also asked him to bring her a cup of coffee and me a glass of milk. We ate fried chicken and light bread for breakfast, with the fruit for dessert.

I had asked the question "Where are we?" so many times since we left Midland, I was ashamed to ask her again, but I did.

"I don't know," became her stock answer.

"How far have we come?" was another favorite question.

"I don't know."

"Will we get there today?"

"I wish you wouldn't ask so many questions," she said, frowning. "I've done nothing since we boarded this train except answer your questions."

"Mother," I said sorrowfully, "you always told me the only way to learn was to ask questions."

48

"Yes, I know I did," she murmured, "but you should give an answer time to digest before you ask for another answer."

She changed the subject by telling me that we had changed conductors during the night. When the new one came through to examine and punch our ticket, I promptly made his acquaintance.

"What are them things up there for?" I asked him as an opening gambit, pointing to an ax, a saw, and a large hammer in a glass case at the end of the coach.

He rose to the bait. "When we have a wreck, we break that glass and get those tools to cut our way out of the coach," he said.

"Are we gonna have a sure-enough wreck?" I wanted to know real quick.

"Son, I hope we stay on the rails tonight," was his reply.

"When will we get to Fort Worth?" I asked.

He glanced at his watch. "We're due there in about an hour," he said.

We reached Fort Worth—the cowhands at the ranch called it "Cow Town"—where we had to change to another railroad. We had an all-night layover.

We stayed at a rooming house near the depot, and ate in a nearby restaurant, where I saw something that made me stare wide-eyed. The men operating it wore their hair in tight braids, which Mother called "pigtails," down their backs. She said they came from China—far away across the Pacific Ocean.

Late that night, Mother awakened me. "There's a fire in the building across the street," she said, her voice shaking, "and I'm afraid the building we're in may catch fire."

The rooming house clerk knocked at our door and told us to be ready to vacate at a moment's notice. We dressed hurriedly and stacked our belongings near the door. Then we watched the thrilling sight across the street from our window.

I had never seen a building on fire before. The only large fires I had ever seen were prairie grass fires sweeping across the Staked Plains. Our house at the ranch, being made of rocks, had never been in danger of burning.

A team of horses pulling a wagon carrying long ladders and several men wearing helmets raced along the street in a dead run. I heard the sharp, insistent clangor of the bell on the fire engine as it stopped nearby. I saw the horses clearly as they stood with their beautiful necks bowed, proudly champing the bits.

People were pouring out of the doors of the two-story burning house and running across the street to congregate below our upstairs window. Some were still wearing their nightgowns. Others were only half-dressed, carrying clothes flung over their arms.

I could see people at the upstairs windows. One elderly man jumped to the ground and lay there until bystanders carried him away. A woman with a baby in her arms stood at one upstairs window until a fireman placed a ladder below the window, raced up, and grabbed the infant. The mother followed him down the ladder to safety.

The heat was so intense we could feel it. We could hear the hissing steam and breaking glass as men holding the hose sent streams of water against the hot window panes. Before long, the roof fell in, sending a shower of sparks high into the air.

When the fire was finally out, little was left of the wooden building. I tingled with excitement as that splendid team of horses turned around and trotted down the street proudly pulling the fire engine.

Day was breaking, and we didn't have time to get any more sleep. We ate breakfast—buckwheat flapjacks swimming in maple syrup—at a Chinese eating house, where I wanted to talk to the man who waited on us and ask him why he wore his hair in a pigtail; but he talked as if he was trying to sing a song, and I couldn't understand him. We checked out of the rooming house after breakfast and caught the train.

As the train sped north from Fort Worth, Mother suddenly said, "Look! We're crossing the Red River."

The water I saw in the river was almost as red as blood from a freshly killed cow. We reached the north side of the bridge. "Now, we are in Oklahoma Territory," Mother murmured.

"This is the part of the country the old cowhands at the ranch call the Indian Nation," I informed her importantly. "They used to drive herds of cattle to the shipping pens at Abilene through here."

She acted amazed at the depth of my knowledge, taking notice that I didn't even ask her a question. Then I had to show my ignorance. "I wonder why it is called Oklahoma, and what that word means?" I mused aloud.

"Well," she answered, "I've heard it is a combination of two words from the language of one of the Indian tribes who live here. The first part of the word, 'okla,' means 'people' and the second part, 'homa,' means 'red.' The two words together mean 'people red,' or as we change the words around, 'red people.' So it is 'the land of red people.'

"When our government gave the Indians this territory," she continued, "they were promised it would be their land 'as long as grass shall grow and rivers run,' and now the government is going back on its promise by permitting white people to move in and settle on their land, the way your uncle did on his claim near El Reno."

I know now that my mother was a woman of great perception and deep compassion.

We stopped at a station, and my heart suddenly stood still! I saw my first real live Indians standing on the depot platform. My cup ran over when an Indian "buck" and his "squaw" got on the train and came into our coach. They sat in the seat across the aisle from us, staring stolidly ahead. The woman was carrying a papoose on her back in a contraption Mother whispered was a cradle, made of what looked like buckskin covered with beads. The woman removed the cradle from her back before she sat down and held it in her lap.

I looked at their hands and faces. *Why,* I wondered, *are they called "red people" when their skins are not even as red as mine?*

"Why are they called red people?" I whispered hoarsely to Mother. "Their skin isn't red. It's brown, like the hands and faces of the old cowhands on the plains."

She was examining a railroad map and timetable and ignored my whisper. The Indian and his wife ignored me too.

Uncle John met us in El Reno with a team and buckboard, and took us to his claim. He had been there almost three years and had a two-room frame house, a well with a handpump, and a small field in cultivation. He also had what he said was a "must" in that part of the country—a cyclone cellar. He told us that settlers in Oklahoma always built a cellar to protect them from cyclones, even before they built a house.

It was a rectangular excavation in the yard near his house, about as deep as an ordinary man is tall, with a dirt-covered roof slightly above the surface of the ground. It was entered through a sloping door that could be securely fastened from the underside. Steps beneath the door led down into the interior. A square wooden vent protruded from the center of the roof.

The second night we were there, my uncle awakened us to tell us that a cyclone was approaching and we must go into the cyclone cellar for safety. As we went from the house to the cellar, a few drops of rain fell on us. Flashes of jagged lightning streaked wildly, and a steady roll of thunder shook the earth. In the cellar, we sat on boxes and waited for—we didn't know what.

The dirt walls of the cellar glowed dimly in the lantern light. Uncle John came down the steps, closed the door, and fastened it with a rope. He sat on the bottom step. "The wind has stopped blowing somewhat," he said, "but I believe it's only a lull before the storm."

Just then a roar and a bang told us that the storm had struck. Objects rattled overhead as they swept over the cellar roof, some striking the ventilator. It sounded as if a herd of stampeding steers were racing across the wooden cellar door. "Just listen to that hail!" Uncle John said in a low voice.

Water dripped down from the ventilator and ran in around the door. The floor soon was covered. Then the light went out, and we were in total darkness.

"I hope this hole doesn't fill up and drown us all," Mother whispered anxiously, lifting me to sit in her lap. "Let's pray the tornado doesn't pick the house up and set it down over the cellar."

I noted real quick that Mother and Uncle used different names for the storm. Uncle called it a cyclone, Mother spoke of it as a tornado. I wondered why.

There was nothing we could do but sit there in that hole in the darkness and listen to nature on a rampage, hoping the roof of the cellar wouldn't be lifted off. The whistling wind whipped toward the center of the storm; hailstones rattled on the door; a deluge of rainwater was gradually filling the cellar; and claps of thunder jarred the earth, sending dirt from the walls down our backs.

Mother said we were like cottontail rabbits trapped in a prairie dog hole by a giant rattlesnake, which buzzed furiously in the hole above.

"I believe the twister has passed," Uncle John said, at last, using an entirely different name for the storm.

He raised the door, stuck his head out, and waited for a flash of lightning to show him what the storm had done. "The house is still there," he told us, "but it isn't where it used to be."

Uncle lighted the lantern, and we came out of the cellar. Hailstones the size of hen eggs covered the ground. The house was rightside-up, but flat on the ground about a hundred feet from the blocks upon which it had rested. The door was jammed, and we couldn't open it. Most of the windows were broken. Uncle helped us in through one of them.

Mother thought we had been on the outside edge of the storm. She was right. We heard the next day that some people were killed and others injured in a community nearby. I learned a lot about such storms during the next few days, listening to Mother and her brother discuss the one we had gone through. They had both seen other storms by daylight. They said the violent rotating wind at the center of the twisting stem of the funnel-shaped cloud was the most destructive of any windstorm known. Mother told me the whirlwinds I saw on the plains were small tornadoes, without clouds, rain, or hail. This was the opening wedge for a question I wanted to ask.

"Mother, why do you call them tornadoes," I asked, "and Uncle John calls them cyclones and twisters?"

"They are commonly known as cyclones," she answered, "but their true name is tornado, which is a Spanish word meaning 'twister.' They were named this because of the whirling and twisting motion of the stem of the cloud."

Uncle John was very busy while we were there, but he found time to take us to visit Fort Reno. The fort was on a hill, with an Indian encampment in a circle around it, and there were soldiers all around. Another time, he took us to El Reno. There were many Indians on the streets. "They received their allotment from the government today," he explained, "and came to town to blow it in."

"When the Indians get their allowance from the government, he said, "they come to town and the merchants get them in their stores, salute them with a 'How,' pat them on the back, and call all of them 'John.' Then they sell them most anything—even things they don't need—to get their money."

He pointed down the street, saying, "There's a good example."

An old Indian perched on top of a hearse drawn by a team of Indian ponies came riding along. His wife and papooses sat on the floor of the glass-enclosed body, proudly waving at other Indians as they drove along.

Mother took me into an El Reno clothing store where she bought me a suit and a complete new outfit. "I want to have his picture taken," she told her brother.

She dressed me in a little velvet suit with gold braid down the front of the coat and around the cuffs. I wore a white blouse with a white stiff collar which spread out over the shoulders. A pair of black button shoes and a stiff straw hat completed my new rigging. Attired in the outfit, I looked in a mirror. What I saw didn't please me. With a frown on my face, I growled: "I don't want to wear these ol' things. They make me look like a girl. I don't want these ol' button shoes or this sissy straw hat. Old Jeff and the cowhands will make fun of me. I ain't gonna wear it!"

"You *are* going to wear that nice little suit and the other things," my mother told me, "and you're going to have your picture taken."

I pouted, "I don't want my picture took nohow! Not with these things on."

She was adamant. "Mother, you let these storekeepers do you just like they do the Indians," I muttered. "Let them get you in their store, talk nice to you, and sell you things for me that I don't *want* and don't *need*, just like they did when they sold that old Indian the funeral wagon we saw him driving down the street a while ago."

She finally softened a little. "Come on now, like a little *man*," she said. "Have your picture taken with them on, then you can take them off."

At the studio, the photographer stood us beside what looked like a big boulder with a hole in it, in front of a canvas with trees, a house, and a fence with a gate painted on it. I was shy and wouldn't look the camera in the face.

"Look right there at that hole and you will see a bird come out of it," he said. I did, and he squeezed a rubber thing in his hand. I heard something click, but didn't see any bird.

We said good-by to Uncle John in El Reno, and went to Guthrie, Oklahoma, to visit one of Mother's sisters, who, with her husband, Edgar Fees, had settled there when it was a tent town. He was a cabinetmaker.

On our return trip, we traveled to Fort Worth over a different railroad.

Mother never got the little velvet suit on me any more. I soon outgrew it and was glad when I did. While going home on the train, I put the straw hat on and stuck my head out of the window. The wind took the hat bye-bye. The last time I saw it, it was rolling on its brim down a steep incline along the track. I considered it good riddance and was glad Old Jeff and the cowhands would never see it, because if they had, my reputation among them as a real *he*-boy would have been irrevocably ruined. They probably would have hung a sissy moniker on me.

8.

The View from the Bank
of the Water Tank

DURING my boyhood days in the 1880's and 1890's, before I was large enough to make a hand, I was never lonesome when Uncle George, Old Jeff, and the cowhands were there. I tagged around after them like a little dogie calf with the "dry" cattle. But when they were away, I had to find some other form of pastime to while away the lonely hours.

From an aerial view, the ranch would have looked like a huge spider web. The house and other buildings, with the windmill and trees, formed the center, and the cowtrails leading off in every direction were the threads of the web.

One of my favorite spots for playing was the dump of the fenced water tank. I would sit on the Bermuda grass in the shade of cottonwood, poplar, and willow trees, watching the cattle and wild range horses come in to water in the heat of the day. After drinking their fill, many of the cattle would walk off a short distance from the troughs to where chunks of rock-salt lay on the ground and lick the salt, then come back to drink some more water. Some of the cows would hurriedly drink all they could hold, then trot back along the trail in the direction from which they had come. "When you see a cow do that," the cowhands said, "you can bet she has a little calf hidden out on the prairie that is too weak to make the trip to the watering place, and she is hurrying back before a sneaking coyote finds and kills it."

The bald-face Hereford, Durham, and other breeds of cattle had not yet been introduced to the plains. The cattle I saw coming in were a conglomeration of colors. There were blacks, browns, whites, yellows, brindles, duns with stripes down their backs, and other mixtures of color. Wild range cattle had horns of every size and shape. Most of the cows carried small sharp-pointed horns. The bulls' horns were mostly rather short and stubby. But the steers' horns were entirely different. Some pointed almost straight out from each side of the head in graceful twists. Others pointed nearly straight out in front of the head and curved upward. Still others pointed straight ahead as if built to kill. One old steer carried a graceful horn on one side of its head, but its other horn, which had been broken, curved around until the point was almost in its eye.

I remember another old steer with an extra-wide spread that kept other cattle horned away from the trough. One day I threw a rock at it and scared it away. Its horns were like the pair on the wall over the fireplace in the living room of our ranch house. I had helped Uncle prepare these horns for mounting by scraping them to a glassy smoothness with broken pieces of windowpane. They measured about eight feet from tip to tip, and these were the horns he used as a rack for his .45–90 caliber buffalo guns.

Once a little dogie, as pot-bellied motherless calves were called, crawled through the wire fence that surrounded the water tank and grazed upon the green Bermuda grass near me. I lay real quiet so as not to frighten it away until it filled its little potbelly with the succulent grass that couldn't be found out on the prairie.

I watched another little dogie as it eased up and put its head between the hind legs of another calf's mother and pilfered some milk from the hind teat while the cow was busy drinking from the trough. I had a sympathetic feeling for them, because Mother likened them to little orphan boys without father or mother to provide for them. Old Jeff told me they were calves whose trifling old daddy had run off with another cow when the mother died.

The cattle on the open range belonged to several different outfits. But even as a child, I learned to tell by the way their ears were marked what brand they carried. As a matter of fact, I learned the letters of the alphabet from A to Z by reading brands on cattle.

The brands were as varied as man's imagination. Some letters were coupled together, and others were inverted or lying down. Some were symbols given special names by their owners. The cow outfits were best known by the names of their brands, such as the LFD, the Turkey Track, and the DZ.

Looking the animals over as they came in to water was like watching a three-ring circus. I especially liked to watch for Uncle George's two old buffalo bulls. They both carried Uncle's brand, and were the only buffaloes left in that part of the Llano Estacado, where so many of their kind had roamed only a few years before.

One walked with a limp, having been crippled when it was branded. Their shaggy humps resembled two loads of hay as they moved along a trail toward the water trough. The range cattle gave them plenty of room. The cowhands said it was impossible to keep them in the roundup when they brought in the range cattle during a circle drive. The buffaloes would leave, regardless of what was in their way.

The crippled buffalo finally died, and Uncle sold the other one to a rancher named McKenzie for one hundred dollars. One day a greenhorn who was greasing windmills for McKenzie saw the old buffalo coming in to water at one of the windmills. He grabbed his rifle, hid inside the water tank, and killed the buffalo while it was drinking. Told he had killed a tame buffalo belonging to his employer, the tenderfoot left the country real suddenly, fearing, no doubt, that he might meet the same fate as the buffalo.

When I first came to the Llano Estacado, buffalo skulls with the horns on were still plentiful on the prairie. Homeseekers coming through in wagon trains often picked them up as souvenirs.

Bunches of range mares, or "broomtails," as the cowhands called them, often came trotting through the herd of cattle to the water trough. In charge of each bunch was a beautiful stallion, who zealously prevented his harem from mixing with other small groups. They were part of a herd of approximately one thousand that Uncle ran on the free grass of the open range. The wilder horses came in to water at night. Many of the range mares were offspring of the mustangs Uncle George and Old Jeff had domesticated. Colts from these mares were sold to ranchers for cow ponies. Others were sold for polo ponies.

Several bunches of Mexican burros, many of which roamed the plains, also came in to water. An old jack would run along in front, ears laid back and mouth wide open, braying. My first mount was one of those little creatures, broken by the cowhands for me to ride bareback before I was given my first saddle. It was a stubborn and ornery little cuss, with a will of its own and the "show me" attitude of a close relative, the *mule!*

The scene from the tank bank was always interesting. In the distance, off on the prairie, heat waves shimmered and danced along the horizon. They might change in a moment, and a distant mirage, resembling a cool lake of water with objects in it all disconnected from the earth, would appear. At other times, several whirlwinds might be seen—slender columns of dust extending upward several hundred feet, funnel-shaped at the top. Sometimes they traveled rapidly, picking up dust as they crossed cow trails and other spots bare of vegetation. Tumbleweeds and other objects too heavy for the wind to pick up rolled merrily along behind the miniature twisters. Occasionally a whirlwind swept over the watering place and caused the tail and wheel of the Eclipse windmill to swing around and fold together and make several complete revolutions.

Once while I lay sprawled out on the grassy bank, I saw our old tomcat mosey out from the house, lie down in the shade, and promptly go to sleep. An old mockingbird that had young ones in a nest in one of the trees swooped down and squawked at the cat, but Old Tom didn't even open his eyes. The cat knew from past experience that it would be a waste of energy to try to capture the wise old bird that had been there several years. The bird was tame and would pick food out of my hand. We wondered where it came from. Someone thought it might have been a pet that strayed from a covered wagon passing through the country.

On this day, Mother's chickens squawked in alarm and fled for cover, and I saw a chicken hawk circling the ranch. Suddenly it dived into a clump of catclaw bushes and came up with an object in its claws. A cottontail rabbit or a quail had been too slow in hunting cover.

Another time, I watched a chaparral cock—the cowhands called it a "road runner"—running rapidly along a trail to the water tank. All at once, it spread its tail feathers to a fan shape, put on its brakes, and slid to a stop. After looking all around, it hopped up on a fence post, then over on the tank dump, and disappeared from view as it walked down to the water edge. It soon came back, perched on a post, and sat watching something on the ground intently. Suddenly it dived down and came up with a green lizard in its beak. I wondered why Old Jeff sometimes remarked that something or someone was "crazy as a road runner." This one wasn't crazy, I thought, judging from the way it caught the lizard.

A person traveling across the plains on horseback or in a vehicle could easily see why the bird was called "road runner." Out of nowhere, one would show up in the road or trail ahead of you and lead your horse or team for long distances, traveling at the same rate of speed you were traveling. I could never find anyone who could tell me why they did that. Jeff said that proved they were crazy. I would agree that they were crazy if I saw one trying to lead a modern automobile down a paved highway today.

A vaquero from Old Mexico who worked at the ranch told me he sat on his horse one time and watched one of those birds kill a rattlesnake. He said the snake was coiled up in a position to strike. The chaparral cock stood off out of reach of the snake staring at it with a fixed look eye-to-eye, moving its head from side to side with a pendulum motion. Slowly it moved in a circle around the snake until it was behind the rattler's head, then suddenly it jumped and struck the snake's head with its beak. After that the snake was at the bird's mercy.

Some lonely days when I would roll over on my back and look at the sky through the branches of the trees overhead, I might spot a dark object against the background of the blue sky or a thunderhead cloud. Traveling in circles, it would gradually become smaller and smaller and finally disappear from view. I knew it was a bald eagle and wondered where it was going. I wondered, too, why human beings couldn't have wings and fly among the clouds in that manner. I thought of pictures in Mother's Bible that lay on the center table in our living room—pictures of angels flying about. Uncle George told me the eagles seen on the Great Plains were mostly bald eagles, whereas the larger ones, known as golden eagles, were found in the mountains to the west. He also said the eagles we saw around our ranch built their nests among the rocks high up on the face of the cliffs of the Cap Rock escarpment along the breaks of the plains because there were few trees on the Llano Estacado large enough to hold their nests.

Old Jeff said the Comanches used the feathers from the bald eagle for plumes to fashion their headdresses. The Indians farther west were able to obtain the gorgeous tail feathers of the golden eagle for plumage in their war bonnets. He said the bald eagle usually preyed upon cottontails and jack rabbits, prairie chickens, and other birds, such as ducks and geese when the surface lakes were full of water. He had also seen them attack young antelopes, but had never known one to try to carry a small calf away to its eyrie to feed to its young.

Once while lying on the bank, I dozed off to sleep and was awakened by voices. Old Negro Ad and another cowpuncher who worked for the LFD outfit were at the water trough leaning over their saddle horns giving their horses free rein to drink. The shade had moved while I was asleep, and I was lying in the hot sun.

"You'd better not sleep in the hot sunshine," the old Negro told me. "It might give you a fever."

They rode around to the windmill for a drink of water out of the barrel, then rode around among the cattle—probably looking for unbranded calves which had been missed in the roundup —then headed north toward Four Lakes.

Mother called me about that time and said to bring her a bucket of fresh water and eat some doughnuts she had just finished cooking. I headed for the house with Old Tom trailing along behind me.

In the spring of the year, hard winds often blew from the southwest for several days at a time, filling the atmosphere with dust so that the sun at noonday resembled a ball of fire. The dust around the watering place where the grass had been trampled off by stock rose in clouds and cut my face like sleet.

During those sandstorms the cattle on the prairie stood with tails to the wind, their heads lowered and their eyes closed. Mules and cow ponies in the horse pasture came in and stood behind the rock corrals and sheds for some protection from the wind and dust. I spent a lot of time on such days in Uncle's room prowling through his relics of Indian-fighting and buffalo-hunting days.

The fine sand sifted into the house, forming a coating over everything. A person could write his name in the dust film on the table top. Mother covered everything she could, but when we ate, we could feel the gritty sand between our teeth.

The hard wind would fold the tail and wheel of the windmill together, and this would stop the wheel from turning. We could hear tin cans rolling across the yard and pebbles striking the doors and windowpanes. When one of Mother's old hens would venture outside the henhouse, the wind would almost turn her wrongside-out.

Sometimes, prairie fires broke out while the sandstorms blew. The winds caused the flames to travel rapidly through the dry grass and across the level plains, doing great damage to the range. Some ranchers protected their houses and watering places from those fires by burning fireguards around the dwellings and other structures.

If a fire broke out when thunderheads were in the sky, it

was blamed on lightning. Other fires started when cowhands dismounted on cold mornings, set fire to dry shoots around yucca plants to warm their feet, and allowed the blaze to get out of control. Many fires were caused by careless campers who left their campfires burning instead of extinguishing them with water or dirt. Sparks from these unattended smoldering embers were carried by the wind into dry grass. Occasionally, fires were started maliciously with intent to do someone harm by burning off precious grass, making it necessary to move whole herds of cattle to other ranges. The red, angry reflection of a prairie fire on the sky could be seen for many miles at night, and the smoke was visible great distances in the daytime. When a prairie fire broke out, everyone turned out to fight it.

One night during one of those windy periods, I was awakened by voices downstairs. I became aware at once that the room was as light as day. Looking out the window, I saw the red glow of a fire that appeared to be several miles from the ranch, in the direction from which the wind was coming. The cowhands had been roused, and were getting ready to go out and fight it. I begged Mother to let me go with them. She agreed, and I hastily dressed, shaking with excitement.

The cowhands hitched a team of mules to a wagon, drove it to the water trough, and put three barrels in the wagon bed and filled them with water. They suspended a full bucket of water in each barrel with a stick that ran through the bucket bail and across the top of the barrel. The stick held the bucket up and kept the water from sloshing out. Tarpaulins were tied over the tops of the barrels.

We gathered up all the gunnysacks, pieces of wagon sheets, tarpaulins, and saddle blankets we could find that would be large enough to beat the burning grass and tossed them into the wagon bed. Two of the men, with me in the spring seat between them, rode to the fire in the wagon. The other men went on horseback. Some of the men on horses went to the lead fire to "backfire" against it, by setting a controlled fire to the grass ahead of the main blaze. The rest of the men went to the rear of the blaze.

63

As we approached the fire, we met cattle, horses, antelopes, jack rabbits, coyotes, and other animals running ahead of the licking flames. Two of the men on horseback roped and killed a two-year-old heifer, cut it open from throat to tail along the breast and belly, then broke the ribs so that it would lie flat on the flesh side. Two men fastened their thirty-foot ropes to the animal's hind feet and the other end to their saddle horns. Straddling the line of burning grass, they dragged the carcass over the flames. The wet side of the carcass smothered most of the fire it moved over.

The other men tied their saddle horses to the wagon and walked. One man in the wagon handed them wet cloths dipped in the water barrels. With these the walking men beat out the flames missed by the dragged carcass. The men with horses took turns dragging the carcass so that the horses could rest from the grueling ordeal and the smoke and heat.

Sometimes the wind fanned smoldering cow chips into a flame and touched off the grass behind us. Then someone would have to go back and beat the fire out before it got out of hand. We worked on up the fireline until we met the LFD cowpunchers who had worked up the other side of the fire, and it was out, but not before it had burned off a considerable portion of the range.

When we arrived back at the ranch, I was lying on the damp cloths on the floor of the wagon bed under the spring seat sound asleep. The cowhands told Mother I was a good firefighter, and I really showed it. My hair and eyebrows were singed, and my face was black with smoke and soot. She took one look at me and hustled me off to a washtub full of soapy water in the kitchen before letting me sit down to breakfast.

9.

Little Red — Horse Trainer

WATERING places on the Llano Estacado in the early days were widely scattered, and the trails that crossed the plains went from water hole to distant water hole. Our ranch with its windmill became a well-known stopping place.

Sometimes on moonlit nights we would see men on horseback ride up to the water trough, water their horses, get themselves a drink of water, fill their canteens, then ride away. "Some *hombres* on the dodge," Old Jeff would mutter.

Often between roundup seasons cowhands who had been laid off at the large ranches would stop at our place while riding the chuck line. They would make the rounds to different cow camps and ranches, staying several days at each one, where their meals cost them nothing, until the next roundup time started and they could return to work.

There was always a job at our horse ranch for any wandering cowboy good at handling and breaking young horses, but he didn't last long if he couldn't break horses properly. The usefulness of a horse depended on the way it was broken and handled from the beginning.

As a rule, the ranch boss could size up a man by his appearance, his belongings, and the way he walked, talked, and sat in his saddle. But once in a while the boss was fooled.

Late one evening, a young man wearing a floppy old black wool hat and custom-made boots with run-over heels rode up to our ranch on a handsome blood bay leading a coal-black gelding that carried his bedroll. The rider asked permission to spend the night and, receiving it, unloaded his bed at the sheds near the corrals instead of at the bunkhouse. He staked one of his horses in the pasture back of the corrals and turned the other one loose.

After supper, he refused an invitation from the other hands to sleep in the bunkhouse. He thanked them and said he would rather sleep in the open.

Old Ad, the Negro LFD cowpuncher, was present, and, believing the boy to be another greenhorn like many others who stopped at the ranch, warned him, "Boy, you'd better watch out, there's lots of polecats hang around them rock corrals and sheds, and sometimes they go mad."

The boy's appearance led our seasoned cowhands to decide he was another "lint" from Central Texas. They claimed cotton lint still hung from the clothing of these wanderers from dragging a cotton sack in the cotton fields.

The man's bedroll didn't look like that of an experienced cowhand, and he was riding a "center fire," a saddle seldom seen in that part of the country. Such a saddle would work forward and cause sores on a horse's withers.

The cowpunchers had just finished rounding up, and the horse pasture was full of young geldings that had been gathered to be broken and sold for use as cow ponies. Our hands had started breaking them a few days before. After breakfast, some of the broncs were brought in and corralled, and the stranger went out to look them over. He spoke to the boss. "How about giving me a job breaking broncs?"

The tough old ranch boss, who had hired many bronc twisters

during his day on the range, looked the boy over from the crown of his old wool hat to the toes of his run-over boots and asked, "Have you ever done any of that kind of work?"

"I've rode a few broncs," the boy replied.

"All right," the boss said. "Come to the house and I'll sign you up."

The foreman got his ledger—in which he kept a record of the hands' names, rates of pay, and other personal information—and asked, "What's your name?"

The boy ran his fingers through his fiery red hair and declared, "They call me 'Red.' "

"That makes it bad," the boss murmured. "I already have one 'Red' on the books; but he is taller than you, so I'll put you down as 'Little Red.' " And thereafter, he was known by that name.

Among the broncs corralled that morning was a black the cowhands had named "Black Panther" because of its color and the way it squealed when a rider crawled aboard. It had thrown every man who had tried to ride it so far. Since it was in the corral, they knew someone would have to try to ride it that day.

When the boss and Little Red returned to the corral, the boss mounted his horse and cut the Black Panther through a gate into the small rock-walled round corral. He dropped a loop around its neck and told Little Red to go down the line and put his hackamore on it.

Old Negro Ad walked up to where the boss was sitting on his horse and whispered, "Ye ain't gonna give that rabbit twister that varmint to ride, is ye?"

"Yes," the boss replied, "I want to see if he can really ride. If he can stay on that horse, I'll give him a steady job." The old Negro shrugged and walked away shaking his head.

Little Red put his hackamore on the bronc, tied a rope around its neck just ahead of its shoulders, then spread a loop on the ground. When the horse stepped into the loop with its left hind foot, Red drew the foot up close to its shoulder and tied it fast. With the gelding in that almost helpless condition, Little Red began making friends with it by rubbing and patting it as he moved around on both sides. Then he jumped up and lay with his stomach across the bronc's back. Later, he swung a leg over and sat on it astride, still patting and rubbing its neck and hips as if trying to create a mutual understanding. He talked to the horse continuously in a low voice.

When Red stood on the ground again, the bronc bit at him. He caught the cheek of the hackamore and held the horse's head while he put his saddle blanket on its back several times. He eased his saddle on its back, cinched it up tight, then removed the boss's rope from the horse's neck.

The other cowhands perched on the corral fence watching the show. "Have you made your last will and testament?" one of them yelled. "Any word you want to send to your best gal?" another asked. The red-headed bronc peeler ignored their wise-cracks.

Little Red asked Ad to help him mount, and the old Negro said, "Ain't you gonna let the hoss pitch around in the corral with just your saddle on before you get on him?" The boy shook his head.

Ad held the horse by both ears, the end of one ear clamped between his snaggled teeth, and covered the bronc's eyes with his forearms. Red removed the rope from the horse's foot, crawled aboard, and settled into the saddle. Then he nodded for Ad to turn the gelding loose.

The black knew what was on its back and ran across the corral into the fence, almost catching a cowpuncher's foot inside the wall. It reared straight up with a vicious squeal and toppled over backwards. Instead of being caught under the saddle horn when the horse hit the ground, Little Red nimbly stepped off as the animal fell. When the horse rolled over on its side, Red placed his foot on the saddle horn and held the kicking horse down for a few moments. Then as the black struggled to its feet, the boy slipped into the saddle and came up with it.

The head-on collision with the fence seemed to have addled the horse's brain. After regaining its feet, it stood spraddle-legged for a few seconds, then started circling the fence trying to rub

68

the rider off its back. Little Red called for someone to open the gate and let them out.

The boss and Ad opened the outside gate, then stationed themselves on either side of the opening to herd the bronc away from nearby barbed-wire fences.

Old Ad built a loop in one end of his rope and double half-hitched the other end to his saddle horn. He was prepared to go to the boy's rescue if the horse should fall or the saddle should happen to turn under the bronc's belly and the rider's foot get hung up in a stirrup.

Circling the corral, the horse saw the opening and went through it, almost dragging the rider off against a gatepost. Little Red tried to hold the horse's head up, but it finally got its nose between its forefeet and fell to pieces.

The antics that horse performed in the next few minutes were called "bucking" by cowhands in some parts of the West, but there it was known as "pitching," and that potro could sure pitch.

The single-cinch saddle sitting slightly ahead toward the withers gave the horse free use of its whole body. It could get a hump in its back, twist and weave without hindrance, and hit the ground with all feet close together like a pile driver.

The wisecracking onlookers perched on the fence, watching with professional interest as the boy made his ride. The Black Panther was

Squealing, pitching, having walleyed fits,
All feet close together, with front feet in the bits.
He fenced rowed, sunfished, changed ends in midair,
Every time he hit the ground, found Red still sitting there,
Watching Panther's movements as he hula danced and turned,
Fanning with his old wool hat, completely unconcerned.

Expressions of amazement and surprise came from the waddies watching the show as they yelled in unison, "Ride 'im cowboy!"

"That cowboy ain't no rabbit twister or cotton picker," one

yelled. "He learned to ride someplace besides on a mule in a cotton patch!"

When the horse quit pitching and started to run, Ad rode alongside, took the hackamore rope, and guided the gelding back into the corral. Then he snubbed the heaving horse's head up close to the saddle horn while Little Red dismounted.

Red continued topping off the horse every few days, and soon had it so docile that he claimed a woman would be safe riding it with a sidesaddle.

Little Red wasn't just a bronc rider, whose only interest in a horse was to be able to ride it till it quit pitching then climb aboard another bronc. He considered himself a horse trainer. Today he might be called a "horse psychiatrist," because he had the knack of diagnosing and administering to mentally disturbed young horses, saving them from becoming hardened outlaws. Little Red was a teacher and the horse was his pupil. He tried to gain a young horse's confidence and companionship by using kind words and gentle methods of handling. He would fight anyone who beat a horse over the head with a quirt or double of a rope. He tried to have enough "horse sense" to be able to teach his pupils "cow sense."

In those days when the herds of horses ran on the open range, there was one type neither he nor anyone else could do much with. These horses ate locoweed, which sapped their vitality and addled their brains. Continually doped, they couldn't be led with rope, hackamore, or bridle. They were dangerous and flighty and would spook at their own shadows, rearing up and falling back with their riders. They were plainly beyond the aid of psychiatric treatment.

After he was given a steady job at the ranch, Little Red moved into the bunkhouse with the other cowhands. But still he was a lone wolf with little to say to anyone, and he kept to himself as much as possible. I tagged around the ranch after him, to the corrals and into the bunkhouse, like a dogie calf following its foster mother.

He had more to say to me than anyone else on the ranch. If

a stranger rode up, he always sent me to find out who he was with instructions to hurry back and tell him. Once I heard Uncle George and Old Jeff discussing his strange ways. But being small, I paid no attention to their talk.

Red's two horses, the bay he called Red Bird and the black he called Nigger, were well trained. He told me he could be asleep on the prairie and if anything unusual showed up, they would snort and, if necessary, nudge him with their noses to awaken him. When he rode one, the other followed him with a pack on its back without a lead rope. He always kept one of his horses staked out in the horse pasture, and when on roundup, they remained in the remuda. He kept a Winchester rifle in a scabbard on his saddle under the right stirrup leather.

Sometimes Little Red rode away from the ranch and disappeared for a week or ten days at a time. When he returned, he never told where he had been, and none of us asked him. He always took both his horses with him and sometimes his bedroll. He usually left the ranch at night and no one knew in which direction he went. I wanted to ask him where he went, but Mother said, "No."

One day when I was sweeping the bunkhouse floor, Red's bed was rolled up but not strapped. I moved it around and it came unrolled. A money belt fell out of his war bag and uncoiled like a snake. Childlike, I peeped in it and saw that it was filled with currency and gold coins—more money than I had ever seen in my life.

That evening while sitting in front of the fireplace in our living room, I told Uncle George and Mother what I had found in Little Red's bed. They sat there staring at the coals in the fireplace and said nothing. I knew they didn't wish to talk about it in my presence.

One day after the fall roundup was over, the hands took the wagons to the west breaks of the plains to gather dead mesquite roots and scrub cedar for our winter fuel supply. Red was away from the ranch on one of his periodical trips, and Mother and I were at the ranch alone. We were eating supper when we heard a horse walk up near the kitchen door and a voice call for help. Running outside, we found Little Red on Red Bird sprawled across his bed still packed on the horse's back. I looked for Nigger, but he was nowhere in sight.

"Help me down," Red whispered. "Into the bunkhouse."

We led his horse to the bunkhouse door. Red slid off, and we helped him inside. I lighted a lantern and rolled out a bed, and we laid him down. Mother held the light close to him, and we saw that his clothes were covered with blood.

"I've been shot below the left shoulder," he murmured faintly.

Mother cut Red's shirt away and found where the bullet had entered his body below the left collarbone. While Mother heated water, I pulled off Red's boots and made him as comfortable as possible. Mother bathed and dressed the wound, using strips from a bed sheet for bandages.

There was little else we could do until the men returned the next day. Mother made him some soup, and I unpacked Red Bird and turned him into the horse pasture.

I took a wash pan out to the windmill and caught some cool water as it flowed from the pipe and washed Red's face and hands. I placed the cold rag on his forehead. "That feels good," he said.

"Who shot you?" I asked him.

"Indians," he answered laconically.

"Oh, Red, you know that ain't so," I told him. "You told me yourself that the Indians are all gone from the plains."

"I'll tell you what you do," he said, sidetracking the subject; "roll me a Durham cigarette and let me have just one puff."

We watched over him through the long night. Toward morning his temperature rose, and I was kept busy placing wet cloths on his forehead to keep his fever down. With her limited supply of medicine, Mother did what she could for him.

"Reckon who shot him?" I asked her.

"I don't know," she answered.

"Do you think he'll die?" I whispered.

"I hope not," she replied.

72

Little Red became delirious and murmured words out of his head. We leaned down close and heard him say something about "Mother."

For a few moments he became rational and asked Mother to write down a name and address—his mother's—and to write to her and tell her about him if he should die.

As day was breaking over the plains, Little Red suddenly stiffened and gasped. Mother had her finger on his pulse. After a moment she looked at me with misty eyes and whispered, "He's dead."

We straightened out his legs, crossed his wrists over his breast, placed silver dollars on his closed eyelids, and pulled the tarp up over his face.

A little while after sunup, two heavily armed men rode up. They told us they were Texas Rangers, and asked if we had seen a man riding a bay horse who might have been wounded.

"He died last night and is lying out in the bunkhouse," Mother told them.

They asked if they could see him for identification. We took them to the bunkhouse. They raised the tarpaulin and one exclaimed, "That's him."

"Where's his black horse?" I asked.

"A black horse was killed," one of them answered.

They mounted their horses and rode off, back toward the Texas line.

When the hands returned the next day, they made a coffin from thick cypress boards that had been bought to build a water trough. Uncle George said that kind of lumber would make a good coffin, being practically waterproof and slow to decay. They placed Little Red's body in it and dug a grave out in the horse pasture.

As the cowhands stood around the grave with their hats in their hands, Uncle George read a few verses from Mother's Bible. Then she led us in the moving words of the Twenty-Third Psalm: "The Lord is my shepherd; I shall not want . . . ."

73

We filled the grave and stacked a pile of rocks on top and around the mound.

Mother wrote the letter Little Red had asked her to write, but she had trouble getting it worded to her satisfaction. When she was finished, she sealed it without showing it to anyone. Gathering Little Red's belongings, she put them in a box with his money and sent the box and letter to the railroad to be mailed to the address he had given her.

One evening about three months later, two men drove up to the ranch in a spring wagon. One introduced himself as an undertaker from Midland, and gave Mother a sealed envelope addressed to her. It contained a letter from Little Red's mother, asking that the bearer be allowed to exhume the remains of her son for shipment to her home.

The visitors spent the night at the ranch. Early the next morning, the two men opened the grave and the men at the ranch helped them lift the cypress casket up and into the spring wagon, where it was securely strapped and covered with a tarpaulin. They then headed southeast toward the railroad.

10.

An Ex-Jingle-Bob Cowhand

BEFORE drift fences were built on the southeastern part of the Staked Plains in New Mexico, the large cattle ranchers on the open range maintained "line camps" where cowhands called "line riders" stayed during the winter months and "rode line" to keep the herds of cattle on the range when the blue northers and fierce blizzards caused them to drift.

A frequent visitor at our ranch was an old man who stayed in a line camp near the west breaks of the plains southwest of our ranch. He rode line toward the east from his camp each day until he met a man riding west from another camp in Texas. After visiting for a while, they then returned to their individual camps.

Our visitor was a man low in stature and heavy set, and was known over the range by his nickname, "Shorty." He often came by our ranch and stopped for dinner. He seemed to like little boys, so I cultivated him as a pal, and many times I coaxed him into spending the night with us.

The main reason I enjoyed having him stay overnight was that he told stories of the early days of cattle ranching along the

Pecos River, where he worked many years for "Jingle-bob" John Chisum, when Chisum was known as the cattle king of the Pecos River.

When he consented to stay, I would unsaddle his horse, feed and water it, then turn it into the horse pasture. I would also feed and saddle it for him the next morning.

Shorty's white mustache and beard were stained from Star Navy chewing tobacco. His white hair hung down almost to his shoulders. "If I don't get my mane roached," he told me, "I'll have to plait it and wear it in a pigtail down my back like a Chinaman."

He was badly crippled with rheumatism and very bow-legged from many years astride a horse. His bowlegs wouldn't allow his footprints to line up when walking, and each foot made a separate row of tracks. This affliction also caused the high heels on his boots to "run over."

He carried two scars where slugs of lead had entered his body. He said they were relics of the Lincoln County War, in which Billy the Kid figured. "When I die," he told me, "it will probably be from blood poisoning."

When he sat at the table eating his meals, his hand shook so badly that at times he would spill much of the contents of his cup before getting it to his mouth, so he usually asked for only a half-cupful. He strained the coffee through his walrus mustache, then pushed the mustache into his mouth with a forefinger to suck out the remaining coffee.

Frijole beans wouldn't stay on his fork, so he always asked for a spoon with which to shovel them up. At times, when stabbing at a hunk of beefsteak in his plate, his fork missed it entirely. Child-like, I enjoyed watching all these operations.

After supper, Shorty and I would go to the bunkhouse and I would hunt up the bootjack to pull off his boots for him. Then I'd go out to the windmill and catch a gourd dipperful of cool water right out of the pipe. He would show me how he could drink it with a cud of chewing tobacco in his mouth without making himself sick, as I did when I tried it one time. Then I would hunt up a tin can and partly fill it with cow-chip ashes for him to spit tobacco juice into while telling me stories of his life along the Pecos River with the Jingle-bob outfit at their head-quarters ranch at Bosque Grande, and his version of "the taming of the Old West."

Settling himself in a broken-down splint-bottom chair and propping his gnarled and bent legs on a rawhide trunk, he would clear his throat, expectorate into the can I had provided, and begin:

"Son, a lot of people nowadays confuse the name of Jingle-bob Chisum with that of Jesse Chisholm for whom the Chisholm Trail was named, which went from Red River up across the Indian Nation to the cattle shipping pens at Abilene, Kansas. They were different men, and their names weren't even spelled alike.

"Jingle-bob John drove herds of Texas cattle across Louisiana before the Chisholm Trail was thought of. He settled where the town of Paris, Texas, is now located. He built the first house there. He also built the first courthouse in Paris, Texas. I was with him when he moved his cattle to the North, Middle, and South forks of the Concho River in West Texas, where Fort Concho was later built to protect ranchers from the Comanche Indians on the Staked Plains to the north.

"In 1867, I helped Chisum drive a herd across that waterless stretch of West Texas from the Concho River to the Horsehead Crossing on the Pecos River. After crossing the river, Chisum turned due north. He was headed for Fort Sumner, New Mexico, where he intended to sell the herd to the U.S. Army to feed the Navaho Indians Kit Carson had rounded up and taken to the Río Pecos.

"Chisum made Bosque Grande, which is about thirty miles south of Fort Sumner, his headquarters ranch. Now, in case you don't know what Bosque Grande means, I'll tell you. It is a big grove of trees on the Pecos River, and in Mexican lingo, Bosque Grande means 'Large Grove.'

"Boy, in later years there were so many durned cow rustlers and hoss thieves hanged from the limbs of them cottonwood trees, the grove came to be plumb ha'nted. Night horses staked out with a rope would get scared, break loose, and run off. And even old chuck wagon mules would hightail and *vamoose*. I've heard cowpunchers claim they could hear chains rattling at night, and sounds like someone gasping for breath with a rope around his neck."

Old Shorty enjoyed telling me his yarns as much as I enjoyed hearing them, sitting bug-eyed on a bedroll beside him. He told about helping Chisum drive herds of beef cattle to Fort Stanton, New Mexico, to the Apache Indian Reservation in Arizona, to the Gila River country, to Tucson, to Colorado, and to Dodge City. He knew and spoke of trail drivers Goodnight and Loving, who also trailed cattle up the Pecos River, and told how Loving was killed by Indians.

Old Jeff and three waddies were sitting cross-legged on a Navaho blanket spread out on the bunkhouse floor playing draw poker, using frijole beans valued at five cents each for counters. They were also listening attentively to Shorty's drawling narrative.

When Shorty mentioned Charles Goodnight, one of the old cowpunchers glanced up at him and said, "I was working for Goodnight when he moved his cattle into Palo Duro Canyon in the Texas Panhandle and started his JA ranch. He told me a lot about Bosque Grande and the Jingle-bob outfit."

My old pal decided to take another "chaw" of tobacco. He had only a few upper and lower snaggled teeth, none of which matched. This made it impossible for him to bite a chew from the plug. He reached in his pocket, pulled out his Barlow knife, picked one of his boots up, whetted the knife blade a few strokes on the instep of the boot, then cut several thin slices from the plug and crammed them into his mouth. Then he asked me to get him another dipperful of water with which to "wet my whistle."

"The Jingle-bob spread covered the west side of the Pecos River country," the old Chisum hand continued, "from Fort Sumner on the north to Eddy [now Carlsbad] on the south—a distance of around 175 miles. His cattle ranged from the Río Pecos to the mountains in the west, and watered along Seven Rivers, the Río Penasco, Walnut Creek, Río Felix, Río Hondo, and on north.

There was no limit to his range east of the Pecos, but there were no running streams to furnish water, and the sandy country between the Pecos and the breaks of the plains made it poor cow country. There was nothing here on the plains but mustangs, buffalo, antelope, and Comanche Indians.

"His spread was so big it was impossible for us waddies to ride the entire range and look after his cows. Many Jingle-bob cows walked out in the Pecos River to drink, got stuck in the quicksands, and drowned. Bands of Comanche Indians from the Staked Plains and Mescalero Apaches from the mountains in the west made raids on Chisum's herds and also swiped many of his hosses."

A young fellow in the poker game who came from Coke County, Texas, that year to punch cattle for the first time, asked Shorty how Chisum's outfit got its name.

"Well, son," the old fellow drawled, "John Chisum's outfit got its name from the way he marked his cows' ears, which was both ears cut with a 'jinglebob.'"

"How is that?" the waddy asked.

"Boy," Shorty replied, "if I had a longeared calf in here, I could show you better and in less time than I can tell you. I marked a lot of them, and Old John liked the way I did it. I cut the ears from the top of a slant down toward the cow's jaw, a little over halfway through. That left the upper part of the ear sticking up in a point, and the lower half dangling like the bob on a clock's pendulum. I don't know why Old John claimed that the bob 'jingled,' because I never heard them make any sounds."

"What was Chisum's brand?" the young cowhand asked.

"His brand was a stripe on the cow's side from shoulder to hip," Shorty answered. "He called it 'The Long Rail.'"

Shorty told about Chisum's building a ranch on South Spring River eight miles south of Roswell, New Mexico, and moving his headquarters there from Bosque Grande in 1873. He set out cottonwood and fruit trees and roses on his new ranch. He also planted fields of alfalfa and irrigated with water from the South Spring River. His niece Sallie and three of his brothers came to

79

live with him. The ranch became a popular stopping place, and all visitors were welcome.

Old Jeff looked over at Shorty. "Rustlers couldn't steal Chisum's cows by *blotting* his Long Rail brand," he said, "but I guess they used other ways of stealing them, didn't they?"

"They sure did," the old fellow replied. "The trouble started when nesters and ranchers with little herds started moving into Chisum's range and settled along Seven Rivers, Río Penasco, and up around White Oaks, Nogal, and Lincoln. They claimed Chisum was trying to keep them off his free grass.

"Many of them settlers brought their milk cows and a few head of cattle with them, and we noticed their herds increased awful fast. We found Jingle-bob mother cows that we knew had been killed for their unbranded calves. Any greenhorn could look at the dead cow's bag and tell that a calf had been sucking her. Around some of them small ranches, we saw as many as three calves following and sucking one cow—one on each side of the cow, and another with its head between her hind legs.

"They also stole a lot of his calves by making them 'sleepers.' You know a sleeper is a calf that is earmarked but not branded. They would cut the calf's ears with the jinglebob so any range rider would think it was branded. Then when the calf was weaned and quit following its mother, they put their brand on the calf and cut off the jinglebob part of the ear, and made an under-half-slope on both ears.

"Many Jingle-bob cattle were stolen and killed for beef. When we stopped at a settler's house and ate beef for dinner and couldn't see any hide hanging on his fence, we were pretty sure the beef had been rustled. I've seen hides with the Long Rail brand on that had been cut up and throwed in the river. I also found some that had been hid in bat caves."

Suddenly, Shorty arose from his chair and started hobbling about the room, complaining of cramps in both legs. Twilight was settling over the High Plains, and the November air became quite chilly after the sun went down.

I stirred up the fire in the fireplace, put some pine boards on it that were rich in turpentine, opened the damper in the chimney, and soon had a brisk fire burning. The old fellow stood in front of the flames with his hands on the mantel, absorbing the heat into his crippled legs. I pulled his chair up in front of the fireplace and he sat down, almost exhausted. He stretched his legs out toward the fire, and the cramps soon left him.

Old Jeff called me over. "Go to the kitchen," he whispered, "and get him a cup of coffee."

I brought him a half-cup of coffee and a cupful of water with which to rinse tobacco juice from his mouth. He dumped the cud of tobacco from his mouth into the can, rinsed his mouth, then sat sipping his steaming coffee and staring into the blazing fire.

The men at the ranch said the old fellow had bought a nice bunch of cattle with the money he saved while working for Chisum. But a dry year, followed by the blizzard of 1886–87, took many of his dogies. He spent most of his money traveling to different places taking treatment for his rheumatic condition.

One morning about a month after Shorty's visit, a cold wind was blowing out of the northeast. As the forenoon advanced, the sky became overcast, the temperature dropped, and snowflakes started falling. By midmorning we knew we were in for a blizzard.

Horses and mules in the horse pasture came in and stood in the shelter of the sheds and rock corrals. That afternoon, I stood at the window watching long strings of cattle drifting past the ranch with heads down and tails to the storm. Snowflakes were falling so thick I could hardly see the windmill, and deep drifts started forming around the house.

As darkness was settling over the plains, Uncle George filled a lantern with coal oil, trimmed the wick, lighted it, and hung it high up in the windmill tower as he always did during those storms.

I climbed the stairs of the rock house that night to my room under the bare rafters and snuggled up in my bed of Navaho and army blankets listening to the storm whistling outside. The fury seemed to increase as the night advanced.

I occasionally heard cattle bawling as they drifted past the ranch. I wondered how far my old line-riding pal would have to follow them after the storm was over to bring them back to the home range. I offered up a little request for his safety in my "Now I lay me down to sleep."

Young as I was, I believed Shorty was too old and decrepit to be compelled to rough it in a winter camp and ride the range in all kinds of weather in order to exist. But in those days, there was no old-age assistance or homes for senior citizens. If an elderly person didn't live with, or near, close relatives who would look after him in his old age, he had to "root hog or die."

When I awakened next morning, I cleared a windowpane and saw that the storm was still raging. With teeth chattering, I went downstairs to dress in front of the fireplace.

Uncle George came in and announced that he had found Shorty's horse, saddled, standing at our corral and feared the old fellow might have frozen to death in the storm. The bridle reins were tied together and still looped over the horse's neck, indicating that the rider might have fallen off. If the rider had dismounted, he would have taken the reins from over the horse's head and held them in his hand to prevent it from getting away.

As soon as travel was possible, the men at the ranch went to Shorty's camp to see his partner, who rode line to the west each day. He hadn't seen the old fellow since he left his camp the morning of the storm. He said he became worried when Shorty didn't return, but thought maybe he had stopped at our ranch, as he often did, until the storm was over.

When the snowdrifts had melted somewhat, the hands found Shorty's body lying on the south side of a clump of bushes with his riding slicker on and a bandanna tied around his head and ears. His hat was missing.

Burned matches lay around, indicating that he had used up what few he had in a vain effort to set fire to a pile of dead sticks and other material in the bushes that pack rats had gathered for a den. Partly protected from the wind by the brush, he had doubtless become drowsy and had frozen to death in his sleep.

They took his body to his camp, made a coffin from rough

pine boards, and buried him on a high point of the Cap Rock escarpment that jutted out from the west breaks of the Llano Estacado. There his spirit could look out across the vast expanse of the Pecos River valley where he had spent so many years of his life. The cowhands gathered flat rocks and built a monument over and around his grave, and let him rest in peace.

I missed the visits of my childhood crony, and it was difficult for me to realize that I would never see him again.

11.

Lawmen and Outlaw Overnight Visitors

ONE of my main pastimes when Old Jeff and the cowhands were away and Mother and I were at the ranch alone was to climb the windmill tower and lie on the narrow platform under the revolving wheel. With Uncle George's powerful field glasses I could look out over the surrounding prairie and see great distances. I could bring objects barely visible to the naked eye right up in front of me. I watched distant herds of antelopes, cattle, and horses, and once in a while I would pick up a coyote or a jack rabbit, or a covey of quail or prairie chickens.

Mother trembled for my safety when I lay on the platform on my stomach for an hour at a time. She was afraid I might fall asleep and roll off or a whirlwind might come along and fold the tail and wheel of the mill together, causing them to whirl around and knock me off my high resting place.

Occasionally, I saw trains of covered wagons headed our way along the trail to Shafter Lake and Midland. They were homeseekers from East Texas on their way to a homestead on the west side of the Pecos River.

Often they camped overnight at our ranch, and Mother usually gave them the forequarter of a beef to fill up their tribe of tow-headed youngsters. I was interested in the boys near my age, and I showed them around the ranch. We also played on the Bermuda grass around the water tank under the cottonwood and poplar trees. Sometimes I found a boy who knew how to play mumblety-peg. When I won, I had the pleasure of driving a peg into the ground and watching my opponent pull it out with his teeth.

Mother was very friendly and enjoyed visiting with those families when they stopped at the ranch. She remembered her own loneliness when she had first come to that remote place so far from civilization, medical aid, and a post office, with her nearest woman neighbor living twelve miles away.

Mother sympathized with those people, many of whom were hard up financially, hauling their worldly possessions in a covered wagon to an uncertain future on a homestead, unaware of the hardships they would have to endure. She did her best to make them realize they were welcome, and feel that her home was theirs while they were there.

She gave them fresh beef to eat and jerked meat to take with them, showing them different ways of cooking it. Some of the women also had Mother teach them the art of fermenting dough for making sourdough bread. She told them of primitive remedies for croup and other child's ailments, instructed them in giving first aid for rattlesnake bites, and warned them of the danger of being bitten by rabid skunks and centipedes when sleeping on the ground at night.

She cautioned them to cover their campfires with dirt when breaking camp to prevent live embers from being blown into grass and starting prairie fires. Visitors always seemed more hopeful when they left the ranch than they had been when they arrived.

One family with a sick horse stopped with us for several days. When the horse died, they told Mother they didn't know what they would do, since they didn't have any money to pay for another horse. She gave them a pony about twenty-five years old that was broken to harness. We called him "WX," which was the brand on his left shoulder.

Early one morning about ten days after this family headed on west, Mother was cooking breakfast and heard a horse walking around in the yard behind the kitchen. She opened the door, and there stood old WX where he was in the habit of picking up scraps of sourdough biscuits. There were no fences between our ranch and the Pecos River, and we never knew how far the old horse traveled on his return trip to the home he loved so well. We never used him any more, and he died about a year later.

Almost every afternoon just before sundown, I climbed the windmill tower with the field glasses to look out over the trails leading in several directions from the ranch to see if I could spot any potential overnight visitors. Anyone approaching the ranch at that time of day would probably spend the night there. If I saw anyone coming, I would tell Mother so she could get supper ready.

One evening, I picked up a small cloud of dust along the trail that led to Roswell by way of Four Lakes. After watching it for a while, I finally made out four men on horseback coming our way and informed Mother that we were going to have four visitors.

I stood in the doorway watching them as they rode up. Two were heavily armed, and I recognized them as Texas Rangers who had stopped at the ranch before. The other two were strangers and seemed to have their hands tied together. They watered their horses at the trough, then rode around to the windmill, where the Rangers dismounted and got a drink of water from the barrel. One of the Rangers came to the house and told Mother that he and the other Ranger had two prisoners and would like to spend the night at the ranch.

"You're welcome," she told him. "Turn your horses into the pasture and make yourself at home in the bunkhouse. I'll have your supper ready in a little while."

She sent me after them when supper was ready. As I showed them the water buckets and tin wash pans just outside the kitchen door, I verified my earlier suspicions, and the discovery made my eyes pop! Two of the men had their wrists connected together with iron bands and short lengths of chain. I had never seen anyone handcuffed before, and I wondered why those men had their arms hobbled together like two chuck wagon mules.

They all entered the kitchen, and the prisoners were ordered to sit at the table. The Rangers told Mother and me to stay back out of the way, and they waited on the men. One of the Rangers took off his belt and six-guns and laid them out of reach on another table. The other officer stood guard just inside the kitchen door. The unarmed Ranger went around behind the prisoners and removed a cuff from one wrist of each man so that he could have use of his hands while eating. Then the Ranger passed the food to them.

The prisoners ate in silence except for the rattle of the handcuffs dangling from one wrist when they struck the table and the tin cups and plates. They spoke in mutters, asking for another sourdough biscuit, another piece of beefsteak, more frijole beans, or another cup of coffee.

One of the prisoners was quite young, with a coat of fuzz on his face. The other was a tough looker with a walrus-type mustache.

When the prisoners finished eating, the handcuffs were snapped back on and they were seated outside the house. Then the officers took turns eating, one standing guard. After they returned to the bunkhouse, Mother and I washed the dishes. Deep in thought, she remarked, "They must be pretty tough men, judging from the close watch those Rangers are keeping over them."

"Reckon what they've done?" I asked. "Maybe they've killed somebody."

"Maybe so." she answered. "I expect they were bad boys when they were small and didn't mind their mothers, and then got with bad company. They might have held up a train or robbed a bank. Now they'll have to go to jail."

"Uh-huh," I said, reasonably sure she was thinking about

how I minded her. She often told me not to smoke cigarettes. Just that morning she had tanned my hide when she caught me smoking a Bull Durham cigarette out behind the corrals.

That night, I stood at a window and, by the light of the full moon watched the prisoners sitting in front of the bunkhouse, wondering what they had done to be treated in such a manner. I thought about the outlaws the cowhands often talked about while sitting in the bunkhouse. I wondered if those two men were real outlaws and had had a gun battle with the Rangers before they were captured.

After a while, all four men went to the windmill for a drink of water. Then the Rangers spread out saddle blankets alongside one of our wagons and placed the prisoners' saddles at one end of the blankets for pillows. The prisoners lay down on the blankets, and the Rangers removed a handcuff from one wrist of each prisoner and snapped it around a wagon wheel spoke. One of the officers went into the bunkhouse to bed. The other one sat in a rawhide-bottom chair tilted back against the wall of the building, on guard, smoking a cigarette.

I asked if I could go out there and talk to the Ranger. "Yes," Mother said, "but don't go around where those prisoners are."

I sat on a box beside the rough, tough lawman with about a two weeks' growth of beard on his face, and asked him what those two men had done to have their arms hobbled together.

"Well, son, one of them is wanted for blotching brands on other people's cattle," he drawled, and took a long draw from his brown-paper cigarette. "The other one is wanted for robbing the passengers on a Texas-Pacific train between Toyah and Pecos City, Texas.

"Oh," I said, "are they real outlaws like Clay Allison and Billy the Kid?"

"I reckon they could be classed as such," he answered, "because they have pretty bad reputations, 'specially the one with the mustache."

"Which one robbed the train?"

"The one with the mustache."

88

"Where did you catch them?" I asked.

"Up close to Fort Sumner," he replied.

"What are you going to do with them?"

"Put them in jail at Midland."

I glanced at his pearl-handled six guns in scabbards hanging from a cartridge-filled belt around his waist. I noticed that the bottoms of the scabbards were fastened to buckskin strings tied around his legs. I asked him if they put up a fight when he ordered them to give up.

"A man who was with them did," he replied.

"Where's he now?" I whispered excitedly.

He knocked the ashes from his cigarette with a little finger. "He was in no condition to ride, and we had to leave him where we found him," he answered sorrowfully.

Much to my regret he changed the subject and asked me about myself. He told me he had a little grandson just about my age, living in Austin.

"Is he going to be a Texas Ranger?" I asked.

"I hope not," he answered, to my utter surprise, because I couldn't possibly imagine any boy, or man for that matter, who wouldn't give up his seat in heaven and sit on the floor for the opportunity of belonging to that colorful and romantic organization of peace officers.

"That's what I want to be when I grow up," I told him, "a Texas Ranger."

"Well, son," he drawled, "it ain't as easy as it sounds. Rangers lead a rough and dangerous life, and they are seldom at home with their folks."

"Oh, that wouldn't bother me none," I told him confidently.

Old Jeff knew many of the Rangers personally in those days. He and I had been talking about them only a few days before, and I had told him I wanted to be one when I "growed up." He had told me what the qualifications were for a person wishing to join those "gun toters," as he called them.

"You have to be brave," he had said, "be able to track and trail, ride a horse like a Comanche Injun, and fight like a wildcat.

You must be an expert with rifle or six gun, a dead shot with either hand, quick on the draw, and be able to shoot from the hip, and never shoot a man in the back. You must be a gentleman in every way, and be civil and polite to everyone, including your prisoners."

"Where's your daddy?" The Ranger asked me, again changing the subject.

"Haven't got any," I answered. "He died three months before I was born, and I never did even see him."

"That's too bad," he murmured.

Neither of us spoke for a few moments.

"Do you ever get lonesome?" he asked.

"I do when the cowhands are away," I told him, "and I'll shore be glad when I get big enough to make a hand and go with them on the roundup."

He asked me what I had to play with.

"Nothing much," I replied, "except something that's alive. I've got five horned toads, a pet prairie dog, a dry-land terrapin, an old tom cat, Old Shep, and two greyhounds. I did have a pet antelope, but it ran off with a wild bunch. Sometimes I lie on the water tank and watch the cattle and horses come in to water. I also climb the windmill tower with Uncle's field glasses and look out over the prairie."

After catching my breath, I continued, "I almost forgot to tell you about my pocketknife Old Jeff gave me that I whittle and play mumblety-peg with. And I'll bet if you'll play me a game, I'll beat you and get to watch you root the dirt from around the peg with your nose, and pull it out of the ground with your teeth."

"If it was daylight, I'd call your bet," he said with the first grin I had seen on his face.

"How's your mother going to send you to school?" he asked, rolling another cigarette. I wanted one, too, but didn't have the nerve to ask him for the makings.

"I don't know," I murmured, "because there ain't no school around here. She gives me lessons every day. I learned my ABC's reading brands on cattle and horses, and can count strings of antelopes when they cross the trail in front of me—you know how they always string out and follow the leader across the road ahead of you when you are traveling across the country."

One of the prisoners called and asked the Ranger to bring him a drink of water. He told me to stay where I was sitting till he came back. He brought both men a drink from the windmill. They then asked him for cigarettes, which he rolled and lighted for them.

Mother called me from the front door of the house, saying it was time all little boys were in bed.

The Ranger shook hands with me, saying, "I'll tell you *adios* now, because you might not be awake when I leave tomorrow morning."

"Come and see me again," I urged, as I held his hand, " 'cause I like to talk to you."

"I sure will when I'm riding this way," he smiled, "and you be a good boy."

I told Mother all about what the Ranger had told me—what the prisoners did, where they were caught, and where they would be put in jail. Then I went upstairs to bed.

Mother went with me to be sure I said my prayers. I had to be careful not to recite the version Old Jeff taught me, which went, "Now I lay me down to sleep, where the bedbugs over me creep."

I lay at the window where I could see that grizzled adversary of cattle rustlers, train robbers, and border outlaws—who was as tough as they make them, but had a warm spot in his heart for little boys—sitting there in the moonlight watching over his prisoners.

The scene made a lasting impression upon my memory, and from then on, when I was tempted to place my brand on another man's calf, or otherwise stray from the straight and narrow path Mother had taught me to follow, a vision of those three men— one on guard and the other two chained to a wagon wheel—would appear before my eyes and cause me to push temptation aside.

12.

Christmas in a Line Camp

CHRISTMAS shopping at our ranch seventy years ago was quite a problem for Mother, since our post office and trading point was so far away. Mother did some shopping from mail-order houses, but usually gave a list of the things she wanted to the drivers of the freight wagons when they went to Midland for supplies about three times each year.

Of course we received our mail more often, because any cowhand riding horseback our way would bring what mail he could carry in his saddle pockets or wrapped in his slicker tied on behind his saddle. But any large packages from mail-order houses had to lie in the post office till the freight wagons went to town.

One winter as the Christmas season approached, Mother decided to go with the freight wagons and take me along. We left the ranch about fifteen days before Christmas, planning to be back by Christmas Eve at the latest.

Two large wagons, each pulled by a team of four mules, made up the freight outfit. Both wagons carried bows and wagon sheets and spring seats. Each wagon carried water barrels on both sides. One was driven by Uncle George, the other by Old Jeff.

One wagon carried a light chuck box at the rear end of the bed. A dry cowhide stretched and fastened under the bed, called a "possum-belly," carried an extra supply of wood, which was scarce along the route. Each man took a saddle horse along, tied and led alongside the team. A plainsman never felt safe without a horse for use in an emergency, such as the mules straying off, or an unforeseen need to travel faster than was possible with a team and a wagon.

The two men threw their bedding together into one roll, planning to sleep in one wagon. Mother fixed a special roll for us, with a heavy tarpaulin, Navaho and army blankets, and one of Uncle's tanned buffalo robes, a relic of his hunting days on the Yellow Houses. We would sleep in the other wagon.

I thought the time to leave would never arrive. When it finally did, we headed the freight wagons toward the south for the four-day trip to the railroad. We reached some windmills, I think in the JAL range, a little before sundown. The men filled our water barrels, moved out to where the teams could find some grass, and camped for the first night.

One man set up the pot rack, built a fire, and started supper. The other man unharnessed the teams, mounted a saddle horse, and drove the mules to water. He then hung the morrals filled with corn on the mules' heads, and as they ate, he tied them with rawhide hobbles and staked the two saddle horses.

Mother made our bed down with the aid of a lighted lantern hanging from a wagon bow. It was a moonlit night, and in the dry atmosphere of the High Plains, the stars were shining very bright. We threw the wagon sheet back, and as we lay looking up at the stars, Mother showed me how to find the North Star with the aid of the Big Dipper.

We heard something moving on the ground, and saw two striped polecats smelling around the evening campfire. A horse nickered, and one of ours answered it. We heard horses' hoofbeats, the jingling of spurs, and the squeaking of saddle leather as two ghostly horsemen rode along the road near the wagons. They went to the windmills and watered their horses, then disappeared from view. Mother said they were probably on the dodge from the law and doing their riding at night. We saw the sheet on the other wagon rise on one side, and knew our menfolks, who were well armed, were watching the strangers.

Day was just breaking when Mother called me. I could hear the mules near the wagon crunching their corn. She was already dressed and was helping one of the men get breakfast, while the other man was harnessing the teams. The aroma of Arbuckle's coffee filled the air as it boiled in the coffeepot hanging from the pot rack, and I could hear beefsteak sizzling in the frying pan. By the time Mother cleaned up the breakfast dishes and put them away in the chuck box, the men had the teams hitched up and ready to go. One of the men took a spade and covered the embers of the cow-chip fire with dirt. We filled the water barrels and headed on south.

We reached Midland on the fourth day. When we were near town, I saw a long freight train with black smoke belching from its stack chugging along the Texas and Pacific Railroad. I asked Mother if it was burning cow chips.

Those were the days before Texas was saturated with oil, and Midland was just a small cow town. It got its name from its location midway between Fort Worth and El Paso. The business houses were mostly one story, with board sidewalks and hitching racks in front. The streets were unpaved and dusty.

The wagons put up at a wagon yard, and the men stayed there and slept in the wagons. Mother and I rented a room in a small hotel, and we all ate at a restaurant nearby. The hotel was one of the few two-story buildings in town. Our room was upstairs and had a window overlooking the street. I spent a lot of time at that window watching the traffic below.

I saw wagons, buckboards, surreys, and buggies moving along the street or standing in front of the buildings with the teams tied to the hitch racks and hitching posts. At times a bunch of cowpunchers would ride down the street in a dead run, slide their horses to a stop, dismount, and "tie their horses loose" with bridle reins dropped on the ground. The horses would stand there till their riders returned.

Mother soon finished her shopping, but we had to wait two days for some ranch supplies to come in on a train. She was worried that we might not get back to the ranch by Christmas. We were in town over Sunday, and Mother and I went to church —the first time she had done so in several years, there being no churches near our ranch.

When the wagons were finally loaded, we got an early start for the return trip. The weather was getting colder and the second morning, when Mother called me, day had not started to break. By the light of the blazing campfire, I could see that the teams were already hitched up and ready to go. As we ate breakfast, the men said they thought we were going to have some bad weather and wished to get an early start in order to get to a line camp near Shafter Lake for the next stop.

Daylight came, showing an overcast sky. A wind from the northeast seemed to penetrate to the bone. As the forenoon advanced, a light rain began to fall and soon turned into snow, the wind getting stronger all the while. By noon a real plains blizzard was howling.

We were headed almost directly into the storm, and the drivers had trouble keeping the mules and horses on the road. The men got down and walked alongside the animals to keep warm. They had tied bandannas around their heads so that their ears would not freeze. They put a tarpaulin over the opening in the wagon sheet at the front of the wagon to keep the wind and snow out, and we wrapped up in army blankets and the buffalo robe, which kept us warm.

All we could hear, inside the wagon, was the clucking of the wheels as they moved in and out on the spindles, the whistling of the wind, the flapping of the wagon sheet, and the voices of the mule skinners talking to their teams.

About noon, the men found a large rat den in a clump of

bushes alongside the road. It was a large collection of cow chips, dry twigs of bushes, grass, and other materials the rats had gathered and stacked there. The men raked the damp material from the top and set the dry material on fire.

They hung the morrals on the mules, and while the animals ate their corn, we boiled a pot of coffee and ate a cold snack. The mules were then given a bucket of water each from the water barrels. Jeff hunted up several rocks, heated them in the fire, wrapped them up in a tarpaulin and placed them in the wagon bed to keep our feet warm.

As evening came on, the storm became worse. Mother said the drivers were having trouble keeping the teams on the road because the snow was getting so deep and drifting. We could see out only through the round opening in the wagon sheet at the rear of the wagon, and at times the snow was falling so thick we could barely see Old Jeff's team following along behind our wagon.

Mother said she feared for our safety if we became lost in the storm. We might freeze to death as many persons had done in the fierce blizzards that region was noted for. But she seemed confident that the two old plainsmen, who had been through many such storms during many years of wandering over the Great Plains Region from the Smoky Hill River in Kansas to the south breaks of the plains in Texas, would pilot us to safety.

As night was falling, we felt the wagon stop and heard voices. We raised the wagon sheet and looked out. We were at a ranch house that we later learned was the line camp at Shafter Lake. The place was known as a "stag camp," where only men stayed.

We were taken into the house to a room that had a large fireplace in which a fire of mesquite roots was blazing, and we soon became warm. On a large hearthstone in front of the fireplace sat Dutch ovens. Pots for boiling coffee and beans were suspended from a rod set in the side walls of the fireplace above the fire.

The only furniture in the room was a small table near the fireplace where the sourdough keg was kept and sourdough biscuits were kneaded. Several bedrolls lay around the room. These were used as seats during the day and rolled out on the floor at night. Several boxes in which canned goods had been shipped were also used for seats or as makeshift dinner tables.

A door led into the only other room of the house, a storeroom, where grain for the line riders' winter mounts was kept. Other camp equipment was stored there too, and such items as chaps, ropes, morrals, gun belts, and clothing were hanging on the walls. Several rifles were stacked in one corner.

The men carried Mother's bed into the storeroom. One of them brought her a kerosene lantern and hung it to a rafter. He also brought in a bucket of water with a gourd dipper in it, a tin wash pan, a towel that was quite soiled, and a bar of soap. He set the water and wash pan on a box and told us to make ourselves at home.

Three men were staying at the line camp, and our two men made five to occupy the other room. It was quite crowded with five beds rolled out on the floor.

The storm was still howling, and the snow was drifting and getting deeper all the while. The men had to shovel a path out to our wagons. Some sheds and corrals and our covered wagons gave the teams some protection from the storm. Mother said we couldn't possibly get away from there until the storm was over and the snowdrifts had melted. Since the next day was Christmas Eve, we would have to spend Christmas Day there.

Someone knocked on our door and said chuck was ready. Supper was sourdough biscuits light as a feather, beefsteak, frijole beans cooked with ripe chili-pepper pods and bacon rinds, and a syrup they called "lick," which was made by melting and browning sugar in a skillet, then adding hot water. We used the lick as a dessert in which to sop our sourdough biscuits.

Only two of the line riders were present. One of them told us that the other man had left early that morning to ride the line, and was probably caught some distance from camp by the storm. They thought he must be having trouble finding camp.

After supper, Mother asked if she might wash the dishes, but the men told her that she was "company," and they would look after cleaning up. She went to her room, but I begged her into letting me stay in the room with the menfolks for a while.

We brought some Dallas newspapers Uncle had got at the railroad out of the wagon and gave them to the men to read. They seldom saw a newspaper in that lonely camp, and they read every-thing—even to the advertisements. They then rolled out a bed and started playing draw poker with a soiled deck, using frijole beans for counters.

They were worried about the man who was missing, fearing that he might freeze to death, but decided it would be useless to search for him in the storm. They compared this storm with others in the past, especially the blizzard in 1887 when so many cattle froze to death. They said a wagon train of homeseekers had stayed overnight with them a couple of days before, and they feared for their safety. They also worried about their supply of wood and wondered if it would hold out till the storm was over and the snow melted. The cow chips were wet and wouldn't burn, and dead mesquite roots were hidden by snow.

Occasionally, we could hear cattle bawling as they drifted with the storm past camp. Sometimes we could hear the yapping of coyotes and the lonesome howl of a loafer wolf.

We heard a horse nicker and thought we heard a voice. One of the men opened the door, and there was the missing line rider, sitting on his horse. The men helped him down and into the house, and pulled off his boots and socks and rubbed his feet, hands, nose, and ears with snow. Keeping him away from the fire, they wrapped him in a blanket and put him to bed.

He was given a small amount of warm beefbroth before he dropped off to sleep. After a while he awakened and told us about his experience. When the snow started falling, he had headed for camp, but the drifting snow soon obscured all landmarks. He had been positive that he knew in what direction to travel and had forced his horse to travel the route he thought would take him home.

After a while he felt that he had traveled at least as far as he was from camp, and figured that he had bypassed camp on one side or the other. He then had no idea which way to go, so he decided to give his horse free rein and see if it would take him home. His horse turned in almost the opposite direction from the way they were headed, and he suddenly realized that it had stopped in front of the camp house. He gave the horse full credit for saving his life by having the better sense of direction.

When we awoke the next morning, it was bitter cold in our room, since there was no way to heat it. Fine snow had filtered into the room and formed small drifts across the bed and floor. I scraped the frost from the windowpane and saw that the snow was still falling. Our bucket of water was frozen over, and Mother told me to get some from the other room to wash up for breakfast.

After breakfast, while some of the men washed dishes, the others shoveled snow and fed, watered, and looked after the mules and saddle horses. They spread a Navaho blanket on the floor of the storeroom, and Jeff and the line riders again started their poker game. Mother told them that if they would turn the large room and fireplace over to her, she would cook dinner for them.

She had Uncle get some provisions from the wagons, among them a large ham, some sweet potatoes, and a case of canned peaches. She baked the ham, candied the yams, and made a giant peach cobbler that filled one of the large Dutch ovens. She also put on a pot of prunes to boil over the fire. Uncle never played cards, so he spent his time reading the newspapers, helping Mother with the fire, and handling the Dutch ovens.

The men didn't eat noonday meal, saying they were saving their appetite for the evening meal Mother was cooking. About midafternoon the wind died down and the snow stopped falling. As darkness was settling over the snow-covered plains, Mother announced that supper was ready.

The line riders appreciated the change in diet and the opportunity—one they seldom had—of eating a meal that was cooked by a woman. Mother told them this would be their Christmas dinner, since we would probably start on our way the following day. She reminded them that this was Christmas Eve, and she thought we ought to hold some kind of services to commemorate the event, even though we were isolated in a line shack far from civilization.

She quoted several verses from the Bible from memory that told about an angel saying, "Fear not: for, behold, I bring you good tidings of great joy . . . . For unto you is born this day . . . a Saviour . . . . ye shall find the babe wrapped in swaddling clothes, lying in a manger. . . . On earth peace, good will toward men."

She sang several hymns and Christmas carols, and some of the men joined her in the singing. Then Old Jeff led the Lord's Prayer.

The flickering fire in the fireplace and the feeble light from a coal-oil lantern shone on the faces of those rough men, tanned to the color of leather from years of exposure to the heat and cold, the wind and rain, and the sandstorms and blizzards of the plains. Some of their eyes were misty, their thoughts probably going back to boyhood days when they sat at their own mother's knee as she read those same verses and sang some of those same hymns.

The man who had been lost in the storm, who appeared to be the youngest of the group, recited what he could remember of "The Night Before Christmas." I liked the poem better than any other part of the Christmas services. I asked Mother several times if she thought Santa would be able to find me there in that strange line camp, in the snowstorm. She said she was almost sure he would find me.

The line rider left out the part of the poem I liked best: "He had a broad face and a little round belly, that shook when he laughed like a bowl full of jelly." I told him so, and he had me recite it for him. He had forgotten the names of some of the reindeer, but I knew them all and told him what they were. I had eight horned toads at the ranch named for those reindeer. The toads were so near alike, a stranger couldn't tell them apart, but I knew each one by its name.

I looked up the chimney and wondered if Old Santa could get down it. But Old Jeff told me confidentially that he believed he could make it all right. He said he would put the fire out before he went to bed so the old boy wouldn't get his whiskers scorched when he slid down.

Mother got me a new pair of stockings, and Jeff drove two nails in the mantel for me to hang them on. He then told me I should go to bed early, " 'cause the old fellow won't come as long as you're awake." I went into the other room, crawled under the tarp, and was soon sound asleep.

Day was just breaking the following morning when I awoke. I eased out of bed and, with chattering teeth, tiptoed over and opened the door just a little and peeped into the room. The men were all still asleep with tarpaulins pulled up over their heads. The one window in the room gave very little light, but I spotted my stockings hanging from the mantel and saw they were filled to the top, with a stick of striped candy showing at the top of one and an apple in the other. I crawled back into bed and whispered to Mother, "Santa Claus did find me."

13.

Wild Plants and Animals
on the Ranch

WHEN I was growing up, it seemed to me that when the Creator made this earth, He put everything that carried a sticker, claw, thorn, stinger, horn, barb, or poison fang here to deal misery to us all.

The limbs of the mesquite bush that grew on the Staked Plains were covered with long, cruel thorns that could penetrate one's flesh quite deeply, the points sometimes breaking off and causing very painful wounds. The *chelatine bush*—commonly called "catclaw"—was also covered with thorns resembling cats' claws. It was disastrous to walk among those bushes when wearing trousers and shoes. The crooked claws would hook trouser legs on all sides and have to be pulled out by main strength. Only boots and chaps gave protection from these thorns.

The sharp stinging needle grass would collect around hems of the long dresses women wore at that time, and in trouser legs and socks. These stickers had to be plucked out one at a time. When spreading bedrolls out on the ground at night and when walking around on the prairie, one had to watch out for the pestiferous sand and grass burs. Their hard, sharp points would go right through a worn boot or shoe sole. Several members of the cactus family were indigenous to the Llano Estacado, the most common of which was the prickly pear.

One of the most abundant plants on the Staked Plains was a member of the lily family known as *Yucca glauca*. It had a cluster of evergreen leaves from one to two feet in length, sharp pointed at the top. In the spring of each year, a stem grew up from the center of the plant to a height of about three feet and bloomed at the top. Cattle liked those blooms, and would run from one to another biting them off. When the bloom died and dropped off, a stick was left standing.

As the leaves of the yucca died, they formed a mass around the base which made a good hiding place for cottontail rabbits, rattlesnakes, Gila monsters, centipedes, and other insects, lizards, and reptiles native to those parts.

Some of the early settlers on the plains called the yucca "bear grass," and others identified it as "soap weed," because when the roots were pounded up, placed in water, and rubbed together, they would form a lather similar to soapsuds. Old Jeff said the Plains Indians used the fiber in the leaves of the yucca for making cords, clothing, baskets, and other items.

When insects were distributed, that part of the country received its full share. The large black tarantula, with the spider family name *Theraphosidae*, came out of its hole in the ground before or after a rain and walked around stiff-legged. Its bite was supposed to cause a person to have a mania for dancing, or tarantism.

Stinging scorpions measuring from two to seven inches in length were plentiful around our old ranch. Of the *Arachnida* family of spiders, they had powerful stings in the tails curved over their backs. Many of them lived in the walls of our rock house. I have lain in bed upstairs and watched a scorpion crawl along a rafter until it was directly over me, at which time it would turn loose and drop. By the time it landed, it always had the bed to itself.

One pest we dreaded and watched out for was the ugly

centipede, which was said to have up to one hundred legs with poison prongs on the two legs just behind its head. It was usually found in dark, damp places, such as under rocks and rotten lumber. Unless disturbed, it did its prowling at night. A visitor who stopped overnight with us told us how a centipede caused the death of a cowhand on a ranch south of our place.

He said the man was building a fence and put his jug of drinking water, uncorked, on the ground in the shade of a bush. A centipede crawled up the jug and dropped down into the water. When the fence builder later took a drink, he partially swallowed the insect. It lodged head-first in his throat, and in trying to pull it out, he tore it in half.

There were big red ants in our yard—hundreds in one bed— and long strings of them came and went in every direction. One day when I was waddling around in the yard, just learning to walk, I sat down in one of their beds.

They covered my body, and my Comanche yells brought Mother on the run. She plucked them off me one at a time, and applied the only medicines she had—Star Navy chewing tobacco and laundry bluing—to the spots on my body where the pinchers had grabbed. For a while after that, I resembled an Indian wearing war paint.

The Llano Estacado had plenty of reptiles. There were several kinds of harmless snakes, such as the bullsnake, blacksnake, king snake, and garter snake. But there were also three different pit vipers with deadly fangs, whose bite was serious unless the venom was removed immediately. They were the ground rattlesnake, the sidewinder, and the diamondback rattler, the most dreaded of them all.

The rattlesnake was not dangerous unless disturbed. It usually gave warning of its presence by rustling its rattles before striking, except during "dog days," from the early part of July to early September, at which time it shed its skin and struck blind. Many cattle and horses were bitten on the nose by rattlesnakes, but the bite was seldom fatal to a grown animal if treated promptly.

There were many kinds of lizards on the Staked Plains, all

said to be harmless except the Gila monster, the largest of the lizard family, which was said to be poisonous. Discovered along the Gila River in Arizona, these reptiles were called "monsters" because some of them were as much as two feet long. They were also known as "mountain boomers."

A member of the lizard family that was abundant was the horned lizard, commonly known as the "horned toad," which had horns on its head and back. It was harmless unless stepped on with bare feet. I used to amuse myself by turning my pet horned toads over on their backs and watching them struggle to right themselves. I also enjoyed teasing them until they were mad enough to squirt small jets of blood from their eyes. I liked to watch them run out their long tongues and capture bugs, ants, and flies.

Larger animals of the plains also wore horns—the range cattle, descendants of those hearty animals brought into this country by the Spaniards who explored the Southwest many years ago. Those animals had horns of every shape and size. Others were the pronghorns, commonly called "American antelopes." They were almost as numerous in the early days as the cattle. But they, like the buffalo, gradually disappeared as civilization moved west. I had a pet pronghorn that I had raised on a bottle. It wore a bell on its neck, but finally answered the call of the wild and ran away with a bunch of other antelopes.

The Staked Plains had a generous supply of plaguy varmints —the wolf, the skunk, and assorted undomesticated cats—whose job it was to worry and torment ranchers and other early settlers.

We had two kinds of skunks. The spotted one was called "hydrophobia cat," because it was believed to be rabid at all times. The other skunk was black with white stripes, and was sometimes incorrectly called a "polecat." Skunks made raids at night on poultry, killing chickens and sucking eggs. When surprised in a raid, they left a sickening odor behind.

There were more striped skunks than spotted ones. These were supposed to go "mad" during the hot summertime, and their bite was believed to cause hydrophobia. The only remedy known for hydrophobia at that time was a "madstone," a porous stone resembling a sponge, which was sometimes found in the stomach of a deer or cow, usually in an albino.

Once, when I was about fourteen years old, I was helping my uncle drill a well southwest of Kenna, New Mexico. Another boy several years older than I was also worked for him. The two of us slept in a tent with our beds spread out on the ground.

One night, I was awakened by a wheezing sound such as an animal makes when being choked by a rope around its neck. Lighting a lantern, I saw my partner lying in bed with both hands around the neck of a striped skunk, trying to pull its teeth out of his scalp.

I grabbed the skunk by the tail, pulled it loose, held it up by its tail, and broke its neck with a J branding iron. It gave out no odor, and my uncle said this indicated that it was rabid.

The boy had an ugly wound in his scalp, and one of the animal's teeth had broken off and was still in the wound when we dressed it.

I saddled two horses and went with the boy to the railroad. He caught a train for Toyah, Texas, where a man was said to have a madstone.

When the boy returned, he described the "magic" stone and the manner in which it was used. The man who owned the stone shaved the hair from the scalp around the wound, then placed the porous spongelike object in a vessel containing sweet milk which he boiled for several minutes. This softened the so-called stone somewhat and made it slightly pliable. After it cooled a little, the man pressed it down firmly on the wound, and the vacuum-type cups of the pores caused the stone to stick tightly to the scalp. The owner said the firm grip the stone made on the skin was a sure sign the animal that had inflicted the wound was rabid.

The boy suffered no ill effects from his experience, but it is impossible to know whether the skunk was really rabid and whether the madstone actually saved the boy from hydrophobia and a horrible death.

Two members of the wolf family lived on the Staked Plains to harass the ranchers and prey upon their livestock.

One was the coyote, a cunning animal with a language of its own and a melodious voice with which it serenaded the moon and countryside at night. Only two animals on the plains were more intelligent than the coyote—the cutting horse and the sheep dog. Coyotes made raids upon the settlers' chicken houses and carried squawking hens off across the prairie. They killed young calves, especially those newly born, when the mother left them out on the prairie to go for water.

The other wolf was the lobo, commonly called "loafer." It was much larger and more vicious than the coyote, being known to kill grown cattle by cutting the hamstring, or tendon above and behind the hock, with its teeth, disabling the animal and putting it at the wolf's mercy.

Wolves killed so many cattle that the ranchers offered a bounty of two dollars each for coyote scalps and twenty dollars each for lobo scalps. Some old cowhands, believing they could make better wages hunting wolves than punching cattle, turned to professional wolf hunting. To claim the bounty on the wolves, it was necessary to display the scalp with ears still intact. The bounty was paid for all ages, from one-day-old pups on up.

Coyotes fed on carrion and were easily poisoned by strychnine sprinkled on dead rabbits, birds, or the offal of cattle. They could also be caught in steel traps, and have been known to gnaw a foot off in order to escape from a trap.

The eating habits of the lobo were entirely different from those of the coyote. The lobo preferred to butcher its own meat and eat it absolutely fresh, seldom feeding upon carrion. Consequently, it was difficult to poison lobos, and they were rarely caught in traps.

One morning, as I was riding across the prairie to a watering place to grease windmills, I came upon a calf that looked as if it had been killed by a lobo the night before. The wolf had apparently gorged itself on the meat of its victim, and I suspected that it was a she-wolf and that she had taken the meat to her den to regurgitate it for her pups.

I circled the carcass and spotted the wolf's tracks in a cow trail. I followed the tracks into the sand hills and found the den in a clump of bushes on a hard spot of ground. There were six small puppies, fussing and fighting over the meat the mother had brought them. I held each one up by its hind legs, gave it a judo chop with my hand at the back of the head, then removed the scalps.

I received $12.00 for that morning's work, which was *some* money in those days, especially since top wages for a cowhand were $1.00 a day for twenty hours' work. With the money, I bought a new saddle with all the trappings from saddle maker Ed Amonett at Roswell.

Two members of the cat family prowled the Staked Plains. One was the puma, also known as the panther or mountain lion. Pumas were scarce and seldom seen during daylight hours. Sometimes, at night, we heard their screech, which was like the scream of a woman.

Once when I was a small child, the cowhands at the ranch roped what they called a panther and choked it to death. They tried taxidermy, skinning and tanning the hide of the cat, then cleaning the skull and mounting it in place, putting in two of my agate marbles for eyes. We used it as a rug in the ranch house.

The other cat, related to the lynx of the northern United States, had a short, stubby tail and was known as the bobcat. It was a fierce, savage animal, that would fight anything that walked on two, or four, legs and usually came out the winner, except when artillery was used against it. I found out for myself just how savage one of them could get when irritated.

I was about sixteen years old, and another young cowboy about my age, whom we called "Wrang," was helping me break a bunch of young geldings to the saddle.

One day we were riding a couple of those potros out on the prairie, teaching them the duties they would perform when they became cow ponies. Suddenly, we jumped a large bobcat. We had chased it some distance, when it stopped, backed up into a bunch of catclaw bushes, and showed fight.

Wrang and I took turns running our horses by the cat and casting the loops in our ropes at it in an effort to catch it. When my mount got too close to the cat, it jumped on the horse's rump behind my saddle and dug in its claws. I've always regretted not having a motion picture of what happened during the next few moments. There were many other places I would have rather been, than riding tandem on a bronco with a ferocious wild cat occupying the rear seat.

The pony squealed like a panther, bogged its head between its forelegs, and went into action. I was hoping it would throw me, and it did, but it threw the bobcat too. I landed flat on my back on one side of a bush, and caught a glimpse of the bobtail as it came down on the opposite side, hitting the ground on all four feet.

Being on the other side of the bush probably saved me from the animal's fury. I had enough presence of mind to lie still and not attract its attention, while Wrang scared it away by throwing the coils of his rope at it.

14.

The First Blacksmith
on the Llano Estacado

R. L. (Bob) Causey, who was the first blacksmith on the Staked Plains, came to live at Uncle George's ranch in the 1880's. He inherited his ability with hot iron and hammer from his father, who also was a blacksmith, and had learned the trade in his father's shop in Missouri.

When the freight wagons went to the trading post at Midland for supplies, Uncle Bob went along and bought a small anvil, bellows, forge, and other blacksmith equipment. He set up a small shop at the ranch and puttered around in it when he wasn't running wild horses, breaking broncs, or branding calves.

Uncle Bob also bought a small stock of flat iron bars. From these he made stamp branding irons for ranchers, along with horseshoes and horseshoe nails. He bought small round iron rods with which he made J branding irons for cowpunchers, pot racks and pot hooks for chuck wagon cooks, and lap links to repair stretchers and chains.

He was also a cabinetmaker and an expert in woodworking,

and this made him a great help to his brother in improving his ranch house and its furniture. He kept the windmill and wagons in repair, and shod the mules and saddle horses.

Herds of buffaloes had roamed the range in that area only a few years before, and a person could go almost any place on the prairie and pick up buffalo horns and even the skulls with horns intact and in good condition. Uncle Bob collected buffalo horns, and in his spare time scraped and polished them with pieces of broken glass, applied a coat of clear varnish, and mounted them upon wooden shields covered with velvet. They were hung on the walls of the living room of the old rock ranch house.

He constructed two chairs for the living room, making the frames from buffalo horns and the seats and backs from rawhide with the hair on it. He mounted two pairs of wide-spread horns from Mexican longhorn steers and several pairs of horns from antelopes.

Associating with ranchers and cowhands, he found they took pride in owning fancy spurs and bridle bits, just as they did in wearing shop-made boots and riding on hand-tooled saddles decked with silver conchos.

My uncle had an idea that he might do well if he opened a shop in a western town and specialized in spur and bit work. Ector County, Texas, was organized in 1891, the town of Odessa on the new Texas-Pacific Railroad becoming the county seat. He went there and opened a blacksmith shop.

In those days before oil was discovered in Texas, Odessa was a small trading point for ranchers in that area. In addition to doing general blacksmithing, Causey served as the town constable. He soon started making spurs and bits, a career that made him famous.

He originated what was known as "gal-leg" spurs and bridle bits with the shank of the spur and side bars of the bits forged and filed into the shape of a girl's leg.

Uncle Bob went to Juárez, Mexico, and brought back a supply of Mexican coins in which the silver was nearly pure, so that it was pliable and easily worked. With a hammer and small chisel, he worked the steel upward along the edge of the legs. Into this he slipped the silver he had beaten out very thin. He then hammered the steel down over the silver to hold it in place. With a small hand tool, he engraved the silver panties, garters, and shoes. Thus the first matched set of gal-leg silver-mounted spurs and bridle bits were finished.

That type of spur and bit was a success from the start. He sold the first set to Sheriff G. I. McGonagill of Ector County, and other sets to Tom Waddell, the Vest brothers, the Dawson and Estes brothers, Cub Roberts, "Two G" Henderson, and other ranchers in that area. After his product was advertised by sight and word of mouth, he received orders through the mail. Texas Rangers bought some of his sets.

After several years in Odessa, Uncle Bob decided to move farther west. In 1895, he moved to Eddy, New Mexico, and opened a shop there. Eddy was a trading point for a vast cattle ranching region at that time. He did a good business there with his general blacksmithing and spur and bit work. Much of his time was devoted to shoeing horses for the ranchers and livery stables, and mules for the freighters who hauled supplies to surrounding ranchers. Bill Morgan, who hauled freight to Roswell, ninety miles north, was a good customer. He drove a team of sixteen mules with a jerk line, and rode one of the wheel mules.

Uncle Bob kept samples of his spurs and bits on display in Sol Schoonover's saloon in Eddy. He usually managed to finish a matched set each week and take them to Sol's place on Saturday evening, when the saloon was crowded with ranchers and cow-punchers, and raffle them off at a dollar a chance.

Another of his side lines was making fancy cases for the faro, monte, poker, and blackjack dealers in the Eddy saloons for their decks of playing cards, and also the racks in which they kept their poker chips. He made small boxes that held several decks of cards by laminating many layers of wood of different colors glued together, highly polished with a coat of clear varnish. The covers of these boxes were carved with the owner's name and a heart, a spade, a club, and a diamond in the corners. He received fancy prices for these articles.

He also polished and mounted horns with a wide spread from longhorn steers, which were still quite plentiful and easy to obtain. One pair he mounted, which had a spread of almost eight feet, hung above the mirror behind the bar in Schoonover's saloon. Many of the horns hanging in saloons in New Mexico in those days were mounted by Bob Causey.

A former Texas cowhand for whom Uncle Bob made a set of spurs and bits was a frequent visitor at his shop. He was Jim White, who rode the range for the Lucas XXX Ranch in the Guadalupe Mountains southwest of Eddy. White discovered the famous Carlsbad Caverns in 1901.

Today the spurs and bits with shanks and side bars shaped like the leg of a girl, in some cases wearing a daring garter, are collector's items. Once it was quite sporty to deck oneself and his horse with those eyebrow raising objects. Uncle Bob made a pair of spurs to order for steer roping champion Clay McGonagill with rubies inlaid in the outer heel bands.

While living in Eddy, Uncle Bob married Agnes Bogle, whose parents operated a boarding and rooming house there. About 1905, he and his wife pulled up stakes and moved to Safford, Arizona, where he continued to operate a blacksmith shop until his death in 1937.

15.

School Days

WHEN Uncle Bob left the ranch on the Staked Plains and went to Odessa to open a blacksmith shop, he invited Mother and me to live with him while school was in session so that I could get formal schooling.

Mother agreed, since there was no school where we lived and she wanted me to have an education. Although she had taught school and gave me daily lessons, she often said she much preferred that I attend school as other children did. So one fall we went to live with Uncle Bob, who was then a bachelor.

We arrived about two weeks before school started. This gave us a chance to get acquainted with the town and its inhabitants. In addition to operating his blacksmith and spur and bit shop, Uncle Bob served as the town's constable, helping Sheriff McGonagill keep law and order. "Pop" Rathburn was postmaster, and Will Mudgett and P. Nobles operated stores there.

On the morning classes opened, we children got acquainted with our new teacher, a man named Mr. Hawkins, whom everyone called "Prof." He taught everything from the ABC's to algebra in the little one-room schoolhouse. To my surprise, he looked like any other elderly male citizen one might meet in Texas. He had the appearance of an ordinary rancher. He wore a vest, and his trousers were stuffed inside his boottops. His mustache and little goatee were discolored by tobacco.

Schoolteachers in Texas in the 1890's received an annual salary of about $250, from which they had to pay board and room. This was for a nine-month school term. They lived the other three months without pay.

One of Professor Hawkins' subjects was "discipline," which he taught with a rawhide quirt that hung near one end of the blackboard. It didn't help the situation for a pupil to put a geography book inside the seat of his trousers, because the professor was wise to that trick, and hit above and below the geography.

As punishment for minor violations of rules, he would have the culprit stand in a corner of the room facing the class and hold his hands high above his head for a half-hour, which I did several times.

Some of my schoolmates were the McGonagill children, Walter, Clay, Bertha, and Minnie. Clay broke my nose in a free-for-all fist fight on the school grounds one day, and it always remained crooked. In later years Clay became a champion in the contests at cowboy reunions over the Southwest, where big steers were roped and tied down.

Other schoolmates were the children from the Waddell, Dawson, Roberts, Atwood, Arnison, and Daugherty families.

I walked almost a mile to school and carried my lunch in a five-pound lard bucket. The school grounds were segregated, the boys' playground on one side of the schoolhouse and the girls' on the other side. At recess, we boys played "town ball," where if a ball was thrown across the base-line ahead of a runner, he was out. We also played rola-hola and "keeps" with marbles. We "spiked" each other's tops while they were spinning, which split many of them wide open. We often played "pop the whip" by all lining up with the big boys at the head of the line, then tapering back according to size, with the smallest boy at the tail end being the "popper" of the whip. We would run a short distance with hands joined together, each one giving a jerk on the boy behind him, and the little fellow at the end usually turned a somersault.

I could wiggle one ear and wink one eye at the same time, or both ears and my scalp. One of the girls could top me, though, by turning her eyelids wrongside-out without touching them with her fingers. And one boy was the center of attention for a while, because his index finger was missing from one hand.

During study periods, I would wink an eye and wiggle an ear at a girl. The girl would turn her eyelids wrongside-out and look like a dying calf. And the boy would put the stub of his index finger to his nose, and appear to have his entire finger up inside his nostril. Everyone would start snickering, and when Professor Hawkins looked around, we three usually were the only pupils studying our books.

The classroom wasn't segregated like the playgrounds, and a little red-headed, freckle-faced girl we called "teacher's pet" sat in front of me. I always had her upset by trying to count the freckles on her face. I would finally give up and say in a whisper, "It's just like trying to count the stars in the Milky Way." She finally begged the teacher into letting her change her seat.

Sometimes when a boy was on his feet reciting and the teacher turned his head, someone toward the rear would place a tack on the boy's desk seat, point up. When the victim sat down, he would let out a squawk and turn the ink bottle on his desk over. Afterwards there was usually a fist fight at recess.

One boy had everyone but the professor standing on desks one day when he turned a garter snake loose on the schoolroom floor. The culprit was up on his desk screaming like a Comanche Indian. The professor had no way of finding out who did it, for it was an unpardonable sin for anyone to tattle to the teacher.

Some of my classmates were known by their nicknames to everyone but the professor, who didn't like nicknames and didn't like to be called "Prof." My best friend was a boy whose given name was "Berry," but because of his very dark complexion and black hair and eyes, his moniker was "Blackberry," or just "Blackie." We were as close, in and out of classes, as two hot tamales wrapped in one corn shuck. We fought each other like bobcats, but if anyone butted in, he had us both to whip.

Blackie lived on a ranch in that area and stayed in town with friends of his family to attend school. Neither of us was very fond of studying, and we were always glad when school was out so we could go back to our ranch homes.

After school hours and on Saturdays, Blackberry and I spent much of our time around Uncle Bob's blacksmith shop. We pumped the bellows that heated the coal fire in his forge, helped him shrink and set tires on buggy and wagon wheels, and held horses while he nailed shoes on their feet.

Every Friday afternoon, Professor Hawkins would tell his pupils to put their books away and prepare for the weekly "spelling match." He selected two of his bright students as captains of opposing teams. They chose sides by first one and then the other selecting a pupil until the whole class was lined up in two rows facing each other.

Blackie and I spelled words the way they sounded or, as he said, "by ear." As a result, we were always the last to be chosen, because neither side wanted us. He usually ended up at the foot of one line and I at the end of the other one.

One afternoon when my turn came, the professor told me to spell "pickle." I spelled it the way it sounded: p-i-c-k-e-l. After I went down, I thumbed quickly through my Webster's Dictionary to learn why the judge had made such an obvious error.

In a match a few weeks later, I was given the word, "nickel," and, recalling how "pickle" was spelled, I said n-i-c-k-l-e.

During another match, Blackie's turn came and the professor said to him: "Spell the word mustache—this thing I have on my upper lip," pointing to the walrus-type growth of tobacco-stained hair covering his mouth.

The boy spelled it exactly the way the teacher pronounced it—m-u-s-t-a-s-h—then went to his seat after the little red-headed teacher's pet, with her nose at a forty-five-degree angle, spelled it correctly.

I went down on the word "restaurant," which I spelled r-e-s-t-u-r-a-n-t. When I went to my seat, Blackie was looking in his dictionary for "mustache," muttering, "The reason you and me will never get very far in school is because we spend too much time looking up words that don't spell like they sound."

He finally found the word, then jumped to his feet, snapped his fingers, and waved his hand high above his head.

"What do you want?" Professor Hawkins asked.

"You didn't pronounce that word right that I missed awhile ago," the boy replied. "You should have called it 'mustake,' because it is spelled m-u-s-t-a-c-h-e, like toothache, headache, and bellyache. If you had pronounced it like it's spelled, I wouldn't have missed it, because I know how to spell 'must' and 'ache.' "

"You remain in your seat when class is dismissed; I want to talk to you," the professor said, giving the boy a look like a registered Hereford bull gives a little dogie calf.

When Blackie came to the blacksmith shop after school that afternoon, he said the teacher had given him some fatherly advice about the pronunciation and spelling of difficult words in our language. The professor told him his purpose in holding spelling matches was to select such words to be pronounced and spelled before the class for the benefit of everyone.

"The professor told me I would find many words in the future that were confusing," Blackie said, and showed me the two words, "need" and "knead," which are pronounced alike, but have different spellings and different meanings.

"You know," he added, "I sorta like that old fellow now. I believe he's a good teacher."

After two winters in Odessa, when we were getting ready to return to the ranch, Uncle Bob told Mother she would have to make other arrangements to send me to school that fall. He was planning to move and settle in some town farther west. When he did so, he said, he would let her know.

A short time earlier, my grandfather—Mother's father—had

shipped a horse to Guthrie, Oklahoma Territory, and made the "Run" in the opening of the Cherokee Strip of the Indian Territory. He won a "claim" at Enid, where he was then living. Mother decided to take me there and send me to school. I attended classes in the first schoolhouse built in Enid.

We lived on a hill above the springs which form the headwaters of Skeleton Creek. Those springs were a watering place in the early days for herds of longhorn cattle being driven north along the Chisholm Trail to shipping pens in Kansas.

To make my own spending money, I used to tie three fish hooks together back to back on a short string at the end of a long pole. Slipping along the banks around those springs, I would locate a big green bullfrog, ease my fish hooks under his chin, and snag him. The owner of a downtown restaurant bought frogs' legs from me at ten cents a pair.

Sometimes I washed dishes in a restaurant owned by the father of one of my chums named Curtis. On Saturdays and Sundays, I solicited subscriptions for the *Youth's Companion*, or stood on a streetcorner with a bundle of Wichita, Kansas, papers under my arm, yelling, "READ ALL ABOUT IT!"

There was a "townsite war" on at that time between South Enid and North Enid, three miles to the north. The Rock Island Railroad wanted the town at North Enid and refused to stop their trains at South Enid. The citizens of South Enid forced the railroad to stop at their station, won the fight, dropped the "south" portion from the name, and became Enid, the county seat of Garfield County.

I didn't like to live in the Indian Territory. There were too many farms with the sod plowed under, too many barbed-wire fences, and no open range where herds of cattle, horses, and antelopes roamed. I yearned to attend school where I could spend the summer on the wide-open spaces of the Staked Plains with Uncle George and my buddy, Old Jeff. I was glad when we received a letter from Uncle Bob, saying he had located in Carlsbad, New Mexico, and I could stay with him there and attend school.

Mother didn't want to go back to the southwestern country,

so I begged her to let me go alone. I told her if she didn't have the money to buy me a ticket, I would "ride the rods" on freight trains or the "blind baggage" on passenger trains.

She finally decided in my favor, with a promise she would join me later. She bought me a ticket over the Rock Island, Texas-Pacific, and Santa Fe railroads by way of Fort Worth and Pecos City to Carlsbad. She had the agent show on my ticket that I was to be in care of the railroad conductors along the way.

She bundled me up and put me aboard the train with a big basket filled with sandwiches, cookies, and fruit to eat on along the way. When they were exhausted, I occasionally bought a sandwich, apple, or banana from the butcher boy on the train. A motherly old lady wearing a sunbonnet rode with me for a long time. She had a basket filled with lunch and saw to it that I didn't go hungry.

I asked the brakeman to tell me when we passed through Odessa, but it happened at night and I didn't see anyone I recognized on the station platform. I became acquainted with all the conductors and brakemen along the way, and enjoyed every minute of the journey.

Mother had sent Uncle Bob a telegram, telling about what time my train was supposed to arrive at Carlsbad, and he was on the depot platform when I arrived. We went to a rooming house where he was living and had a cot in his room for me. Of course I missed Mother, but he was a real father to me.

It was summer when I arrived in Carlsbad, and there was no school. I made Uncle Bob a hand in his shop and learned a lot about blacksmithing before school started that fall. I learned how to drawfile and polish hand-forged spurs and bridle bits to a glassy smoothness with emery cloth, how to cut and shape spoke and saw-tooth spur rowels, and how to inlay the silver plates.

My uncle taught me how to use a hammer, chisel, and file when working on a piece of metal clamped in a vise; how to trim a horse's hooves, fit the shoes, and nail them on; how to use a sledge hammer, flatter, cold cutter, and other tools when drawing out, shaping, and cutting red-hot metal; and how to weld two pieces of white-hot metal together.

I learned how to "temper" steel chisels and other tools used for working metal, to a certain "hardness" by heating them in the forge, holding them in the air, watching the color change to a certain hue, then quickly dousing them in cold water.

I was also taught to repair buggy and wagon wheels, inserting new spokes and applying new felloes. I learned how to measure the circumference of the wheel and the inside of the tire to determine how much to "shrink" the tire to make it a tight fit on the wheel.

My best friend during schooldays at Carlsbad was a boy who reminded me of my old buddy Blackberry at Odessa. He also was very dark complected, with black eyes and coal-black hair, which gave him his nickname. Instead of being called "Soot" from his color, he was known as "Sut" or "Sutty."

Sutty's father owned a small ranch north of Carlsbad on the Penasco River and brought his son to Carlsbad each fall to attend school. Sutty roomed and boarded at the same place Uncle Bob and I were staying. When school opened, we were in the same class and became inseparable in or out of school. After school hours, we both worked around the blacksmith shop. My uncle helped us both with our homework at night and otherwise looked after us like an old hen with two chicks.

Uncle took us with him almost everywhere he went. Sometimes we went into saloons and gambling houses where youngsters weren't allowed unless accompanied by a grownup relative.

"I believe it is better," he explained, "for someone to show boys such places and explain their evils than for them to sneak off and go by themselves."

Carlsbad was originally named "Eddy," but when it got the reputation of being a tough little town, its name was changed. The residents later forced the saloons, gambling houses, and red-light districts to move outside the city limits. The businesses reopened about two miles south of Carlsbad in a large barnlike adobe building with everything under one roof. They named this den of iniquity "Chihuahua," and things were plenty lively out there at times.

Uncle took Sutty and me out to Chihuahua one night, when a shooting commenced in the saloon and gambling part of the building. The lights were shot out, and the room was plunged into darkness. Sutty and I fell flat on the floor and crawled behind some whisky barrels. I could hear the sound of glass breaking as bullets struck the mirrors in the bar fixtures and the bottles and glasses.

The girls in the dance hall screamed. Chairs and gaming tables crashed as they were overturned. Gold and silver coins and poker chips tinkled as they struck the floor and rolled across the room. A silver dollar rolled between the fingers of my outstretched hand on the floor.

Then I heard the dull thud of a falling body. I could hear my heart beating against the floor, and Sutty breathed heavily as he lay alongside me. The scent of burned gunpowder filled my nostrils.

From where I was lying, I could look through the front door and see the dim light outside the building. The swinging doors opened and closed violently as fleeing patrons dashed through them like bats coming out of a cavern at sundown. Then I heard hoofbeats of horses as their riders left in a dead run.

Someone stumbled over my outstretched legs and fell headlong, cursing in Spanish as he hit the floor. There was a crash of glass in a window as someone went through it.

Suddenly everything became still. Someone struck a match and held it high above his head as if testing the situation to determine whether it was safe to light a lamp. When the lamps that were not broken were lighted, Sutty and I eased up and peeped over the barrel through the smoke-filled room. A dead Mexican was slumped against the barrel opposite us. Whisky was spurting from the barrel through a bullet hole and mixing with a pool of blood on the floor beside the dead body. The wrecked room looked as if an Oklahoma cyclone had passed through it.

Uncle Bob located us, and we slipped out through the swinging doors into the fresh night air and headed toward town. No one spoke a word until we were almost there. Then Sutty looked me in the face and said, "You sure were scared, wasn't you?"

"Guess you weren't," I answered.

"Naw," he shot back. "I like the smell of burnt gunpowder, and the crack of a six gun is music to my sunburned ears."

"Oh, yeah?" I jeered. "If you weren't scared, how come you lay down behind that whisky barrel?"

"Oh, just 'cause you was laying there," he said.

As the Christmas season approached that year, Sutty talked my uncle into allowing me to spend the holidays with him at his father's ranch on the Penasco River. I was glad to have the opportunity to be out on a ranch in the wide-open spaces again, among cattle and horses, away from the humdrum life of a boardinghouse.

Sutty was the only boy and the youngest child in a family of six children. The family lived in a sprawling ranch house originally constructed of adobe bricks, with some log additions built around it. The father and mother were real pioneers, who seemed to enjoy having me visit them and made me feel at home.

Sutty's dad came to the Pecos River country with Jingle-bob John Chisum. Chisum's cattle ranged on both sides of the Pecos River from the breaks of the Staked Plains on the east to the Tularosa Valley on the west, and from Seven Rivers on the south to the Canadian River on the north.

Sutty's father worked on that vast range until Chisum's death in 1884, at which time the Jingle-bob outfit folded up. He then established a ranch of his own. I enjoyed hearing him tell of the wild times during the early days along the Pecos and about the Lincoln County War.

About a month before school was out the following year, Sutty was notified that his father had been shot and killed by a cattle rustler he had caught stealing one of his unbranded calves. Being the only male member of his family now, Sutty immediately headed for home to look after his mother and sisters.

123

Water was scarce in the Carlsbad area in those days, and good drinking water was a problem. Much of the city's supply was hauled into town in railroad tank cars. Most of the water for other domestic use was piped into town from an open-top standpipe located in Dark Canyon several miles southwest of town.

One summer a typhoid epidemic hit the town, and about sixty persons were stricken with the fever. I was one of the victims. It was said the epidemic was caused by using water from the open-top standpipe, which had become contaminated from having no cover to protect it from the filth of birds, bats, mosquitos, and other insects.

I was confined to my bed in the rooming house for three of the hottest months of that summer, much of the time in feverish delirium. I was told later that I was given up for dead at one time, but thanks to the close attention given me by my nurse, Uncle Bob, I finally took a turn for the better.

When the fever left me, I was skin and bones, and afflicted with bedsores on my back, hips, and the insides of my knees. All my hair had fallen out, and I had to learn to walk again. I was told I resembled a young mockingbird with no plumage.

The only nourishment the doctor would let me have for some time was freshly churned country buttermilk, which was delivered by a milkman about daylight each morning. I would awaken real early and lie there in bed in an upstairs room, listening for the rattle of that milk wagon and the clip-clop of the horses' hooves, bringing my buttermilk, which tasted better than anything else I have ever drunk, before or since.

After I regained some strength, and was able to navigate, I headed for the Llano Estacado, my education in the public schools having come to a dead end.

16.

Yesterday's Horse Roundup

COWPUNCHERS on our ranch on the Staked Plains sixty-five years ago looked forward with eagerness each year to the horse roundup, at which time they would round up and corral herds of broomtails that roamed the open range, brand that year's crop of colts, and geld some of the males for the bronc twisters to tame.

It was a change from the humdrum routine of the cow roundup, carried on in the wide-open spaces without the aid of corrals, the crew continually moving from place to place each day over the range. During the horse roundup there was no "day herding" or standing guard around a herd at night, and the waddies put their feet under a table in the ranch kitchen when they ate and slept in the bunkhouse at night.

The large corrals at the ranch, where most of the work of the horse roundup was done, were built of *caliche rocks*. A long rock wing extended out in a V-shape from each side of the main gate, making it easier to crowd the broomtails in.

The hands rode the best "drive" horses in the remuda—those having long wind, stamina, and endurance for long runs—to round up the wild mustangs on the prairie and herd them into the corral at breakneck speed.

When a bunch was corralled, mares with colts were worked through a gate into a small round corral with a snubbing post in its center. Then men on foot "forefooted," hog-tied, and branded the colts. At that time they roached the colt's mane and bobbed its tail so range riders could tell from a distance it had been branded without having to run the bunch down again.

Cowhands saved the fine, soft hair, and in idle periods pulled it apart a few strands at a time, letting it fall into small piles. Then one man would turn the crank on the ranch grindstone while another held one end of a few strands of the hair, tied at the other end to a hook in the end of the wooden shaft in the stone. The hair was pulled out of the bundle as the shaft turned, creating one long continuous twisted line. The single line was then doubled and twisted again.

They used those skeins of soft hair to make saddle girths, claiming it was less apt to cause "cinch sores" on a horse than cotton girths. They also made it into stake ropes, because weather did not affect it. Some cowboys laid hair ropes in a circle around their beds, claiming rattlesnakes wouldn't crawl across them, but I doubted this.

The men were always careful when working the wild horses through the gates from one corral into another. If the horses were crowded, they often "knocked down" their hips against gate posts, which caused them to be "hipped" for life and practically useless except for breeding.

The young stallions and geldings were cut into a separate corral, where they were kept overnight. After the rest of the herd had been released and were well out of sight back on the range, the broncs were turned into the horse pasture. Thus they were not tempted to run through wire fences trying to rejoin the herd.

After the roundup was over, the bronc peelers began breaking the young geldings. They rode them seven or eight times—first with a hackamore, then with bits—until the horses were considered broken. They were then turned into the remuda or sold to other cow outfits for cow ponies. As a rule, the cowboys named them, and the names they gave them often stayed with them for life. The young stallions were castrated and kept in the pasture under close supervision until all danger of screwworms was past.

Part of a cow pony's education was to learn to be staked with a rope, for many were ridden later as "night horses" around a herd of cattle on the bed ground at night. As a rule, white horses were never broken for night horses, because a cowhand believed he was more likely to be struck by lightning while riding a white horse.

Most broncs "pitched"—or "bucked"—when first ridden. But occasionally one was found that seemed to have been raised as a pet. I remember a beautiful black with a white star on its forehead that the peeler named "Navaho." It was gentle from the start, and after having been ridden a few times, could be caught anywhere on the prairie. It was gaited and would alternate with a pace or a single-foot.

The herds of mares running on the open range were a mixture of colors—blacks, browns, bays, sorrels, whites, flea-bitten and dapple greys, pintos (piebald) of different colors, shades of roans from the strawberry to blue, blends of duns from light yellow to the dark buckskins with a stripe down the back, some albinos with pink eyes, and occasionally a mouse-colored grulla with vertical stripes down its shoulders.

During wet years when grass was plentiful and surface lakes were full of water, the Staked Plains was a horseman's paradise. But when the droughts came, causing the scant forage to wither and the lakes dry up, thus making it necessary for the herds to cover a large territory to get sufficient grass and water, it was a different story. When the grass died down, locoweed remained green, and once a horse got a taste of it, the animal would continually walk and hunt for it, until its vitality was sapped and its brain addled from eating the poison plant.

Many of the old mares were found with "witch knots" in their manes and tails, caused when some object such as a cocklebur or a twig got caught in the hair. This gradually formed a matted mass that eventually became so large that when it got between the animal's hind legs and swung from side to side, it prevented her from running. When a mare was found in the corral in that condition, she was roped, a hind foot was tied up, and the knot was removed.

The horses' hooves were almost as hard as the *caliche* rocks that covered the range they roamed. They went through life without trimmed hooves or shoes. The hard life they lived gave them stamina, staying power, and intestinal fortitude. They had to be tough to endure the blue northers, fierce blizzards, and summer heat. There were no ravines, bluffs, or timber to provide shelter from the north winds and the heat of the blazing summer sun. In the winter when blizzards howled, they had to paw the snow that covered the grass to get something to eat.

Horse breeders of today claim their animals are far superior to those of sixty-five years ago, and maybe they are in some ways. Raising horses, like raising beef cattle from the lean and lanky longhorn to the bald-face Hereford and the Shorthorn Durham, has improved.

In the past, the horse pulled the vehicle. Now the vehicle pulls the horse in a semienclosed trailer to protect it from the wind as it travels along the highway at seventy miles an hour.

I find horses today finer looking than those of yesteryear. They should be. From the time many of them are foaled in a modern "horse maternity ward," they are pampered and coddled in sheds and barns, allowed to graze only in modern fenced and cross-fenced pastures of alfalfa and clover, and on top of that, fed plenty of good oats and hay. They are rubbed down, curried, and combed by makeup artists. Their hooves are cleaned and they are shod by experts.

But are they superior in every way? I doubt it. A modern horse can be hauled from the shade of his barn, or from his lush alfalfa patch for a march around the parade grounds or a quarter-mile run on the track, and look magnificent. But if he were ridden on one of those grueling circle drives in a horse roundup, running unshod at breakneck speed for miles across a rocky range covered with badger holes, I'm afraid he just couldn't take it.

Putting a majority of modern horses through such paces would be like taking a modern ten- or fifteen-round pugilist from his air-conditioned quarters for a finish fight in a ring under the broiling sun, with bare knuckles and no Marquis of Queensberry rules, against an old-time champion like John L. Sullivan.

There was nothing smarter in those days than a good cutting hoss. A sheep dog was second, with a college graduate next in line. The top waddies with the large outfits on the open range always had three cutting horses among their regular mounts that they rode in the roundup. They thought a lot of them, and usually trained those horses themselves. Man and horse were a team.

The modern cutting horse puts on a fine show in the arena before the grandstand as it is ridden in among a few cattle. It dutifully brings one out, turning and dodging with a free rein, blocking the calf's every movement.

The horse—and probably its rider—would be lost if ridden into a roundup of three thousand cattle on the open range, with alkali dust boiling up from the roundup grounds, to start a cut of cows with calves following, without separating the calf from its mother, then start another cut of big, wild Mexican steers. That's when a horse has to use its skill. If the modern horse were turned out onto the open range to shift for itself, it would have a difficult time doing so. I am not belittling the horse of today—far from it. I love anything that resembles horseflesh. But I do believe yesterday's horses were more self-reliant than today's.

On circle drive during a horse roundup one year, when the hands were bringing a bunch of extremely wild mares to the ranch, Uncle George was on the right "point" when some of the herd broke out in an effort to get away.

As he rode furiously to turn the animals back, his horse fell. Seeing the horse struggle to its feet and limp off a short distance without the rider, the other men rushed to the scene and found him lying unconscious. It was apparent that the horse had stepped into a large badger hole partly covered with grass, and had broken its foreleg. Humanely, they put it out of its misery. They placed the injured man on a mattress in the rear part of a buckboard to be taken to the ranch. With his head resting in the lap of one of the men, they headed for Roswell, by way of the LFD Ranch at Four Lakes, where they changed teams. Thirty miles farther west at Mescalero Springs, they changed teams again. One man had gone straight through to Roswell on horseback to get a doctor and bring him back to meet them.

The doctor found that Uncle George's spinal colum had been severely injured and put him in a hospital at Roswell. Later, he went to a sanitarium at Kirksville, Missouri, for several months of treatments, but without getting much relief. From there he went to other clinics in the East and North, where his condition seemed to improve somewhat.

When he returned, he sold his old ranch and most of his stock to pay doctor and hospital bills and traveling expenses. He married his nurse, a German-born graduate in her profession, named Johanna Feuson, and built a small ranch a few miles south of Kenna. After that, Uncle George took a turn for the worse, and at times seemed despondent. One morning while eating breakfast at his ranch, my brother Ralph and I heard a muffled gun-shot. Running into his room, we found him lying in bed with smoke coming from under the covers. Raising the blanket, we found a .45 Colt clasped in his hand. He was buried in a cemetery at Roswell.

Thus ended the career of a widely known pioneer of the Llano Estacado, who led a rough and dangerous life during the years he helped settle that region.

After the tragedy, I saddled a horse, rode to Four Lakes, and hired out to Bud Wilkerson for a job punching cattle and breaking broncs for the LFD outfit.

PART THREE
Adventures of a Young Cowpuncher

17.

The Littlefield (LFD) Outfit

MAJOR George W. Littlefield and his nephews, Phelps and Tom White, were among the first of the Texas cattle barons to move their herds of cattle to the Staked Plains for pasturage. But they did so unintentionally, not planning to establish a ranch there at the time.

While moving large herds of cattle from South Texas up the trail to shipping pens in Kansas in the mid-1870's, they arrived at Dodge City with a large herd and found the market glutted and prices unfavorable. They moved their herd, branded LIT, back south to the Texas Panhandle plains and grazed them along the north side of the Canadian River near the site of the future pioneer town of Tascosa. Liking the wide-open free range, they established a temporary ranch there.

When John Chisum moved his headquarters from Bosque Grande on the Pecos River south of Fort Sumner to his new Jingle-bob Ranch on South Spring River south of Roswell, Littlefield and the Whites decided they would move to a new range farther west.

They sold their LIT herds to the Prairie Cattle Company and established a new ranch at Chisum's abandoned Bosque Grande location. Their new cattle brand was LFD on the right hip, side, and shoulder, and their earmark was an under-half-crop, both ears.

Major Littlefield retired from active participation on the range and settled in Austin, where he engaged in the banking business. He turned his cattle-raising operations over to his two nephews, and made Phelps White—the elder of the two—general manager.

White wasn't satisfied with the water and range conditions along the Pecos River. When he heard that George Causey, with whom he was acquainted, had discovered that a plentiful supply of good water could be had on the Llano Estacado by digging or drilling wells to a reasonably shallow depth, White immediately headed for that region to investigate the report.

As he rode across the plains to Causey's camp at the OHO he could see that the plains would be good range during wet years, with surface lakes full of water, and grass knee high. But when dry years and droughts came, it would be a different situation. He realized that watering places would have to be established before a large herd of cattle could be brought there.

Phelps White and his LFD outfit bought George Causey's water rights and improvements at his OHO and Ranger Lake locations. White also made a deal with Causey to buy a well-drilling rig and drill for him at several locations over the plains at points about ten miles apart. The drilling rig was powered by a team of mules, walking in a circle, turning a large flat gear and pinion, which was keyed on the shaft leading to the drill rig.

Everything to improve the new ranch had to be hauled from the Texas-Pacific Railroad more than one hundred miles to the south. George Causey, joined by his younger brothers, John and Bob, hauled well-drilling equipment from the railroad and started putting down wells.

Causey also put his bull teams and wagons into service, hauling material such as well casing, water pipe, windmills, and the lumber for windmill towers and water troughs, fence posts, stays, barbed wire, and other items needed to improve the watering places. He helped the Whites throw up dumps for surface-water tanks for storage, which they fenced. Water was piped into troughs on the outside where float valves controlled the flow of water. Causey and his men helped White establish his headquarters ranch at Four Lakes and build a ranch house of rocks.

In the early 1880's, when everything was ready, the LFD outfit moved their cattle from the alkali flats, gyp hills, and quick-sand bed of the Pecos River southeast across the Mescalero sand hills and up on the Llano Estacado to a cattleman's dreamland on the free government range of southeastern New Mexico.

There were no sloughs or quicksands for their cattle to bog down in. And the animals would not have to walk off their flesh making long hikes to and from water, as they did on the Pecos.

Very little of the virgin range had ever been grazed by any-thing other than herds of buffaloes and antelopes and bands of mustang horses. About the only drawback to the new range was the blue northers and fierce blizzards during the winter months, which caused cattle to drift long distances, and the prairie fires, which broke out at times and swept across the level land almost as fast as a horse could run, burning off large areas of precious grass.

The LFD outfit dammed up Mescalero Spring (located un-der the cap rock about twenty miles west of Four Lakes), fenced it, and piped water to troughs outside. The men built a one-room adobe house there, and used it as a horse camp for their remuda of cow ponies branded Bar F on the left hip.

Major Littlefield's brother, "Bill" Littlefield, established a ranch at San Juan Mesa about ten miles west of the present town of Kenna, New Mexico. The LFD built the T71 Ranch at Kenna and a dam across Long Arroyo just north of that town. They also had an open watering place at a lake, known as Curlew Lake, just south of Railroad Mountain southwest of Kenna.

The original LFD range was from the Pecos River on the west to the Texas–New Mexico state line on the east, a distance of about eighty-five miles, and from where Kenna is located on the north to Monument Spring on the south, about ninety miles. The LFD became one of the most famous of the large cattle outfits in New Mexico. LFD cowpunchers branded about thirteen thousand calves a year, and ran their herds there on the open free range for over twenty years before being crowded out by small ranchers, nesters, plowed ground, and barbed wire.

Several of the old cowboys who came to the Staked Plains with the LFD outfit had been with them since trail-driving days, when they had helped Major Littlefield drive herds of longhorn cattle to the rail heads in Kansas.

Among them were Bud Wilkerson, Joe Champion, Charlie Walker, and his brother Walter Walker, who was known as "Big Spider," or "Tarantula," on account of being so crippled up with rheumatism that he walked stiff-legged, like one of those big spiders.

Others were "Shorty" Carrington, John House, Doc Sears, Ben (C Hop) Baker, Bruce Conner, Dave Howell, George Urton, Captain Tom York, Will McCombs, Max Tabner, Fate Beard, Charlie Abers (who was known as "Bill Nye"), "Rain-in-the-Face," Bob Honley, John Cole, and three other nephews of Major Littlefield's—"Big" George Littlefield and Edgar and Victor Harrell.

Another was Harry Robertson, who was known to everyone as "Old Man Harry." He had deserted an English ship on the Texas Gulf Coast and spent some time on Padre Island before crossing over to the mainland. He was with the Major at Tascosa and Bosque Grande before coming to the Llano Estacado with White. He finally settled on a small spring under the west breaks of the plains south of Mescalero Spring, built a little one-room rock shelter, acquired a small bunch of cattle, and started ranching on his own.

One of the most important personalities with the LFD outfit during its entire operation was the bookkeeper, "Cat Head" Smith, who looked after the finances, kept the cowhands' time, and issued them their checks.

Another member of the LFD crew was Old Negro Ad, the

most famous Negro cowpuncher of the Old West. He had been with "Marse" George Littlefield since Emancipation days. He was an expert horseman, a good rider and roper. He was very bow-legged from a lifetime spent in the saddle. He was a good cowhand, but because of the custom in those days, never became what was known as a "top" hand. In later days, Old Ad enjoyed telling of the time "Black Jack" Ketchum and his brother Sam were working for trail-driver Charlie Walker on the trail to Dodge City.

It was before the Ketchums started robbing trains in northeastern New Mexico. They were harassing a tenderfoot boy Walker had hired by making him dance to the tune of their six guns, the .45-caliber slugs knocking up the dust around his feet. Charlie Walker caught them in the act and told them if they wished to make someone dance, to try him on and he would get them both. They meekly put up their guns and didn't bother the boy any more.

Some of the common waddies who worked on the LFD range on the Llano Estacado were Charlie Fairweather, who formerly mustanged for George Causey; Luther Swanner; Ralph and "Buster" Whitlock; Johnnie Formwalt; Harve Harris; Otto and Valpo Douthitt; and Walter and "Wrang" White.

Bill Morgan stayed at the Mescalero Horse Camp. "Arizona" Bowen lived at the Keenam east camp and oiled windmills on that part of the range. After the death of George Causey, George Jefferson was at the 7HR south camp oiling windmills on the south part of the range.

Some employees with duties other than punching cattle were Dick Miller, the windmill man, and his two assistants, Fred Fairweather and Master Lewis. Their responsibility was to repair and keep in constant operation the windmills at about fourteen watering places over the range.

Others were the chuck wagon cooks, John Fuson, Hayden Manning, and Curly the Crow, who claimed to be a Crow Indian and a one-time scout for General Custer but was absent from the Battle of the Little Big Horn River.

Next to the wagon boss, the cook was the most important man in a cow outfit. With a poor cook and bum cooking, the morale of a bunch of cowhands was soon ruined and everyone had a grouch, from the boss on down to the horse wrangler. A cook had to know his business to be able to move camp twice a day and cook three meals for twenty-five or thirty hungry cowhands, especially when the cow chips were wet.

In addition to being a good cook, he also had to be a good mule skinner. For it was he who had to drive a team of four, six, or eight mules hitched to the heavy chuck wagon with tarpaulin-wrapped bedrolls stacked on it to the top of the wagon bows. He drove across all kinds of terrain, much of which had no roads.

There were two Tom Whites on the Staked Plains, which made it necessary to use their brands in connection with their names to distinguish one from the other: "T Bar T" Tom White and "LFD" Tom White. T Bar T Tom White ranched with the Heard brothers at the High Lonesome Ranch in the southeastern part of the LFD range.

Around 1898, when the Pecos Valley & North Eastern Railroad (PV&NE) built their line into the Pecos Valley from Amarillo, the LFD changed its trading point from Midland to Roswell. The outfit did business there with the Jaffa-Prager and Joyce-Pruitt stores.

The freight-wagon road went west from Four Lakes, and down off the Staked Plains at what was known as the Gap, then across the Mescalero Sands and Long Arroyo, fording the Pecos River at the Juan Chaves Crossing.

The Littlefield outfit bought a large farm a few miles east of Roswell, planted it in alfalfa, and irrigated it with artesian wells. They turned its management over to Joe Champion. In February of each year, they rounded up their remuda of saddle horses at the winter camp at the breaks of the plains and drove them to the lush fields of alfalfa. By the time the spring roundup started, the horses had shed their winter coats of hair and were fat and frisky.

LFD Tom White was a great conversationalist. The only

man on the Staked Plains who could beat him was "Massa" John Beal, former manager of the old Jumbo Ranch on the Double Mountain Fork of the Brazos River southeast of Lubbock, Texas.

One day, Massa John came to Four Lakes on his way to Roswell and spent the night at the ranch. During the evening, White couldn't finish a sentence or get a word in edgewise without Beal's drowning him out.

They slept in the same room, and the last thing White said before dropping off to sleep, was, "As I was going to say awhile ago . . . ." Beal cut him off before he could finish.

White awakened about daylight the following morning, raised up on his elbow, looked over at Massa John, and said, "As I was trying to tell you last night . . . ."

But Beal again interrupted, and Tom White never did get to finish what he was going to tell.

The LFD leased the Z Bar L Ranch, located at the east side of the Staked Plains, in Crosby County, Texas, to use as a steer ranch. Since the rough terrain was partly covered with brush, good protection from northers and blizzards, it was an excellent pasture for cattle.

During the fall roundup each year, the men gathered their yearling steers and trailed them across the Llano Estacado to the Z Bar L pasture. When the fall cow work was finished, the day herd in which the yearling steers were kept as they were gathered was rounded up and the young steers were cut out to themselves. Then the trouble started.

Many of the yearlings were still following their mothers, and a lot of them weren't even weaned. The cows in the roundup could hear their calves in the cut bawling, and the yearlings in the cut could hear their mothers in the roundup bawling for them. It was very difficult to keep them from getting together. When the cutting out was finished, the new trail herd immediately headed east toward the Texas line.

During the first two nights on the trail, the yearlings were very hard to hold. Everyone but the cook had to stand guard around them in order to hold them on the bed ground. Natural instinct caused them to want to return to the place where they last saw their mothers. They would stand in a mass, looking back in the direction from which they were driven, bawling as if their little hearts were breaking.

Sometimes, one would break through and hightail it in a dead run. If a rider followed it, several more would break through at the same place. Then part of the crew would have to return to the roundup ground the following morning, where they would find all the calves with their mothers.

After the third night on the trail, the little steers were perfectly contented and lay on the bedground peacefully chewing their cuds throughout the night, without giving any trouble.

The trail boss had orders to gather a herd of larger steers at the Z Bar L pasture and trail them to shipping pens at Bovina, Texas, for delivery to steer buyers from Kansas. That procedure prevented overstocking the steer pastures.

The LFD foremen and top hands had steady employment and were never laid off. In addition to receiving their regular wages, they were allowed the privilege of running a small bunch of cattle of their own on the LFD range without cost or obligation.

This fair play by the employer caused the employees to be loyal and to jealously guard the interests of the employer against cattle rustling and other such cow-country activities.

Top hands led groups of riders when making circle drives, dropping a rider off at intervals to drive what cattle he might find to the roundup grounds. They also rode their cutting horses into the roundup when it was formed, working cattle out into different "cuts." The common hands rode herd on the cuts, and stationed themselves around the roundup to hold it together.

When changing mounts four times each day, top hands walked around in the remuda roping the horses for the men holding up the rope corral as the names of horses they wished to ride were called out.

When neighboring outfits such as the DZ, Bar V, Turkey Track, Hat, JAL, and others started working their ranges, one LFD top hand—known as a "rep" or "outside man"—with his mount of horses went to each of those ranches and worked with them, gathering cattle belonging on the LFD range and brought them home. Top hands spent the winter months riding grain-fed horses in line, horse, and bog camps and other winter quarters, constantly riding the range and looking after the stock.

The most unpleasant assignment—especially during cold weather—was "riding bog" along the Pecos River. Two men together rode up and down the river each day looking for cattle that had waded out in the water to drink and, by the time they had their fill, were mired in the quicksand so deeply they couldn't extricate their legs. If not rescued, they would gradually sink farther and farther until they drowned. When a cow was found in that condition, one man would pull off his boots and wade out and tie the other man's rope around the animal's neck in a knot that wouldn't slip and choke. Then, as the waddy tramped around the cow's legs and loosened up the sand, the other man, with rope tied to his saddle horn, would pull the cow to dry land. They would then "tail up" bossy, but sometimes she didn't appreciate the treatment given her. She would "get on the prod" and show fight, fall down, and have to be tailed up onto her feet again.

If it hadn't been for four old chuck wagon mules belonging to the LFD outfit, the following event involving mustangs might never have occurred. It makes a story an old horse lover and wildlife enthusiast doesn't like to think of, much less put on paper. The only reason I am including it here is to record the passing of the last bunch of mustang horses from the Llano Estacado in southeastern New Mexico.

The four old chuck wagon mules were as contrary and hardheaded as any that were ever driven by a cook from one roundup ground to another. They were cunning, crafty, and almost as smart as a cutting horse. They took great delight in sneaking out of the remuda at night and being absent-without-leave the following morning. Bells around their necks solved the problem for a while. But they soon discovered that if they eased along real carefully, they could keep the bells from ringing.

One fall when the outfit tied up for the winter at the Four

Lakes headquarters ranch, the mules were turned into the horse pasture to be fed grain during the winter months. They usually came to the corral for their feed, but if they didn't show up, someone rode out and brought them in.

One morning when the mules didn't come for their feed, I rode out after them. There was some rough terrain, including some of the lakes, in the large pasture. I explored every corner but found no mules. I rode around the pasture fence and found the staples missing in several posts and all strands of the wire lying on the ground. I made a close examination of the ground and found tracks where the mules had crossed over the wires.

I followed the tracks for some distance but lost them on a rocky ridge. I then made a complete circle of the ranch, but saw nothing of the old "hardtails." The foreman sent several men in all directions from the ranch to make a wide search. No success. The mules had really "gone over the hill" this time.

Late that afternoon, "Buttermilk" Smith, who kept the south camp on Newman's DZ ranch to the north, showed up at Four Lakes. He told of seeing four mules with a bunch of mustangs that ranged in the sands to the north, between the LFD and DZ ranges.

The following morning, the boss sent me up into the sand hills to hunt up the wild bunch, cut the mules out, and bring them home. I found the mustangs with the mules among them. But, pardner, those old mulas were wilder than any mustang in the bunch. With their "make me" attitude, they defied me and really showed me that I couldn't separate them from the horses. They would run along looking back on one side, then the other, emitting an occasional "hee-haw," as if laughing at my efforts to handle them. I ran them until my mount was almost exhausted, then returned to the ranch, admitting defeat.

The following morning, the range boss sent five of us cowboys up into the sand hills with explicit orders to bring the mules back. We were all riding strong, long-winded, grain-fed horses, capable of making endurance runs.

We located the wild bunch in their usual haunt, with the

mules among them. We "took stands" about one mile apart along the direction in which the herd ran when disturbed.

The first man took the herd at a rapid rate of speed to the second man, who, mounted upon a fresh horse, took up the chase and turned them over to the third rider, and so on. By the time the fourth man fell in behind the running mustangs, the old mules became tired of playing that kind of game, meekly dropped out, veered off to one side, and headed for the ranch, perfectly innocent and docile.

The wild bunch was pronounced a nuisance, and orders were issued for their disposal. It was a task that none of the waddies wished to participate in, but orders had to be obeyed. The old cowpokes often made derogatory remarks about the wanton slaughter of the buffaloes, and now they were ordered to do likewise to the last of the mustangs.

Later, those orders were carried out. But those who took an active part in the operation would never discuss how they did it. Thus, a whim in the minds of four old mules to "go wild" brought about the severe decimation of those colorful horses that had roamed the Staked Plains for many years.

18.

Cattle Brands

HISTORIANS tell us that for hundreds of years, ownership of animals has been determined by brands burned into the skin with red-hot irons. They also say that in some instances in the past human beings were marked by that same method for identification by their owners. Cortés, who is credited with being the first person in America to place a brand on his cattle, is said also to have so marked his Aztec slaves.

Although almost all of the old Spanish missions in the Southwest had herds of cattle, very little is known about the brands of these early-day ranchers. One mentioned quite often is the "*Cabeza de Vaca*," or "Head of a Cow," brand ꙮ . The records show that Don Nicolas Saez branded his cattle ℣ before 1800.

The White Ranch located in southeast Texas between Beaumont and Galveston was probably the first ranch started by an Anglo-Saxon. James Taylor White located there in 1819 and grazed his cattle branded W (crossed W or WX), over Chambers, Liberty, Polk, and Jefferson counties. That ranch is still operated by the White family.

Another early rancher in that part of the Lone Star State, was William McFaddin, whose herds branded M6 ranged in Jefferson County, Texas, as early as 1837. Daniel Shipman, who was a member of Stephen F. Austin's colony, ran his herds branded DS around 1822. And Thomas O'Conner started branding his cattle ⅄C about 1837.

Some of the famous brands that were well known to the waddies who rode the ranges on the Great Plains region sixty or more years ago were Slaughter's ∽ (Long S lying down); Kokernot's O6; the ⊶D (Spade) brand that was started by Evans and later owned by Elwood; the Cowden brothers' JՈL ; Robertson and Scott's TX; Littlefield's LFD, LIT, and –F (Bar F) on cow ponies; the Espuela outfit's Ո (Spur), Matador outfits ∿ (Matador V), McNulty's ⋀ (Turkey Track) outfit located near the old Adobe Walls ruin; Newman's DZ; Sanborn's –O (Frying Pan); Bates and Beals' LX; Lee and Reynolds' LS and LE; Halsell's ⊂⊃ (mashed O); Joe Sneed's ∿ (Pot Hook); and McElroy's J Cross outfit on Sulphur Draw in Yoakum County, Texas.

Some of the early brands in the south part of the Llano Estacado in Texas and New Mexico, besides the LFD, were the Mallet; the Beal outfit's ⌒⌒ (Lazy B); ⌒ℓ (hat); VVN; –V (Bar V); HUT; WAX; RAT; Crossed Links ⊕ ;HX△ (HX Triangle); the 8o outfit; Brownings J96; the Herd Brother's Crazy J's; and George Causey's JᗺB (JHB connected), on cattle and Ո (roundtop open A) on his range horses.

Each brand carried a certain earmark, such as Littlefield's herds that were marked with an ⊂⊃ (under-half-crop, each ear). Cattle bearing certain brands were more easily identified in a roundup by the manner in which their ears were marked, especially in the spring of the year when their hair was long.

To further identify their cattle—in addition to the earmark and the brand on shoulder, side, or hip—some ranchers placed a brand on the animal's jaw, such as the "G" that Cortés was said to have burned upon the cheeks of his slaves. Some ranchers also burned a stripe across the back of the animal's legs above the hock, to make brand blotting more difficult for rustlers. Some ranchers used what was called the "dewlap." This was made by slitting out the dewlap toward the top in the animal's skin under the neck and letting a short portion hang down.

The Prairie Cattle Company was probably one of the largest outfits in the West, ranging their herds in three states, using the JJ brand in Colorado, the Cross L brand in New Mexico, and the LIT brand they bought from Littlefield in the Texas Panhandle around Tascosa. Charles Goodnight and his cowpokes chased the buffaloes out of the Palo Duro Canyon, moved his (JA connected) herds in there, and established one of the oldest ranches in that part of the country.

When Ab Blocker, the South Texas trail driver who drove herds to the railheads in Kansas for his brother John, delivered the first herd of cattle to Barbecue Campbell, manager of the XIT at their headquarters ranch at Buffalo Springs, cowhands who were with him said Blocker asked Campbell what their brand was. Campbell replied, "We have no brand."

"What! No brand?" Blocker asked. "If you don't have a brand, you don't have a ranch."

They said the two men squatted down in a corral and, making marks in the dust with sticks, designed the XIT brand that made the ranch famous from the Canadian border to the Gulf of Mexico. They thought they had designed a brand that couldn't be "burned" or "blotted" by rustlers. But XIT hands used to tell how they found cattle upon which the XIT had been changed to a "five-pointed star with a cross made of the I in the center."

Although most of the ranches of the Old West were known by the brand their cattle carried, this was not so with "King of the Río Pecos" John Chisum's cattle empire. Instead of being known by the "Long Rail" he burned on his cattle's side, it was known by the "jinglebob," the way the ears were marked—slit out in such a way that one part of the ear pointed upward and the other pointed down. A big, longhorned, wild Mexican steer marked in that manner made a gruesome sight.

Brands were sometimes used to specify persons bearing identical names, as in the case of "LFD" Tom White and "T BAR T" Tom White.

When a new brand appeared on cattle on the open range, rustlers immediately started trying to figure out a way to change it—by adding something to it, or by "blotting" it so that the original brand could not be identified. As a rule, cattle to be driven up the trail for a long distance through other ranges were given what was called a "road brand," usually one letter or one figure by which they could be easily identified if they became mixed up with other cattle in a stampede.

Most of the original brands were applied with a "stamp" branding iron. But the altering was done with a "J running iron," which cowhands carried on their saddles as part of their standard equipment. They used it to brand "mavericks," "sleepers," and large unbranded calves that had been overlooked during the regular roundup.

Sometimes during the winter, rustlers would come across a large unbranded calf still following its mother. They would "pick" the brand carried by the mother on the calf, by pulling the long hair out of the skin in such a way that it appeared to be branded, and then "mark" the calf's ears in the same way the mother's ears were marked. When the calf was weaned, and the "picked" brand disappeared with the shedding of the winter coat, the rustler would place his own brand on it and alter the earmark.

When rustling became widespread, the ranchers organized the Texas and Southwestern Cattle Raisers Association and hired "brand inspectors" who—from long and wide experience—were experts in that line to look after their interests. The inspectors made a close check of cattle being loaded in the shipping pens and of trail herds passing through the country for any cattle bearing brands belonging to members of the association, and for any evidence of brand altering or blotting. They were particularly interested in cattle belonging to members of the association which they represented.

There is a case on record of an inspector's becoming suspicious of the brand on a steer that was loaded at the shipping pens.

He followed it to the stockyards at Kansas City, then on to the slaughterhouse, where he got the hide and brought it back to be used as evidence in a court trial. The flesh side of the hide showed very plainly what the original brand was before it was altered. On this evidence, the thief was convicted.

It is unlawful in most western states for a person to place a brand on stock unless the brand is properly recorded. This story is told about a circuit-riding district judge who was holding his first term of court in a newly organized West Texas county:

After the newly elected sheriff walked to the courthouse window and announced to the world at the top of his voice, "Oh, yes! Oh, yes! The honorable district court of————County is now in session," the judge impaneled the first grand jury and told them to hold up their hands and be sworn in. Some of them held up their right hands, some held up their left hands, and one old boy held up both hands.

When he gave members of the new jury their instructions, the judge told them, among other things, "Gentlemen, it is a violation of the law for anyone in this county to place a brand on cattle or horses unless it is properly recorded. You gentlemen will investigate any violation of that law that may be brought to your attention." It was whispered around the courthouse that afternoon that when court adjourned for the noon recess, several of the grand jurors and some of the spectators in the courtroom sneaked into the office of the newly elected county clerk and placed their brands on record.

While sitting around campfires or in the bunkhouse, Old Jeff and the old waddies who were with Major Littlefield when he was holding his steers along the Canadian River around Tascosa used to tell how the early ranchers in the Texas Panhandle hired John Poe—famous peace officer, former U.S. marshal, and former town marshal of Fort Griffin who was with Sheriff Pat Garrett the night he killed Billy the Kid at Fort Sumner—to look after their interests and track down rustlers who came over from the Pecos River country and made raids on their cattle.

They told how Poe followed a long trail of those rustlers

across the Texas–New Mexico line and across the Pecos River to the Tularosa Valley near the White Sands in New Mexico, where he found cowhides hanging on a rancher's fence bearing brands of several Panhandle ranchers whom he represented. He was instrumental in arrests made and indictments returned for cattle theft.

Back in the days before law and order came to the plains, only one crime was considered more heinous than cattle rustling, and that was stealing a man's saddle horse. They used to tell of necktie parties in the bosques along the Pecos River where cottonwood trees were used to "string 'em up." But on the treeless Llano Estacado, windmill towers and guy wires stretched across the tops of gateposts in barbed-wire fences were used for that purpose.

The old-time cattle rustler with his cow pony, rope, running iron, pocket knife, and cow chip branding fire, is almost as extinct as the longhorn breed of cattle he used to rustle. But a new type of rustler has taken his place. He drives a large truck with an enclosed body, and with his rifle and butcher knife goes to lonely spots away from the beaten highways where he kills and skins an animal and loads the meat on his truck. Before the crime is discovered, he is many miles away, selling the meat to some butcher who neither questions nor cares where it came from.

19.

Barbed Wire

ALTHOUGH barbed wire was not invented in Texas, it is as Texan as cattle brands, the longhorn steer, rawhide, and the road runner. It did its part in helping settle West Texas, and changed the mode of ranching from the open range to enclosed pastures. There was probably more barbed wire used on the High Plains of West Texas than in any other area its size in the world. The Panhandle plains and the Llano Estacado were tied together with mile after mile of barbed wire.

Historians disagree about who first introduced barbed wire to the Lone Star State. One claims that the first known to have been brought to Texas was sold in Gainesville in 1875 by H. B. Sanborn, who founded the town of Amarillo, Texas. Another says John W. Gates introduced the first barbed wire to Texas when he put it on display in the San Antonio area. According to available records, barbed wire was invented by J. F. Glidden of De Kalb, Illinois, who received a patent on it in 1874. Shortly thereafter, he was joined by I. L. Ellwood, with whom he obtained a patent on a machine for making the wire. They built a factory at

De Kalb for manufacturing it and employed H. B. Sanborn as their agent and salesman to put the product on the market.

All three of these pioneers in barbed wire made fortunes from its manufacture and sale. Sanborn invested his funds in the 125,000-acre Frying Pan Ranch, and a few years ago some of the first barbed wire to be strung in the Texas Panhandle was still hanging on the posts bordering that ranch.

I. L. Ellwood invested his profits in land and cattle in the Lone Star State. He established ranches near Colorado City and on the South Plains of Texas. On these ranches he ran herds of cattle bearing the famous "Spade" brand which he bought from John F. Evans in Donley County, Texas, in the 1880's.

Probably the largest sale of barbed wire to one ranch was to the 3,000,000-acre XIT Ranch that covered all or parts of ten counties in the Texas Panhandle.

XIT cowhands used to brag that theirs was the largest fenced ranch in the world, the west line running down the Texas–New Mexico border for about 150 miles without a turn. About 1,500 miles of wire was used to cut up the ranch into seven divisions, each division having several smaller pastures. They said a man named Collins, who owned a mercantile business at Channing, Texas, sold the XIT outfit thirty carloads of barbed wire (900,000 pounds) at one time.

When the buffalo hunters hauled the last of the bleached buffalo bones from their old killing grounds to Colorado City, to sell for fertilizer, they loaded their wagons with barbed wire, fenceposts, and stays for the return trip to the Staked Plains.

Although Glidden's invention changed the mode of ranching in the West, it was not a peaceable change. Some ranchers fenced large tracts of land enclosing smaller tracts owned by small ranchers, cutting them off from public highways. This practice started the famous "fence-cutting wars" of West Texas. Governor John Ireland called a special session of the legislature, and a law was placed upon the statute books making fence cutting a felony. This law was enforced by Texas Rangers.

Barbed-wire drift fences were built to take the place of the

151

line riders, but although drifting cattle were indeed stopped by those fences, they died along the north side of them by the thousands. Barbed wire merely changed cowhands from line riders to fence riders, who rode the north side of those fences trying to keep cattle from "balling up" along them. It was claimed that barbed wire ruined more good cow ponies than anything else except locoweed, because it cut them badly and crippled them up.

To measure the distance covered by the length of their fence, to determine the amount of wire they would have to buy, LFD officials took the circumference of a rear wheel on a buckboard vehicle and, with a string tied to one of the spokes of the wheel, counted the number of revolutions the wheel made on a trip across the plains where the fence would be built. This gave them a close figure on the length of the four strands of wire they would need to complete the line. The survey also helped them figure the number of fenceposts and stays they would need to haul in.

After a few years, the nesters filed on their quarter-section homesteads and moved in with a few head of cattle to start "dry-farming." The cowhands said the government was betting them 160 acres of land against their filing fee that they couldn't make a living on the land, and some of them couldn't.

Some of the nesters filed on the watering places and the free ranges were soon cut up with barbed-wire fences. The grass was plowed under, and the cattle barons had to hunt other ranges.

20.

Yesterday's Cow Roundup

A person who has never slept or eaten around a chuck wagon with a large cow outfit, who has never gone on circle drive, ridden a well-trained "cuttin' horse" in a roundup, day herded, roped or flanked calves around a branding fire, or stood guard around a sleeping or milling herd on the bed ground when an old-time cow roundup was in full swing, has missed some of the most vivid experiences of the Old West.

One of the sweetest sounds in a cowhand's life is the chuck wagon cook grinding coffee in the coffee mill fastened on the side of the chuck box early in the morning. Peeping out from under his tarpaulin that has been stiffened by the morning dew, the cowhand glances at the surroundings lighted up by the blazing campfire. Then, if he doesn't crave a few more winks of shut-eye, he watches the cook empty the contents of the coffee-mill tray into the pot hanging on the pot rack over the fire. The cook pours part of the foaming contents of the sourdough keg into a dishpan partly filled with flour and kneads the dough for the biscuits, pinching off small hunks and putting them into Dutch ovens sitting on beds of coals. He covers the ovens with lids that have been heated over the fire, and spreads a shovelful of glowing coals on top.

A few minutes later, the cowboy hears a sound like the buzzing in a beehive. It is beefsteak or sow bosom sizzling in the skillet hanging over the fire, and he knows "it won't be long now."

Squatting down on the opposite side of the fire, squinting through the smoke that partly obscures his grizzled, tanned, and weather-beaten face is one of the cowhands. He is smoking a Bull Durham cigarette and taking sips of coffee from a tin cup between puffs. His night horse stands just behind him with bridle reins trailing on the ground. He is on last guard around the remuda and has the horses rounded up nearby, so that the hands can catch drive horses as soon as breakfast is over.

He has filled and hung the morrals on the heads of the four chuck wagon mules, and they are crunching their grain, standing near the front end of the wagon. When they finish eating, by tossing the morral up to get the last grain of corn, they do not wait to have the bag removed, but put a forefoot on it and pull back, breaking the string. Then they mosey back to the remuda.

Here and there in the tarpaulin-covered beds around the wagon, tousled heads of sleeping cowhands can be seen where the wind has blown the tarp back. Their Stetson hats lying on the ground have boots and spurs on the brim to keep the wind from blowing them away.

Day hasn't started to break as yet, but across the sleeping herd of cattle on the bed ground, the morning star is shining like a diamond, close enough to touch. The cook yells, "Come and get it or I'll *throw it out!*" and tarps are thrown back. As you pull on your boots, you are greeted by the delectable aroma of boiling coffee. Beds are rolled, strapped, and loaded onto the wagon by hands working in pairs, the one on the ground pitching them up to the other on top of the wagon.

The water barrels carried on each side of the wagon bed don't hold enough water for an overnight camp and thirty cowpunchers to wash their faces and hands, so no one washes his hands but the cook, and it is sometimes doubtful that *he* does.

As a rule, many of the older cowhands eat very little breakfast, taking only a cup of coffee, while some top off their breakfast of biscuits and meat with a helping of "lick."

As the waddies finish eating, they drop their tin cups and plates into a dishpan on the ground under the chuckbox lid, then harness and hitch the mules to the wagon. While the cook washes the dishes, some of the hands put the skillet, pots, ovens, and pot rack in the rawhide "coosie" or "possum belly" swung beneath the wagon, and it is ready to roll. Cook then climbs on top of the bedrolls stacked to the top of the wagon bows, gathers up his lines, and clucks to the mules. The heavily loaded, broad-tired wagon, with its sloping chuck box in the rear, lumbers off across the prairie toward the watering place where that day's roundup will be held.

The hands stretch their ropes around the remuda, and the horse ropers walking among the horses neatly drop loops around the necks of those the men call for by name, brand, or color. Then the wrangler moves his remuda off along the trail taken by the chuck wagon. The wagon boss gives his drive leaders instructions, and the first phase of the daily roundup is in progress.

The LFD outfit was rounding up and branding calves. It was a wet year that made range conditions good. The cattle were fat, and there was a good calf crop. To help the regular top hands, a number of lints had been brought out from Roswell to punch cattle for the first time.

When the roundup started, a number of "outside" men from the surrounding ranges such as the DZ, Bar V, Diamond A, Circle Diamond, Turkey Track, VVN, HAT, Crazy J, and others showed up with their mounts to work through, gathering cattle bearing brands they represented, and holding them in the day herd to be taken back to their home ranges when the roundup was finished.

They rounded up at the West JIM windmills on the Staked Plains, and as the cattle started coming in from the circle drive, the wagon boss and other hands who drove straight in from camp that morning held them up a distance from the watering place to form the roundup, where they would be worked.

As the men came in, many loped up to the chuck wagon, left their coats, and went to the chuck box and got sourdough biscuits, a hunk of baked beef, and an onion. Then they loped on off to the roundup. When the drive was all in, the horse wrangler brought up his remuda, and the hands changed from sweat-covered drive horses to cuttin' horses, then started working the roundup.

Most of the cattle bore the LFD brand, and the top hands started a cut on one side of the roundup of LFD cows and calves. On the opposite side of the roundup a cut of cows bearing mixed brands was started. Into this went other brands belonging to that outfit and the men working for them, such as D Diamond, WAX, HUT, Cross Links, HX Triangle, and strays from other ranges.

Keeping the brands separated made things much easier for the calf ropers when branding started that afternoon, since there was less danger of placing the wrong brand on a calf. When that did accidentally happen, the calf had to be "counterbranded." For instance, if LFD was placed on a calf whose mother bore another brand, another LFD would have to be burned on it under the first brand, then the proper brand applied. Some counterbranded calves' sides resembled a map after everything was burned on them.

Cows with calves were cut out first to keep them from becoming separated in case the animals started milling. After these, dry stuff and strays that went into the day herd were cut out. It was then the cutting horses had a chance to show their skill. They brought the wild ones out between the men sitting around the edge of the roundup and headed them toward the cut. The horses showed pride in their work, and their riders were proud of them. Ears working, the horses dodged and "turned on a dime" as they brought an animal out of the roundup, then champed the bits as they turned and started back into the roundup.

After the roundup was worked and dinner was over, roping horses were caught, and all hands except those on day herd went out to the cow and calf cuts to start branding. Expert calf ropers, such as "Doc" Sears, George Urton, Ben "C Hop" Baker, and "Fate" Beard, would start "draggin 'em out."

At the calf branding fire, common waddies held the cut near the fire while top hands rode their roping horses into the cut, roped the calves around their necks, dragged them out to where cowboys on foot went down the rope and flanked them, then removed the ropes and held them down.

The calf flankers worked in pairs, taking turn about reaching over and catching the calf's dewlap with one hand and its flank with the other, bouncing along on the animal's back until all four feet were caught off the ground, then laying it on the ground. One man then placed his knee on the calf's neck and held a foreleg, while his partner grabbed one hind leg and, sitting flat on the ground, placed his other foot above and behind the hock of the other leg. When the calf was held that way, its whole side was exposed for branding. If the wrong side was up, the animal could easily be turned over.

The ropers called out the brand to be applied on each calf as it was dragged up, the brand corresponding with the one on the calf's mother. The roundup boss, seated on the ground nearby in the shade of his horse, with tally book and pencil kept his record. Other top hands who were acquainted with all brands on the range handled the branding irons.

A grassy spot was usually selected for the branding to keep down the dust. But three kinds of smoke and odor filled the atmosphere. They came from the burning of hair, the searing of flesh by the red-hot irons, and the scent of the smoke coming from the cow-chip fire.

Other top hands who were acquainted with earmarks corresponding with each brand handled their sharply whetted pocket knives. They cut the animals ears with the proper markings, and castrated the bull calves.

Many of the old cowpokes would drop those "mountain oysters" taken from the bulls into the embers of the cow-chip fire to roast. During lulls in the branding they would fish those tasty morsels out of the ashes and devour them with smacking lips. The younger hands would refuse to partake of these delicacies.

Cowboys of those days led lonely, rough, and very dangerous lives, lacking altogether in the kind of romance shown in movies and on television. Instead of cowpunching for the fun of it, most of them did it because it was the only work available there at that time. About the only amusement they had when in camp was joking among themselves or playing tricks on each other.

My old school friend, Sutty, who worked for the LFD outfit at the same time I did, was full of devilment and was always playing practical jokes on the other cowhands. The young lints were innocent victims of many of his tricks, and even the wagon boss was not immune from his pranks.

One evening he played an old joke on one of the new waddies. He caught a little cottontail rabbit and put it inside his shirt bosom. When the tenderfoot rolled out his bed that evening, Sutty slipped the little rabbit way down between the blankets. As the boy was about to get into his bed, Sutty began, in a loud voice, "There're shore lots of rattlers around this camp. I'll bet I saw thirty right around camp while I was bedding down the herd awhile ago." Then he added, "Cook, how about lettin' me sleep in the chuck wagon tonight?"

The boy got into bed, and Sutty laid a dead sotol on the fire so that its blaze would light up the surroundings. When the boy stretched out and his feet touched the rabbit, he threw the tarp and blankets back full length, almost stampeding the herd of cattle on the bed ground. "Rattlesnake!" he yelled, at the top of his voice, and, too late, saw the little rabbit scamper away into the darkness.

Another evening Sutty caught two horned toads, wrapped them in his bandanna handkerchief, and put them in his inside vest pocket. The wagon boss rolled out his bed, and while he was catching night horses, Sutty put the horned toads inside his pillowcase, then folded the end of the case under so they couldn't get out of it.

When the boss turned in, the toads evidently started scratch-

The first blacksmith on the Llano Estacado. R. L. (Bob) Causey, wearing a leather apron, stands in front of his blacksmith shop in Eddy (now Carlsbad), New Mexico, in 1900. The teenager on the left, wearing a Stetson hat and galluses, is Vivian Whitlock, the blacksmith's apprentice.

The Bob Causey home in Odessa, Texas, in 1893. *L.* to *r.*: Bob Causey, G. W. Causey, Vivian Whitlock, George Causey, Rose Causey, Ralph Whitlock, Eliza (Causey) Corwin, Mrs. G. W. Causey, and Nellie (Causey) Whitlock.

Courtesy of Joe W. Wilcox

The T71 ranch house, a short distance north of Kenna, New Mexico, as it looked when it was built in 1884 and as it appears today. The ranch was an early-day livestock watering place on the LFD range.

Courtesy of Emmett McCombs

Cowboy's "bedroom." A nighttime scene around an LFD chuck wagon in 1901, made with early-day photographic lighting equipment. The waddy at the left in the foreground is Doc Sears. At his left is Will McCombs.

Ralph Whitlock bulldogging a steer with his teeth at a Miles City, Montana, roundup in 1915. A judge is checking the hold the 'dogger has on the steer's upper lip. Whitlock started mustanging for George Causey in the 1890's, as soon as he was big enough to straddle a horse. He worked for the LFD outfit before moving to Montana.

Clay McGonagill, Sr., on his dark sorrel roping horse, Kelly, at a steer roping contest in Dewey, Oklahoma, July 4, 1911. The judge is checking the tie he made of the steer's legs. McGonagill was World's Champion Steer Roper in 1903.

Ol' Waddy mounted on his roping horse, Puddin, in Roswell, New Mexico, in 1907.

All that is left today of a house built with rocks by John Causey in 1903 at a spring below the west breaks of the Staked Plains. This old ranch was on the freight wagon road from Roswell, New Mexico. The Cap Rock escarpment is visible in the background.

The George Causey ranch on the Llano Estacado as it appeared in 1963. Built in the 1880's, it is still in good condition, having modern lean-to additions. The present owner is Mason Graham, who has lived there since his birth in 1903.

Ol' Waddy and his bride, the former Zelma Beal of Bronco, Texas. Born in Snyder, Texas, Mrs. Whitlock has always been known among her relatives and close friends as "Bob" and is called "Mother Bob" by her great-grandchildren today.

Mr. and Mrs. J. D. Earnest, who managed the Mallet Ranch, were George Causey's nearest neighbors in the 1880's. This photograph was made around 1898.

Courtesy of Raymond F. Waters, Hobbs, New Mexico

The historic High Lonesome ranch house, photographed in 1963. It was established as the Mallet Cattle Company's headquarters in the 1880's, and is one of the most famous of the early man-made livestock watering places on the South Plains. Once called the Mallet Ranch, it is twelve miles from the George Causey ranch, where Ol' Waddy grew up.

ing inside the pillow case. He raised up and struck a match and looked under his pillow and all around on the ground at the head of his bed. He lay back down and must have put his ear on one of the toad's horns. Sitting up again, he struck another match and looked inside the pillow case, got one of the toads and tossed it to one side, then pulled the case off the pillow and found the other toad.

"If I find out what scissorbill put these toads in my pillow," he growled, "I'll put him on day herd the rest of the summer."

Although Sutty and I were bosom pals, we would fight each other like two bobcats, but if anyone butted in, he had us both to whip. We were always together—on day herd, on circle drive, standing guard—and we teamed up when flanking calves at the branding fire. Neither of us had much bedding, so we threw our suggans into one roll and slept together.

At the branding fire one afternoon, Sutty and I paired up as usual, first one then the other going down the line to big mosshead calves as the calf ropers dragged them up, and flanking—or running those too large to flank—across our legs. A big calf with nubbin horns about an inch long got me down and tramped all over me—tearing my jeans and skinning my legs with its sharp hoofs.

"Let me at him!" Sutty yelled. "I'll show you how a shore 'nuff flanker can lay him down."

He bounced along on the calf, holding its dewlap and flank, catching it just right and laying it on its side. Then he started razzing me.

"I always told you I was a better flanker than you. I can also beat you roping and riding. I can beat you playing poker and drink more likker than you can. I'm better looking than you and can take your gal away from you, and if you don't like what I'm telling you, I can lick you 'fore a cat can bat its eye."

"I can't help it 'cause you're better looking than me, with your black curly hair that makes the gals hang around you like ants around a sugar barrel," I growled. "But you can quit bragging about it, and rubbing it in."

Sutty was a friend of all dumb animals, especially little dogie calves. Quite often around the water trough, he would maneuver a dogie around to where a cow was drinking from the trough so it could put its head between her hind legs and steal some milk from a hind teat while she was drinking.

A roper came dragging a little dogie, and Sutty yelled, "You take him 'cause he's just your size, but don't let him get you down."

"Poor little dogie," Sutty said as we held it down. "It can't help it 'cause its mommie died. And now it has to have that old big LFD brand that's 'most as big as it is, burned on its side, and its ears marked."

We finished branding and rode by the windmills to water our horses on our way to the chuck wagon. As we approached the water trough, I dropped behind Sutty, and when he leaned over the saddle horn giving his horse free rein to drink, I lifted his horse's tail and slipped my quirt handle under it close up.

The horse jumped the trough with head bogged, and Sutty grabbed at everything, but failed to make connections. His landing stained him up considerably.

"What happened?" he yelled. Then looking at his horse crow hopping off with the quirt handle still under its tail, he started throwing everything he could get hold of at me.

"You were telling me just a little while ago that you could ride anything that walked on four legs and wore hair," I sneered. "And here you let an old gentle roping horse pitch you off. Aren't you ashamed of yourself, bragging like you do?"

He finally promised he wouldn't fight if I'd catch his horse, but I knew I'd have to watch him, for he'd try to get even with me some way; and if anyone could study up a plan, he could.

The next morning when the cook yelled, "Chuck!" I raised up and looked over at where Sutty should have been, but wasn't, then looked all around to see where he was, but he wasn't anywhere in sight.

I put on my hat, then slipped on one boot. The sock on my other foot was open at both ends and I pulled it down over my toes as far as I could, then folded my jeans over and pulled on the boot.

160

Something inside it seemed to reach up and wrap itself around my bare toes. I jerked the boot off—throwing it as far as I could, and yelled, "What is it?" I saw a big hunk of sourdough sticking to my foot, all squashed in between my bare toes.

I heard someone snicker and saw Sutty squatting down on the opposite side of the wagon grinning at me through the spokes of the wheels. While I was getting on my boot, I heard him telling the cook, "You ought to be more careful where you throw your dough and not get it in the boys' boots."

We finished rounding up on the plains, then dropped down the cap rock and rounded up along the Pecos River. Then we went out on Long Arroyo at Curlew Lake south of Railroad Mountain. The next day we crossed the sand hills and rounded up at the T71 Ranch near the little town of Kenna.

That was to be the last roundup of the season, after which the outside men would cut their cattle from the day herd, put their bedrolls on a pack horse, and head their "cuts" toward the home ranges. The LFD outfit would then head south across the sands to headquarters at Four Lakes, where they would disband and "Cat Head" Smith, the LFD bookkeeper, would pay off the lints.

The ranch manager came up from Roswell that day on the train and brought the boys a couple of jugs filled with "refreshment." When they called Sutty and me to stand third guard, one of the jugs was sitting on the lid of the chuck box. As I rode off to the herd, I saw Sutty standing at the chuck box getting an eye-opener.

When a cowhand is standing guard around a sleeping herd of cattle, under big bright stars and a full moon that make the range almost light as day, with a trusted and sure-footed night horse as a companion, he feels about as close to Mother Nature and his Maker as he can get. And as he rides around "singin' to 'em," his mind has a chance to go back over his past life and think of things he should, or shouldn't, have done.

He thinks of several letters from his mother in his war bag in his bedroll that he has thoughtlessly neglected to answer. His conscience brings up a mental picture of her disappointed face each day when the postman blows his whistle but fails to leave a letter from him, and he resolves to write to her more often in the future.

Sutty and I were riding in opposite directions around the herd. The only sounds were the tinkle of a bell on one of the old chuck wagon mules, the yapping of a coyote off on the prairie and another one answering from the opposite direction, the hoot of a prairie-dog town owl in a dogtown nearby, the grunts of the cattle belching up their cuds and contentedly chewing them, and Sutty's voice floating across the herd singing a song to lull the longhorns to sleep.

He was singing a song all the old cowhands sang when they were lonesome for home and loved ones: "I'm going to see my Mother when work's all done this fall." He chased away some stray cattle that were trying to get into the herd, and, as he rode back with spurs jingling, he sang a little ditty that he made up himself: "I'm punching cattle for the LFD, and duty I'll not shirk. They're paying me a dollar a day, for twenty hours' work."

Flashes of lightning in a dark bank of clouds hanging in a semicircle along the horizon to the northwest toward Fort Sumner warned us that all hands but the cook might be out helping hold the herd before daylight if one of those fierce electrical storms struck us.

The wind changed, coming from the direction of the cloud, and fanned the smoldering embers of the campfire near the chuck wagon into a blaze. A night horse staked near the wagon that had been lying down with saddle on, got to its feet and shook the saddle, causing some of the cattle near the wagon to jump to their feet. Several of the big wild steers slowly walked to the edge of the herd, raised their noses in the direction the wind was coming from, and drew in deep breaths of the rain-scented air.

Sutty and I were sitting on our horses on the opposite side of the herd from the wagon when he suddenly said, "I'll run you a race to the wagon, and the first one there will drink from the jug, and the other one smell the cork."

"O. K.," I said, "let's go." He circled the herd in one direction and I in the other. We slid our horses to a stop near the campfire and hit the ground running, but he jumped over the pot rack and beat me to the chuck box, grabbed the jug, pulled out the cork, and handed it to me.

A few minutes later he challenged me to another race, but when we arrived that time, the old wagon boss was sitting up in his bed, yelling, "This ain't no kindergarten! You buttons get back to that herd and stay there, or I'll give you both your walking papers!"

We restaked our horses when we came off guard and squatted down beside the campfire. After a while Sutty looked at me with a grin on his face and asked, "Do you know what I am?"

"Yeah, I know exactly what you are," I answered, and didn't hesitate to tell him.

"I'm a tumblebug," he continued, ignoring me and glancing at the beds scattered around the wagon with cowhands in them sound asleep, "and I'm gonna roll up some of this stuff around camp."

He pulled off his boots, then backed up to a bed on his hands and knees, working his toes under the tarp, and rolled the bed up with his feet, the sleeping cowhand still in it. He backed up to another and did the same thing to it.

"You'd better not try to tumblebug that one," I warned, as he backed up to the third bed. I knew from experience that the old waddy inside it would awaken at the first touch of his tarp, and come out fighting.

He took no heed of my warning and started working his toes under the edge of the bed. The tarpaulin was thrown back and a grizzled face with a walrus-type mustache raised up with a frontier-type Colt six gun in his hand. The hole in the barrel looked as big as a badger hole. "You just try an' tumblebug my bed, you dadgummed scissorbill," he growled, "and I'll pistol-whup you."

Sutty looked around at me with a sheepish grin on his face and said, "Can't do anything with this pile. It's too old and won't ball up."

21.

Early-Day Rodeos

ACCORDING to available records, the first rodeo took place in 1883 in the little West Texas town on the Pecos River known in those days as Pecos City, but now shown on maps as Pecos.

On July 4 of that year, the cowhands from the surrounding ranches gathered in that small cow town to compete for prizes by giving exhibitions of their skill in doing things they did in everyday life. There was no admission fee.

The cowboys who competed in those early-day riding and roping contests were real cowhands and riders of the open ranges, with the alkali dust of the roundup grounds along the Pecos River still in their ears. The wild steers they roped and tied were right off the range, and the horses they rode in the riding contests were real outlaws led in from the remudas belonging to ranchers in the area.

Those outlaw horses were notorious and bore names that were known far and wide. In some parts of the West, the gyrations those horses went through with a rider aboard were called "bucking." But Texans have their own vocabulary, and they called it "pitching." Could some of them pitch! This writer was wearing long breeches and going to square-dances with the nester gals before he ever heard that a horse could "buck."

These events, called "roping and riding contests" in the early days, were not known as "rodeos" until many years later—around 1915. Bulldogging, bull riding, bareback horse riding, and calf roping came later on. And the cowboys rode only their "cuttin' horses" in the roundups. The Humane Society eventually stopped, to a certain extent, the roping and tying of big steers, because so many of the animals' legs and horns were broken. It was then that "calf roping" made its start.

The term "saddle-bronc riding" as used in rodeos today is misleading. In the parlance of the range, the word "bronc" or "bronco" means a young unbroken gelding, and the men who rode those young unbroken horses were called "bronc, or bronco, busters." The so-called broncs that are ridden in rodeos today are misnamed. They are horses that are trained to buck with a rider.

Some of those affairs were held in connection with other events and were known as "carnivals." In different parts of the country they were known as "cowboy reunions," "stampedes," "cowboy tournaments," "roundups," and "frontier days." They usually lasted for three days, elimination contests being held the first two days and the winners competing for the grand prize on the last day.

When an old Texan pronounces the word "rodeo," the native sons of California roll their eyes toward heaven. They then, condescendingly, tell the old Longhorn exactly how to pronounce it, with the heavy Spanish accent on the "de"—*ro-day-o*. But the old Longhorn continues to resist that pronunciation. Californians say theirs is the correct pronunciation in English for the Spanish word. I tell them Longhorns don't speak English—they speak Texan.

There were no flashy exhibitions in those early events, such as Sheriff's Posses mounted on matched palomino horses, wearing silver-mounted trappings and costly, highly decorated saddles.

No women had participated until Miss Lucille Mulhall showed up on the scene around the turn of this century.

There was always a barbecue, the merchants in the town where the carnival was held furnishing the trimmings and the ranchers donating the beef to be broiled by the chuck wagon cooks over pits filled with mesquite-root coals.

The cowhands "swung their pardners" on a temporary platform with a shade over it as the old-time fiddlers sawed the catgut and patted their feet. It took a good floor to stand up to the rough treatment when the fiddler struck out on "Cotton-eye Joe" and the dancers hopped in unison.

There was almost always a table with some tubs on it where the cowboys were supposed to escort their gals after dancing a set. A man stood there dipping out liquid as he droned, "Red lemonade, made in the shade, stirred with a spade, by an old maid."

Some of the men usually had bottles staked out under their saddle blankets, and would go out after a nip now and then. But they usually had some Sen-Sen or a few grains of coffee to kill the scent, for if their best gals smelled liquor on their breath, it was too bad.

Sometimes added attractions would be Molly Bailey's Dog and Pony Show, or one of those forerunners of the merry-go-round called "flyin' jenny," which had seats hanging on ropes tied to a circular framework, with an old mare hitched inside to furnish the horsepower to pull it 'round and 'round. A fun-loving cowpoke with a bottle of high-life in his pocket took a seat next to the old mare one night. When the seats had been filled and the manager clucked to the mare to get going, the cowhand dumped the contents of the bottle on the old mare's rump, then unloaded.

The old mare started running and kicking as high as she could reach. The driver was yelling, "Whoa! Whoa there!" The passengers, who were holding on to the ropes—since their seats stood almost straight out, making it impossible to unload—were screaming "Hold-er! Stop-er!" The mare finally kicked clear out of the harness and ran out into the darkness. The guilty cowpoke knew better than to stay there, because those angry passengers would have strung him up to the nearest windmill tower. So he headed out where the "woodbine twineth" and the "whang-doodle mourneth."

Bronc peelers in those days had no chutes in which to saddle and mount their horses. Each horse was saddled and mounted out in the open while another waddy eared it down, and many horses' ears were "gotched" from being pulled through a cowboy's teeth. The riders dreaded to get a horse that wouldn't "pitch," for there had to be plenty of action or they had no chance to win the prize.

Broncs we see in present-day rodeos do not pitch the way the old outlaw horses did. They just don't seem to get their noses bogged as far down between their front feet as those horses did. Nor do they have the humps in their backs that made the backs of the saddle skirts stand almost straight up as the horses sunned their sides, fence rowed, climbed to the moon, changed ends in midair, and struck the ground with all four feet together, squalling like a panther and shaking like a hula dancer. Pardner, those horses were natural-born pitchers and needed no training in technique.

Horses probably pitch differently today because of the flank cinch, which is pulled up tight far back of the flanks. This rig practically puts a horse in a straitjacket, so that the animal no longer has free use of its body. It can't get a hump in its back, or twist and weave at will, or hit the ground with all feet together. To show its skill, a horse should have an even chance with the rider. That cinch far back on the flank denies the horse such a break.

There was no eight- or ten-second rule, whereby a whistle blast would stop the ride, in bygone days. You rode the horse— if you could—until it quit pitching, even when you lost control of your neck muscles, and your head got to nodding, and you could feel blood trickling from your nostrils.

Hobbled stirrups, swell-fork saddles, and a slicker rolled and tied across in front of the peeler's knees were taboo. He had to "ride 'im clean" without "pullin' leather," and the judges made their decisions according to the amount of daylight they could see between the rider and the seat of his saddle.

One of the most important events at those carnivals was the roping and tying down of big steers. Cowhands practiced their skill and trained their roping horses for these contests by roping cattle out on the range, on circle drive, around the roundup, at the branding fire, and on day herd. Many animals, of course, were crippled.

The contest was an exhibition of teamwork between a man and his highly trained horse, who understood each other from long experience. More depended on the horse than on the rider, for all the man had to do was cast the loop and hogtie the steer when the horse threw it. When roping and tying were discontinued, one of the best exhibitions of the horses' skills was eliminated.

Cowboys who competed for championship crowns before the turn of this century had no nationwide organization to keep official records, like the Rodeo Cowboy's Association of today. The "tournaments" and "reunions" were more local affairs than they are today. Those waddies working for $30.00 a month weren't financially able to travel to distant events. They led their horses or traveled by rail, whereas today they put their roping horses in a trailer hooked on behind a powerful auto and glide along a paved highway at sixty miles an hour.

One exhibition of skill at those early cowboy get-togethers was expert rifle shooting by Captain Tom York, an old LFD cowhand who traveled for the Winchester Arms Company. Another attraction was fancy roping and loop twirling by a grinning, gum-chewing, wisecracking cowhand from up in the Cherokee Strip of the Indian Territory named Will Rogers, who at that time called himself "The Cherokee Kid." Later, along with some of the contestants of those early roundups, Will joined a Wild-West show and climbed the ladder of fame as he twirled his loop and joked his way into the hearts of his countrymen.

One of the most impressive sights in parades at those reunions was a beautiful horse bearing an empty saddle and empty boots in the stirrups to commemorate the old waddies who had "headed out over the Great Divide" and were waiting for the "Last Great Roundup."

Back in 1903, the ropers of West Texas, New Mexico, Arizona, and Oklahoma gathered at the Cattleman's Convention at El Paso, Texas, to hold their carnival and compete for the world's championship crown held by Clay McGonagill, who had roped and tied a steer a couple of years before at Tucson, Arizona, in the record time of twenty-three seconds. It seemed as if that time would go unbeaten. Whenever waddies gathered in the Southwest, their main topic of conversation was the time in which Clay had tied his steer, and many of them believed the record could be beaten.

Many of the top ropers of the West gathered at Washington Park that day in 1903. Among them were Ellison Carroll, Tom Vest, Lee Nations, Billy Connell, "Little Joe" Gardner, Ace Draper, Mossman, Hopkins, Withers, Houghton, Tom Crow, Wilson, Borjorquez, Barksdale, and Raleigh Conley.

The first woman roper, Lucille Mulhall, from the Mulhall Ranch up in the Indian Territory's Cherokee Strip (properly, Outlet) was there to compete. Clay McGonagill was there to defend and try to better his record. He felt confident that no one would beat it.

There were three prizes that day. First money was $1,000; second, $500; and third, $250—big money for those days.

When the drawing was made for positions in the steer-roping contest, Raleigh Conley drew first place, which meant that he would be the first to rope and tie a steer. Conley was a small, wiry, dark-complected cowhand about twenty-seven years old, who was ranch boss for McElroy's J Cross outfit along Sulphur Draw.

Conley had roped in carnivals before but had never showed much speed, and nothing brilliant was expected of his performance by the crowd. McGonagill, Carroll, Gardner, and Barksdale were the favorites of the audience.

Conley's roping horse was a short-coupled, powerfully built white horse that he had trained himself. It was part Steel Dust and was very fast for a cow pony. From long experience, they understood each other. Conley had led the horse the one hundred miles from the J Cross Ranch to Midland and shipped him to El Paso by baggage car, riding along with him in the car.

The roper rode out to the starting line in front of the corral gate where the steers were, carrying his piggin' string, with which he would tie a steer, in his teeth. He wore no chaps because the extra weight might hinder fast movements in dismounting and running to the steer. He built a loop in his rope, which he held out away from his side, with bridle rein, and coils of rope in his left hand, the end of the rope being double-half-hitched to his saddle horn. The horse stood perfectly quiet with ears working back and forth and eyes taking in every movement. It knew as well as the roper did what was going on. The corral gate swung open, and a wild Mexican steer almost as large as the roping horse came charging out.

The cow pony seemed to crouch for a spring, as a runner in a foot race might do. When the steer crossed the deadline and a shot signaled the stop watches to start ticking off the seconds, the roper leaned forward, and the horse, with ears laid back, ran onto the steer like a white streak of lightning.

Conley had time only to swing his loop twice around his head before he was close enough to make the cast. The loop dropped neatly around the steer's horns, and the roper jerked it tight. Then he threw the slack in the rope over the animal's rump and dropped over in the saddle with his weight in his left stirrup. The horse swerved to the left, and the steer hit the ground with a thud directly in front of the grandstand.

Conley's feet hit the ground almost simultaneously with the steer's fall. With a command to his horse to "hold him down," he started running down the rope, sliding it through his left hand, with his tie rope in his right hand. The horse dug its hooves into the dirt, straining every muscle in its body in an effort to drag the big steer along and hold it down till the roper reached it.

The cowhand slipped the loop in his tie rope over the steer's forefeet, reached and grabbed a kicking hind leg, and took three wraps around the three legs, with a half-hitch around one leg. Finished, he threw up his hands as a signal for the timekeepers to stop their watches. One of the judges rode up and inspected the tie, then waved his approval.

The people in the audience held their breath as they waited for the official announcement of the time, for they knew they had seen some fast work. When the time of 21½ seconds was announced, they went wild, for they knew a world's record had been broken.

Conley gave his well-trained horse full credit for his success, because of its fast getaway from a standing start and the speed it made in getting him to the steer. He declared that all he did was throw the loop and tie the animal. But experienced ropers knew better. The throw of the loop and catch were perfect, and the tying was with the speed of lightning.

Ellison Carroll placed second by tying his steer in 30 seconds. "Little Joe" Gardner roped and tied his in 40 seconds. Tom Crow's time was 45½ seconds. Nations and Borjorquez used 55 seconds, the rest of the ropers' times being one minute and over.

Barksdale caught his steer almost as fast as Conley did and had a good chance to place second, but before he could tie the steer, his horse got a foot over the rope and the animal got on its feet, pushing his time over two minutes. Lucille Mulhall wasted three loops, missed her steer each time, and finally gave up, but she was given a great hand by the crowd, which admired her horsemanship and grit and the gallant effort she made in behalf of women.

Those two champion steer ropers of the early roundups in the southwest—Clay McGonagill and Raleigh Conley—were both residents of the Llano Estacado.

McGonagill was fatally injured later in an accident in Arizona, and Conley is buried in a cemetery between Los Angeles and Long Beach in southern California.

22.

A Horse Named Cut-Throat

OFTEN a cowhand will tell you he would much rather someone would take his best girl away from him than to take a certain one of his horses. He knows he could easily find another gal but probably never another horse like the one he is so fond of. This old bronc twister had owned several such horses during the past sixty-five years, but one in particular.

That one was among 120 head of broncs the LFD outfit bought one summer from Tom Pridemore, manager of the Block outfit that ranged around the Capitán Mountains northwest of Roswell. The broncs were as much as six years old and had not had a rope on them since they were gelded.

After the spring roundup that particular year, the outfit moved into the headquarters ranch at Four Lakes and tied up. The bosses laid off a bunch of "lints," and I thought I might get it and have to ride the chuck line till the calf-branding roundup started, but I was mistaken.

Another young fellow and I were sitting on our bedrolls at the chuck wagon one day waiting for the verdict. We saw roundup boss Charlie Walker riding toward us and the other kid punched me and said, "Here comes bad news."

Walker pulled up his horse and said, "You two boys get a couple of horses each, one to ride and another to pack your bedrolls on. I want you to go down to the 7HR Camp and break a bunch of broncs that are in the horse pasture down there. Old Negro Ad will go with you to help you handle them."

The old Negro was an expert horseman who claimed he could look a horse square in the eye and almost tell what it was thinking. But at that time the wool on his head was almost as white as snow. He was considered to be too old and crippled up to take an active part in riding the young unbroken horses. He was going along with us to help us handle the broncs—guide them away from the wire fences when we were aboard them and catch them when they threw us off and high-tailed with our saddles.

My pardner was a young fellow who wrangled horses when he first started working a couple of years before. He was nicknamed "Wrang" and always went by that name. He was a good rider, and the boss was giving him a chance to become a bronc buster.

We headed south on our thirty-mile trip to the south camp where Old Jeff was staying at that time, greasing windmills. Arriving after dark, we found that Old Jeff had already gone to bed. We staked a couple of horses to rustle horses on the next morning, warmed up a pot of frijole beans, hunted up some cold sourdough biscuits, ate supper, and went to bed.

The following morning we rounded up a few of the broncs and put them in the large square corral. Next, we worked two broncs at a time through a gate into a small round corral with a snubbing post in the center, where we handled and rode them the first couple of times. This round corral had a gate through which we rode out into the wide-open spaces.

Wrang had bad luck the second day when a horse fell with him and broke some bones in one of his insteps. Ad and I helped him to headquarters to be taken to a doctor at Roswell.

The boss sent another boy named Swanner back with us to

take Wrang's place. He was just a kid, but having been raised in the saddle on a horse-ranch and being a good rider, he proved to be an expert in breaking young horses.

He and I earned our thirty dollars a month that summer, for some of those potros were *mucho malo!* We made outlaws out of several, and they were known far and wide in the future as "buckers." Many lints from East Texas who came out to "run 'em" had their first experience with horses of that kind after these were issued to them in their mounts.

Some families think they do a great job when they select names for seven or eight children. Their task is minor compared with ours of giving those 120 horses names by which they would be known for life—names the cowhands holding up the rope corral around the remuda would call out so the horse ropers would know which horse they wished to ride on circle drive, around the roundup, at the calf-branding fire, on day herd, and when catching night horses to ride around the herd at night.

Negro Ad was a great help in that task. He knew every horse in the Bar F remuda by name, just what individual characteristics it had, and for which job it was best suited. He named many of them for horses he had known, broken, and ridden in the past.

We named some of them according to their color. One was a grulla, and was given that name. It had a sort of "mouse color" that was almost blue, with a dark line over its shoulders. It made one of the best cow horses the LFD owned.

One that was a dunnish color, with dark mane and tail and a dark stripe down its back, was named "Coyote" because it looked somewhat like that varmint. A "buckskin dun" was named "Buck." Ad told us that almost all large remudas had a "Yellow Fever," and a light dun in our bunch was later known far and wide by this name.

A big sorrel was named "Pridemore" for the man from whom the horses were purchased. A light bay that put everyone on the fence when it was put in the round corral was named "Carrie Nation" for a person who was touring the country about that time. Some were named for their gaits. Two were pacers and were called "Sop-an' Tater" and "Rockin' Chair."

One had a hip that was slightly knocked down, and we called it "Hippy." One bay had white spots below its ankles and was known as "Speckled Feet."

Ad was earing one down for me to saddle and mount, holding both ears with one ear between his snaggled teeth. When the horse swung its head, pulling its ear out of Ad's teeth, the ear was slit clear to the end, and the horse was named "Gotch." The potro that busted bronco buster Wrang's foot was named "Wrang" and was issued to him as his mount when he returned to work.

Every man in a cow outfit except the cook had to have a horse to stake out and stand guard on around the herd at night. We broke some of the most docile among them to stand staked with a thirty-foot rope tied around their necks by a knot that wouldn't slip and choke them, the other end of the rope being tied to the rim of a large wagon wheel lying flat on the ground out in the horse pasture.

The wheel would rotate so that the rope wouldn't wind up when the horse went around it in a circle. The wheel also had a certain amount of "give" to it when a horse ran double the length of the rope and hit the end. Some horses were able to drag the wheel at times but not very far.

We always staked two broncs at night to rustle horses on the following morning. I staked Carrie Nation one night, and the next morning when I was saddling up and reached under to get the cinch, the horse pawed me in the belly, tearing my only pair of trousers. I kicked at its nose, and my spur hung in the hackamore. The horse dragged me across the prairie, making left jabs at my head with a hind foot, but luckily my spur leather broke.

One of the broncs was a beautiful chestnut sorrel with flaky mane and tail, stockings on the front legs to the knees, a blaze face, and one glass eye. It became tangled up in barbed wire when I was breaking it, cutting a gash under the neck. I named it "Cut-Throat." That was a wicked name, but no sign the horse was mean.

From the start, it never pitched, but seemed to have been born gentle. I soon had it doing tricks, such as counting by striking the ground with a forefoot, lying down and rolling over, coming in from the pasture when I whistled for it, and getting down on its knees and praying for a lump of sugar or a cold sourdough biscuit. I believe it would have "savvied the cow" and made a good cutting horse if I hadn't lost it.

LFD Tom White, manager of the outfit, saw me put Cut-Throat through its tricks, and being a lover of smart horses himself, knew Cut-Throat and I were in love with each other. He told me that since the horse had not been branded as yet with the outfit's horse brand—Bar F on left hip—I could work a month for nothing and he would give it to me. I shook his hand real quick to seal the bargain.

After we finished breaking the horses and drove them to the horse camp at Mescalero Springs, I rode Cut-Throat over to Roswell to blow in some of my summer's wages. I had to stop at the LFD farm where "Cat Head" Smith was staying and get him to write me a check before going on into town.

On my way back to the plains, I was crossing Long Arroyo when I glanced back and saw a man on horseback following me in a long lope. When he caught up with me, I saw that his horse was covered with lather, and so near "give out" it had the "thumps."

He was a tough looker, carrying a beltful of cartridges and what looked like a .30–30-caliber saddle gun in a scabbard under his right stirrup leather. I could also see a six gun sticking down in the waistband of his trousers. I didn't have as much as my J branding iron on my saddle.

As he came alongside me, I suspected what was going to happen. "Hey, Buddy," he said, "let's trade horses."

I glanced over at his horse, which was almost ready to drop from exhaustion, and shook my head. ""Huh-uh," I murmured, "I don't want to."

"We'll trade anyway," he growled. "Get off, and be damn quick about it."

I unloaded in nothing flat. "Get your saddle off," he yelled, "and keep away from me, 'cause I don't want to have to hurt you." I knew he was desperate, so I did as he said.

He saddled Cut-Throat, jumped on, dug in his spurs, and headed north toward San Juan Mesa. I stood there watching him, hoping the horse would bog its head and throw him so high the jay birds would have time to build a nest on the seat of his pants before he came back down. But Cut-Throat wasn't that kind of horse.

There I was, miles from water with a give-out horse. Fearing he might get so stiff he couldn't walk, I put my saddle on him and started down the road, walking and leading him. I hadn't gone far when I saw two men coming from the rear carrying rifles. They were Sheriff Fred Higgins of Chaves County, New Mexico, and one of his deputies. They said the horse thief had killed a man in a card game in Roswell that morning. I told them which way he went, and they went after him.

After the horse had rested and cooled off, I mounted and rode in to horse camp that evening. The nag I fell heir to turned out to be a very good horse, but nothing compared to my Cut-Throat, which I never saw again.

23.

A Winter at the Bar-F Horse Camp

ONE fall, the LFD outfit returned to headquarters ranch at Four Lakes to disband for the winter after shipping a trail herd of about three thousand B-Heart steers from Amarillo that they had bought from Governor Terazzas in Chihuahua, Mexico, four years before when the animals were two years old.

The lints were laid off, given their checks by "Cat Head," and furnished with horses to ride to the nearest railroad. A few of them had their own horses and rode them back to their homes in Central and East Texas, or spent the winter riding chuckline over the ranges.

Top hands were being sent with their mounts to stay in line and other winter camps over the range, and to "bog camps" along the Pecos River.

Range boss John House rode up to where Sutty and I were sitting on our horses around the remuda and said, "You two scissorbills take the remuda over to horse camp at Mescalero Springs and stay there with them this winter." We roped a couple of gentle horses and led them to the chuck wagon, unrolled our beds and prepared them for packing with the blankets and war bags equally distributed in the tarpaulin so as to not have more weight on one side than the other, tied them on the horses' backs with ropes and the diamond hitch, then turned the horses loose in the remuda.

We ate some cold sourdough biscuits and hunks of beefsteak and an onion, then rounded up the remuda and drove them to water. As we came back by the chuck wagon on our way, the boss yelled, "Hey! You buttons keep them horses under the breaks away from the locoweed on top the plains."

We turned and started to ride off, and again he yelled, "Hey! Wait a minute till I give you the rest of my orders. I want you to ride up and down under the breaks and skin any cattle you find that fall off the cliff and are killed, and drag their hides to camp and hang them on the corral fence so the freight wagons can pick them up. Maybe you can save enough hides to pay your wages this winter."

Horse camp was an excellent place for horses to stay during the winter. There they could find protection from the fierce blizzards that came out of the northeast, since the camp was under the west breaks of the plains. The northeast wind caused cattle to drift and bunch up along the cliff, and many fell or were crowded off to death on the rocks below.

It was around the first of November, and it had been a hard year on the cow ponies. The roundup had been going on almost constantly since it started in the spring. We had worked up the Pecos River, bringing back to the range cattle that had drifted south during the winter storms. Then there had been calf branding, and later on gathering fat stuff to ship to market and yearling steers to drive to the steer pasture at the Z Bar L Ranch in Crosby County, Texas.

The Mexican steers in the trail herd were as wild as those traditional "rats" and stampeded several times going up the trail. The cow ponies were poor and jaded, and many had sore withers and cinch and kidney sores.

I was glad Sutty would be my companion during the winter,

for he was good company, a good cook, and a willing worker. Some waddies become cowhands by accident, but Sutty seemed to have been born for the saddle. He was a good roper and rider and an expert horseman. Since his ancestors had been cattlemen and trail drivers of the brush country of Southwest Texas who knew no other livelihood, he naturally made a top cowhand.

Neither of us said very much as we drove the remuda on the eighteen-mile trek to the cap rock. Once Sutty remarked, "I'm shore glad I'm staying in horse camp this winter, and not in a bog camp on the Pecos pulling poor old cows out of the sloughs, and tromping them out of the quicksands, ain't you?"

I agreed.

Several times during the trip, I noticed him sniffing the breeze that was blowing from the northeast, like an old steer smelling the air from an approaching rain cloud, and looking at a blue haze lying along the northern horizon. "Smells to me like a blue norther's coming," he said.

Suddenly we rode up to the breaks of the plains. Regardless of the number of times a person rides up to that bluff, after the monotony of seeing nothing but the level prairie month after month on the Staked Plains, he is stunned by the vast panorama that unfolds before his eyes.

Looking off to the west from that five-hundred-foot-high cliff across the Mescalero sand hills and Long Arroyo, one can see the outline of the Pecos River Valley. To the northwest beyond Roswell is majestic Capitán Mountain. Due west are the White Mountains, more than one hundred miles away, and through the haze across the white sand hills to the southwest are the outlines of the Sacramento and Guadalupe Mountain ranges.

We worked the horses off the cliff to wend their way down the steep and winding trail, then sat there on our horses for a while looking out over the land. I thought of the bands of Indians who formerly traveled that trail with bunches of horses taken from settlers on the east side of the plains during roving expeditions. They had probably sat there as we were doing, looking across to the mountains in the west, where their homes were located. I thought of the scouting expedition Uncle George had made years ago on which he had found signs around Mescalero Spring showing Indians had camped there.

Sutty hooked a leg over his saddle horn, rolled and lighted a Bull Durham cigarette, and sat gazing through the haze at the Penasco River. He reminded me of pictures I had seen of the Apache chief Geronimo sitting on a horse on a high hill after his capture, looking out over his old hunting grounds. I had an idea the boy was thinking about his home over there on the Penasco where his mother and her other children lived, and of a cross on a knoll back of the house where he had helped bury his father.

We rode on down to the watering place. The water from the spring ran into a fenced tank to be piped to troughs for the stock. After catching our pack horses, we drove the remuda out on the mesquite flats and turned them loose. Then, leading our pack horses, we rode up a hill about halfway to the top of the bluff where the one-room adobe camp shack stood.

It wasn't much of a house, but thick adobe walls and a dirt roof made it a warm place in winter. It had one door and one window with all the panes broken out, which was covered with rawhide. There was no furniture except a small table, on which the sourdough keg sat, and some shelves, where the grub was stored. Cooking was done at a large open fireplace with a hearthstone in front where bread was baked in Dutch ovens.

Dead mesquite roots being plentiful under the breaks, we didn't have to cook with cow chips as we did on the plains. Long ago prairie fires had burned and killed the mesquite bushes, and the partly exposed dead roots could be lifted out of the ground with a pick. Many of them looked like octopuses, their branches extending out in several directions from the main center. They were easily broken up and made excellent fuel, especially for a fireplace. Scrub cedar found along the bluffs made good kindling wood to start the mesquite roots burning.

The freight wagons from Roswell had left us a supply of

flour, spuds, frijole beans, "sow-bosom," sugar, a bucket of "lick," a case each of canned corn and tomatoes, a can of coal oil for our lantern, and several sacks of grain for our winter mount of horses.

The door had a latch with a leather string hanging down outside, and was never locked. If no one was home when a visitor arrived, he was welcome to cook and eat all he wished as long as he cleaned up his mess afterwards. That old "stag" camp was one of the most famous places in that section of the Staked Plains–Pecos River country. There were few cowhands who worked very long in that region without eating at least one meal there or stopping overnight in the old adobe shack. It was just a day's ride from Roswell. Anyone leaving town usually did so with the intention of spending the night there. Those going into town usually stayed the night there before riding on the following day.

Freight wagons hauling supplies for the ranches on the plains from Joyce-Pruitt or Jaffa-Prager stores in Roswell always camped overnight there, then went north around the point of the cliff and climbed to the level plain by way of "The Gap," now known as "Cap Rock." This was the only road across the Mescalero Sands for many miles to the north or south.

Sometimes, wagon trains of homeseekers from Central and East Texas, hauling their worldly belongings in covered wagons to homesteads west of the Pecos, stopped there for several days to let their teams rest up before tackling the sands. We usually killed a sucking calf to feed them and their youngsters. Sometimes a family would stop on the way back to the wife's kinfolks and the sharecrop cotton fields of Texas, broke and very discouraged with what they had found in the promised land on the west side of the Pecos.

Many horsebackers we had never seen before stopped overnight, and we never knew who they were, since it was very impolite in those days to ask a person his name or where he was from. Sometimes on bright moonlit nights we would hear horse's hoofbeats and the squeaking of saddle leather, and see a ghostly horseman ride up and water his horse at the trough, then fade away into the distance. The next day a ranger or some other officer might show up, hot on the fugitive's trail, and borrow a fresh horse to continue the chase.

Our nearest neighbor was "Old Man" Harry Robertson, who lived alone, looking after his little herd of cattle at his small spring a few miles to the south. He had the first, and only, phonograph in that part of the country at that time. Quite often, Sutty and I would stop at his place while making our rounds, and he would play his collection of records for us. Later that evening, Sutty would get his French harp out and practice the tunes he had heard.

Sutty was a good singer. He was always making up little ditties and asking me how I liked them. He made up and added many verses to old songs about "Frankie and Johnnie" and "Nellie the Milk Maid," many of which were unprintable.

One evening after singing several songs, he said "I'm goin' to make an actor out of myself and go on the stage. Don't you think I'd do all right?"

"Yeah," I answered, "but the way you act at times, you might wind up by finding yourself at the end of a rope following an organ grinder around."

Some evenings, we had no kerosene for our lantern, and all the light we had came from the blazing mesquite-root fire in the fireplace. After supper Sutty would get out a soiled deck of cards and we would play "Canfield solitaire." He would give me fifty-two frijole beans for the deck, and I would give him five beans for every card he put in piles above the spread. We would keep track to see who would win if the beans were real dollars.

We had some hot arguments as we lay on our beds during the long winter nights. We seldom agreed on any subject, and for pure cussedness and to be ornery, one of us would express his views, then the other would take the opposite side. One evening we had an argument about the different church denominations. "I'm like old Maria," Sutty said, "that old Mexican midwife who helped bring me into this world. She and Mother were of different faiths, but she told Mother they were just on different trails that led to the same place."

After a while, he continued: "Them different denominations

remind me of a big watering place out there on the plains where a large number of cattle come into water. Cow trails lead in to the windmills from every direction, and cattle can be seen coming along all them trails looking for the same thing, life-giving water. They all meet at the same place and drink from the same trough. The different religious trails all lead to the same promised land, and people who travel them hope to find the same spiritual water at the end of them.

"Cattle wander away from the beaten trails, and coyotes and lobo wolves get them and they never reach the water. Some people who are following the other trails stray away in search of things they shouldn't. Many covet their neighbor's calves and can't resist the temptation of putting their own brands on them, and they never reach the promised land."

I told him that, instead of an actor or a monkey following an organ-grinder around, I believed he should try being a sky pilot, judging from the sermons he could preach.

A number of objects around the shack reminded us of Bill Morgan, a well-known character along the Pecos River who had stayed at the camp before going back to his old occupation as a freighter. Before the Pecos Valley and Northeastern Railroad was built from Amarillo to Roswell and on down to Eddy, the end of the line from Pecos, Morgan hauled freight with a sixteen-mule team from Eddy to Roswell.

He rode a wheel mule which he drove with a jerk line, and he took great pride in showing how he could turn that team and wagons around in the main street of Roswell. He was a member of the posse that shot it out with Black Jack and Sam Ketchum across a ravine in northeastern New Mexico. Sam was "gut-shot," and later died of lead poisoning. When the P.V. and N.E. built on down to Eddy, it put his freight outfit out of business.

A number of deer ranged in the area of the white sands a few miles southeast of camp, and Sutty got to craving some venison. He went over to headquarters and brought back two rifles, and we rode to the white hills and killed a buck. We could have killed more than one, but we knew we couldn't eat all the meat before it spoiled.

The only vegetation in the sand hills was large cottonwood trees. One could dig down in the low spots among the hills and strike water, which was the way deer got their water. The wind caused the loose sand to shift continually. Sometimes the roots of a tree would be visible, but the next time one saw the same tree, the sand would be halfway to the top.

"It looks like we're gonna have some bad weather," Sutty said one morning. "We'd better get up a supply of wood."

We took a pick and rode down into the flat toward the sands. We lifted a lot of mesquite roots out of the ground, tied onto them with our ropes, and dragged them up near the door of the house. Then we broke up a lot of them and stacked them in the shack on one side of the fireplace. That night just before we went to bed, Sutty looked outside. "The wind's changed to the northeast," he said, "and it's spitting snow. Guess we'll be snowed in for a while."

When we crawled out from under our tarps the following morning, we found a real blizzard howling. We fed and watered our horses and were glad to get back into the house and in front of the fire.

Looking up through the falling snowflakes, we could see a herd of antelopes and a long string of cattle huddled along the edge of the cliff. Two animals, partly covered with snow, had already been crowded off and had fallen to their death near the shack. There was nothing we could have done about them, for it would have been impossible to drive them back against the storm. I told Sutty we ought to be able to skin enough cattle to pay our winter's wages after the storm was over.

The storm lasted for several days, and then we had to wait till the snow partly cleared off before we started skinning, but we managed to take almost a hundred hides before the carcasses became too decomposed to handle.

Old-timers claimed it was the worst storm they had seen since the blizzard of 1887, the blizzard that almost destroyed the cattle business over the Great Plains region from Charles Russell's range in Montana to the Llano Estacado in Texas. We heard after the storm was over that around two thousand sheep belonging to Ike Gronski drifted over the bluff south of us and the herder who was caught out with them froze to death. Several other herders in that section of New Mexico also died from exposure.

Almost everyone coming our way from Roswell brought our mail from the post office. One night Sutty was looking through some letters in his war bag. "Today's my birthday," he murmured, "and I thought shore I'd get a letter from Mom 'fore now."

We had just crawled under our tarps when we heard a horse nicker. Outside, we could hear Old Negro Ad's big Mexican spurs jingling as he rode up the hill to the house.

He dismounted and handed Sutty a letter and a small package. "The postmaster tole me this letter and package was there for you, and knowing who it was from, I thought you'd like to have it, so I brung it to you."

After reading the letter, Sutty opened the package. It was a small Bible, and on the flyleaf I saw a notation that said, "Happy Birthday. With love from Mother."

Grinning from ear to ear, the boy crawled back under his tarp, murmuring, "Uncle Sammy did come, didn't he?"

24.

The Cowboy Plays Shepherd

TWO of man's best and most loyal friends are his horse and his dog. No matter what happens to a man, his dog won't desert him. If he has to sleep in the gutter, his dog will lie down beside him in an effort to keep him warm.

One of my earliest recollections of our old ranch on the Llano Estacado is of a shepherd dog and two large greyhounds the cow-hands used to chase wolves and antelopes and to protect the ranch from sneaking coyotes. They would stand at the kitchen door and catch sourdough biscuits we threw to them the way a World Series baseball player catches fly balls in center field. They never made an error.

Those dogs had many fights with wolves right around the ranch house at night when Mother's chickenhouse was being raided. After dark one evening when I was alone in the house, they got into a fight with wolves near the kitchen door. I opened the door and let the dogs come inside and had closed the door before discovering there were too many dogs in the room. A wolf had come in with them. I climbed on top of a table and managed to reach over and open the door so that the dogs could run the wolf out.

Who doesn't admire an old potlicker-hound coon dog, as he howls along the trail through the swamps on a bright moonlit night after a coon or possum? Then there are squirrel dogs, bird dogs, bulldogs, hog dogs, deer dogs, and seeing-eye dogs.

A cattleman or cowhand will claim that the cutting horse is the smartest animal alive. A sheepman or his herder will contend that a sheep dog is smarter. I think they have about the same level of intelligence.

A fine example of animal loyalty and devotion to duty is seen in this story concerning a sheep dog:

Another cowhand and I were staying in camp at the old T71 Ranch a few miles north of Kenna on the old P.V. and N.E. Railroad (now the A.T.&S.F.). We were riding the range looking for calves that had missed being branded in the roundup. In the sand hills on our way to Curlew Lake, we rode up on about two thousand sheep, with no herder in sight. A shepherd dog came running around the herd to meet us, barking as if to attract our attention. He would jump up beside our horses and almost touch our hands, then run off, looking back to see if we were following, then come back and bark some more. We followed the dog to the top of a hill and looked down on the herder's camp, which was in a draw. There we found Juan, the herder, lying on a suggan in the shade of a bush, delirious with fever. One leg was swollen to twice its natural size, probably from a rattlesnake bite.

The dog licked the Mexican's face, then looked up at us with tail wagging and trotted off in the direction of the sheep. He knew from long training that its responsibility was with the herd, to protect it and keep any of the sheep from straying away. It was summer and the weather was hot and snakes were shedding their skins and striking blind without warning. Juan had probably walked up on one and was struck before he knew what was happening.

We bathed his face and hands and laid a wet rag on his forehead, then examined the wound and found marks the two fangs had made on the skin. We cut a cross in the flesh where the two fang marks were and my pardner started to place his mouth over the cross to suck the venom from the wound. I asked him if he had any bad teeth or any kind of a sore in his mouth. He said he had a rotten wisdom tooth. Having no sores in my mouth, I did the sucking and spitting in an effort to remove all the venom I could get from the wound.

Being many miles from a doctor, we wondered what we should do. I had no desire to herd sheep, but I told my pardner we would load and tie the Mexican on my horse and he could take him to Kenna and put him on the first train going either way—north to Portales, or south to Roswell. I decided to stay with Shep and look after the woolies until another herder came.

About sundown the dog brought the sheep to the bedground and bedded them down for the night by rounding them up into a small bunch and walking around them till they lay down. He came and smelled of Juan's suggan, then looked up into my face. I told him in Spanish that his pardner Juan was okay. He lay watching me as I fried some tortillas, boiled a pot of coffee, heated up the pot of frijole beans, and fried some bacon. The dog probably had not eaten anything for two days and was very hungry. He and I had a good supper.

I gathered enough dead mesquite roots and sagebrush to keep a fire burning all night. As I lay on my slicker looking up at the Milky Way, with Shep lying on Juan's suggan beside me, I admired the intelligence and loyalty of the animal. At the slightest movement from the sheep, he was alert and on his feet. He would trot out and circle the herd, then come back and lie down at my side. I thought of Mother reading to me out of her big Bible with the pictures in it when I was a child. She read about the "Ninety-and-nine that safely lay" and the shepherd who went out into the perils of the night to search for a lamb that had strayed away from the fold so that it might not be devoured by lurking beasts. In my mind I saw Shep playing the role of the shepherd tending the flock.

I thought of the lonely life of a sheepherder, and wondered if those herders who had watched over their flocks around Bethlehem had the same kind of life this herder had. Of the many evils in the desert country, two of the worst are thirst and loneliness. Thirst means a few days of wandering around on the desert with swollen tongue and parched lips, chasing imaginery lakes of water in a mirage. When someone finds the body, the arms are buried in the sand up to the elbows where the victim tried to dig to water in his last hours of delirum. Loneliness is a different kind of thirst, a never ending yearning for companionship, for someone to talk to, even someone who speaks an entirely different language.

At that time, nearly sixty years ago, it was said that there were more sheepherders in the insane asylum in the Territory of New Mexico than men of any other occupation. Shepherds seldom saw anyone except the camp tender, who came at certain times to bring a supply of corn meal, sow bosom, and frijole beans, and move the camp to another location. Some of them had a sheep dog for company, or maybe a burro to carry bedding and camping equipment, but many had neither.

They seldom saw a woman. They would begin to have hallucinations and to talk to themselves. When the camp tender came, he sometimes found a raving maniac who had been driven crazy by the loneliness of the desert and the constant ba-ba-ing of the sheep.

Coyotes started yapping, and Shep sprang up with a growl and ran to the herd. In a few moments I heard what sounded like a fight between Shep and a wolf. Grabbing Juan's .22-caliber rifle, I ran around the flock in time to see a coyote slit a lamb's throat with its teeth. When it came out of the flock, I was about fifty feet away. I shot at it, and it ran a short distance before falling. I was not an expert marksman, so I felt very lucky.

Shep was tangled up with a wolf farther around the flock. It was hard to tell in the dim light which was the dog and which was the wolf as they wrestled in the sagebrush. I was afraid that if I shot at them, I would hit the dog. I shot several times into the air as I ran toward them, and by the time I reached Shep, the wolf had high-tailed it over a sand hill.

When Shep and I had rounded up the sheep and got them

quieted down, we went to camp. Examining the dog, I found a slit in one of his ears and a shoulder gash. I washed the wounds with coal oil from a lantern and applied a coat of bacon grease to them. I could only hope the wolf wasn't rabid.

It was almost sundown the following day when the owner of the sheep drove up in a buckboard with another herder to relieve me. He took me on to my camp. As we rode along, he told me the doctor thought the Mexican would live. He thought the first-aid we gave him probably saved his leg and possibly his life.

25.

Frontier Towns Along the Pecos River

IN the spring of each year the LFD outfit went to the Texas line south of Carlsbad and worked up the east side of the Pecos River to Fort Sumner, rounding up at a different place each day, gathering cattle that had drifted south during the winter storms and holding them in a day herd to be brought back to the home range.

When camped opposite the small towns located on the west side of the river, the cowhands who were not on duty would ford the river and spend a few hours in those little frontier villages. About all the entertainment to be found there was in the saloons, gambling houses, and brothels. Many of the men would have sought better entertainment if such could have been had, but, since there was no other place to go, they naturally drifted into those places.

Almost all the restaurants in those small towns were owned and operated by Chinese. After cleaning up, we usually went to one of those places and ordered "ham-'n'-eggs," which was never served at a chuck wagon and gave us a change of diet. Some cowboys liked their eggs with their "eyes open," but others asked for theirs to be "shipwrecked" (scrambled).

Some of the hands wouldn't eat greens of any kind, saying, "They look too much like locoweed, and they might have the same effect on me that loco has on horses." Some of the boys liked any kind of fruit pie, but others craved no other kind than custard with "calf slobbers" over the top. In some parts of the South, rice was served with some kind of gravy over it, but there we ate it as a dessert with cream and sugar. Sometimes an order for "graveyard stew" (milk toast) would be given, and if we wanted breakfast, we ordered one or maybe two stacks of hot cakes with plenty of butter and "lick" over them.

Regular Chinese dishes such as noodles and chop suey were available to anyone who liked that kind of food. It was amusing to watch a cowhand wrestle with a grain of rice or a noodle with chopsticks, while back in the kitchen a Chinaman could be seen using the same kind of tools, as easily as we could use a fork. It was said among the old cowpunchers that Chinese ate cats, and when a stew was served containing small rib bones, the younger hands wondered if that was really what it was. The cooks said it was lamb, but most cowhands would as soon eat cats as sheep, claiming eating lamb was too much like eating human flesh.

All the Chinamen wore their hair in pigtails. A barber once told about one coming into his shop and requesting that his pigtail be removed. When asked by the barber why he wished to have it cut off, the Chinaman—who had recently married a disreputable white woman—grabbed his pigtail and, jerking on it, said, "My woman give it too damn much yank!"

Chinese seldom ever got into trouble with white people. It was said that if they committed a crime, they were punished by members of their own race, who kept them in jail in their own quarters. At times one of them would disappear, and no one knew where he was, but after a while he would show up around his usual haunts. Sometimes a new one would make an appearance, but where he came from, nobody knew. They lived in the back rooms of their restaurants and laundries, and because a Chinese woman was never seen around these places, the cowhands often wondered if any were there.

Most of the Chinese had plenty of money and were fiends for bucking the faro games, doing most of their playing late at night when everything was quiet. One of them would "keep cases" while the others did the betting. Many of them also played "draw poker," and no one ever had a better "poker face."

After their visit to the restaurant, the riders of the open range moseyed into the saloons with gambling tables at the back. Some of the men stopped at the stud, senate, and draw poker tables, some at the keno, klondike, crap, roulette, and blackjack games. Others went to the faro table, where a female "lookout" usually sat in a chair on a raised platform at one side of the dealer, intently watching the spread as the dealer slipped the cards from the case, one at a time. In some places, the dealers "banked" their own games, but in others, the person who owned the saloon did the banking and paid their dealers a salary.

The back door of the saloon opened out into an enclosure, called a "bull-pen," with a high board fence around it into which customers were thrown who became drunk and unruly. They stayed there until they sobered up. Sometimes they were relieved of any money they might have in their pockets.

From the saloon, the denizens of the wide-open spaces would meander down to the "red-light" district, where the main attraction was the "parlor house" operated by a "landlady," or "madam," who ruled the joint like a one-eyed captain might rule a pirate vessel on the high seas. She always had a few "bouncers" to help out when things became too tough for her to handle. Beer in quart bottles was the beverage, and it sold for one dollar a bottle.

There were shacks in the "district" cut up into single rooms, in each of which one female plied her trade. The doors to those "cribs," as they were called, were in two sections. The female would lean on the bottom section of the door with her head sticking out. There was a smile on her face, but not much of anything covering the rest of her body. She would try to coax the cowhands to stop as they passed by. Old cowpunchers referred to these women as "snake charmers."

The girls in the parlor houses were supposed to help the landlady relieve the waddies of their money by inducing them to buy beer, and it didn't take long to get the rider's hard-earned roll at a dollar a bottle. The girls were supposed to get the punchers drunk while staying sober themselves. "I'd just as soon try and fill a prairie-dog hole with water," one boy said, "as to try and fill one of them gals with beer."

Connected to the parlor house was a dance hall in which a bleary-eyed man played the piano. He was said to be a "hophead," and the waddies were supposed to buy him a drink after each request he played for them.

Girls of all colors, races, ages, shapes, and sizes were found in those places. Many of them had seen better days and were victims of circumstances. Some of them, said to be addicted to drugs, were called "snowbirds." Syphilis and other venereal diseases were rampant.

When a puncher drank too much and fell by the wayside with his "head under him," the landlady put him to bed. He awoke the next morning with a hangover and was lucky if he had a thin dime in his pocket. He would then go back out on the range and "rough it" in all kinds of weather, staying in the saddle eighteen hours a day. After a few months, he would draw his pay, go back to town, and "blow" it again.

Many of the older cowboys never drank or gambled. Some of them never took the Lord's name in vain and had no use for anyone who did. They used their influence to keep the young men out of trouble in town, and took them back to camp when they got to drinking too much and trouble started brewing.

Many of them had seen life in the raw in the frontier towns of Texas, the Indian Nation, Kansas, Colorado, and the territories of New Mexico and Arizona. Some of them were qualified to have notches cut on the handles of their six guns, but frowned upon such practice and looked askance at anyone who kept that kind of record and bragged about it.

They never hunted trouble, but were capable of handling it if it came. It was dangerous to start anything with such men. They had very little to say, but spoke their minds when necessary and were usually ready to back up what they said at any cost. Many of them would take a liking to a young puncher who had "come west to run 'em for the first time," and would look after him like an old hen with one chick. At times this guiding influence kept the young man from "going bad." Many an eastern mother never knew the debt she owed some hard-bitten old cowpuncher who kept her "darling boy" from going to the penitentiary or sleeping through eternity in an unmarked grave with his boots on.

Ofttimes after a rain, when one of those old fellows would roll out his bed and spread the blankets out to dry along with the contents of his war bag, a worn Bible or New Testament wrapped in oil cloth to keep it dry was there among his personal belongings.

One spring, the LFD outfit was working north, up the east side of the Pecos River, and the chuck wagon made an overnight camp a few miles east of Carlsbad. That afternoon, I rode into town with a cowhand named Jim who worked for the Cowden Brothers JAL outfit along the Texas–New Mexico line east of Carlsbad. Jim had a weakness for playing monte, and bucking the games kept him broke.

A gambler known as Sam had opened a new monte game in a saloon in Carlsbad the day of our visit. Jim asked me to "put in" a dollar with him and said he would play the new game. I handed him a silver dollar and he sat down and started playing. Sam had opened his game with an $800 bank roll. Jim was lucky from the start, and in a short time he relieved Sam of his entire roll.

Jim divvied up his winnings and handed me four hundred smackers as my half. Then we moseyed over to see Sol Schoonover who ran a monte game with the inviting motto: "The Sky's the Limit." As we walked through the swinging doors to the scene of action, Jim asked if I wished to "put in" with him to play Sol's game.

"Huh-uh," I grunted. "I'll keep what I've got."

Schoonover's saloon and gaming house in the little cow town

on the Pecos River was a show place with an excellent reputation for giving its patrons a square deal in every way, and its owner strove to protect its good name. The house banked all the games and employed dealers to operate them.

Jim went the round of monte tables and watched the play at each one, then took a seat at one where the chips on the table were of only two colors—blue chips worth one dollar, and yellow chips valued at five dollars each. One dollar was the least bet that could be made. This showed that he was planning to do some plunging.

Lady Luck seemingly had her arm around the cowpoke's shoulder guiding his hand as he placed a bet on a card on one side of the spread, then on one on the opposite side. I had a hunch that Jim was "right" and began to wish I'd put in with him. Sometimes I would place a few of my "frogskins" alongside his chips and did real well.

As the deals went on, Jim became reckless, and his bets became larger and larger. He soon had all the chips on the table, and bets were paid off in gold and currency.

All other activities in the saloon ceased, and the crowd gathered around the monte table sweating the game in silence. The only sounds were the voice of the dealer as he called the cards, one against the other, the low voice of the cowhand as he placed his bets "barring the door" or when he bet his "alce," the silken swish of the monte deck as the dealer shuffled the cards, and the exciting clink of gold coins as bets were placed or paid off.

The crowd dwindled as the night advanced, and the only other game in progress was between two Mexicans at a poker table who were playing kun-kan for four bits a game and two bit tabs. A cowhand who had been leaning against the bar all evening mumbling to himself was stretched out on a pool table snoring fit to choke. The swamper was stacking chairs on tables, rolling up mats along the footrail in front of the bar, cleaning spitoons, and mopping the floor.

The bartender was wearily polishing the bar, the glasses, and the large mirror, above which hung the pair of highly polished steer horns my Uncle Bob Causey and I had polished and mounted during my school days.

Having no customers to wait on, the barkeeper walked over to the monte table and stood behind the dealer to watch the game. He was portly and dignified in appearance, with a handlebar mustache twisted to sharp points. A diamond on his right hand that matched another in a stud in his stiff shirt bosom twinkled like the morning star.

I heard the faint crow of a rooster, and, looking out of a window, I saw day breaking above the trees along the river. I whispered to Jim that I was going to camp, but he asked me to wait till he made one more bet.

It was the start of a new deal, and the first spread showed a seven-spot against an ace. The range rider moved a lot of his winnings in on the seven, and without counting it said, "I bet $2,000 alce on the seven." (Alce is the only bet during each deal when a player has an even break with the game. The best monte players make their play for a cleanup on alce.)

The dealer looked a little sick. He laid the deck face down on the table and placed a stack of silver dollars on it, saying, "I'll not turn for it. You're just too durn lucky."

"Buddy, you'll have to turn for it," the waddy smiled. "Ain't you kinda forgot that this is a no-limit game? Read your sign hanging up there behind you."

The dealer called Pedro, the Mexican swamper, saying, "Go upstairs and get the boss. Damn if I'll turn for this bet without his say-so."

Presently, Schoonover showed up in his sock feet and half asleep. "What's the matter down here?" he growled.

"This man bet a $2,000 alce, and I won't turn for it," the dealer explained.

"Get up and let me set down there," muttered Sol. "I'll turn for it. I didn't get this game to where it is by turning down bets."

The hard-bitten old gambler who had been in many predicaments such as this looked over the spread and removed the stack of silver dollars from the deck. Then without a second's hesitation, turned the deck face up—and the cowhand's seven-spot was "in the door."

Sol and Jim made an inventory of the winnings, and found that the cowhand had won $7,600 off a single dollar he started with the evening before. Jim turned almost all the amount over to Schoonover to deposit in the bank for him, for which Sol gave him an IOU. We then went to the livery stable, got our horses and rode hell-bent for that day's roundup grounds. Later, men who worked with Jim said that he bought a small herd of cows and never gambled again.

I hadn't done badly myself. I lumped my winnings along with what I'd saved from my salary punching cows and breaking broncs for the LFD outfit, and bought some yearling steers. I had visions of becoming a cattle baron like the Whites and Little-field.

26.

A Ghostly Night in the Sand Hills

ONCE when I was working with the LFD outfit up the east side of the Pecos River, I had a weird experience. We were rounding up at some windmills on Long Arroyo between Roswell and the Staked Plains. On circle drive that morning, the drive leader had dropped a cowhand the punchers called "Britches" and me off in the Mescalero sand hills to drive what cattle we found to the roundup grounds at the windmills.

My companion had been given the nickname "Britches" by Old Negro Ad because he wore bib overalls when he started working for the outfit. Seldom seen on a cowhand on the Staked Plains in those days, the overalls were quite conspicuous. Ad first called the boy "Bib Britches," then cut it to "Britches" for short.

Up in the sand hills, we noticed that the cattle, strung out along a road ahead, would stop when they reached the top of the high sand hill and, after looking at something, would split up and go around on each side, returning to the road at the next hill.

"What are them cattle looking at?" Britches wondered.

I told him I didn't know, but whatever it was, it wasn't moving.

"If it was," he replied, "it would have showed up on top of the hill, because I've been watching the cows doing it for quite a while."

When we reached the top of the hill where the cattle had been stopping, we saw a covered wagon standing in the road with four mules hitched to it, all lying dead in their harness. Another mule was standing near the wagon, and when it saw us, it brayed and came to meet us.

Two men were sitting in the spring seat of the wagon in unnatural positions. When we got close, we saw that they were dead. One man had slumped over with his head in front of his knees, still holding the lines. The other man was leaning against the wagon sheet with his head thrown back. As we sat there looking the outfit over, Britches wondered aloud what could have happened.

I told him it looked to me as if they had been struck by lightning. I reminded him that while standing guard a few nights befor, we had seen lightning flashing in this direction. If I was right, the tragedy had occurred three nights before. Britches allowed from the way things smelled the wagon had been sitting there for at least that long.

He wondered what we should do. I told him I would remain there with the bodies while he went to the roundup and told the boss what we had found and asked him what he wanted us to do. He grunted an okay, rode around the wagon, and headed for the roundup grounds in a long lope.

I dismounted and climbed up to see whether I could recognize the men by their faces. I didn't know either of them.

Although the bodies were protected somewhat from the hot sun by the wagon sheet, decomposition had set in. The bodies of the mules were in the same condition.

Inside the wagon I found grain and provisions and supplies of all kinds, such as a freight wagon belonging to a ranch would carry. The barrels on each side of the wagon were full of water. I filled a bucket I found on the coupling pole with water for the mule. It was gaunt and almost famished, and drained the bucket without raising its head. I filled the bucket for it twice more.

"Just like a durned hard-headed mule," I told it. "You'd stay with your partners and starve to death, before you'd leave them and hunt for water."

After a while, Britches returned and said the boss had sent a man to Roswell to notify the law and told him that we should stay with the bodies until the officers came. There was only one thing to do—make ourselves as comfortable as possible and obey orders.

We unsaddled our horses and staked them out to graze. Then we laid our saddles in the shade of the wagon with the saddle blankets spread out beside them, and, using the saddles for pillows, went to sleep.

When I awoke, the shade had moved and I was lying in the hot sunshine. The flies were so bad around the wagon, a person couldn't rest, and the odor from the bodies was very strong. There was no other shade from the noonday sun. It was a choice between remaining in the shade of the wagon with the odor and flies to contend with or moving out into the hot sun and sand. We decided to remain in the shade of the wagon.

Late that afternoon, Britches asked if I was hungry. I told him I sure was and suggested that we see if we could find something in the wagon to eat.

With a sickly grin, he told me he had been thinking about looking for some food in the wagon, but didn't feel that he could swallow anything he might find there.

In a small chuck box in the wagon, I found a coffeepot, frying pan, some ground coffee, and a hunk of bacon. Among the supplies I also found canned corn and tomatoes and a box of crackers. We built a fire, boiled our coffee, fried some bacon, and had a good supper.

Night came on, and we drew water from the barrels for our

horses and the mule, and gave the mule some grain in a morral.
Our horses had never eaten grain.

As dusk settled over the sand hills, we moved our saddles to
the side of the wagon from which the wind was coming, gathered
up some sagebrush and mesquite roots, built a large fire, and lay
down on our saddle blankets to spend a lonely night.

"I've seen places I'd rather stay at than here," Britches
drawled as he rolled over, spitting a cud of Star Navy chewing
tobacco into his hand and throwing it out into the sagebrush.

I shuddered. In the ghostly light of our campfire, the whole
layout looked spooky.

The fire died down, and Britches got up and put some wood
on it, then sat down cross-legged. "I'll bet them fellows have got
a couple of widows and a bunch of kids waiting for them to come
home," he said. "I feel sorry for the kids."

We agreed to take turn about, one sleeping while the other
stood guard. I told Britches to hit the hay and I would stand first
guard. He turned over with his back to the fire and was soon
snoring.

There was no moon. By the flickering light of the campfire,
I could see the wagon covered with its white sheet and the four
mules lying sprawled in the road in front of it. Off to one side,
I could see our cow ponies grazing at the end of a thirty-foot
stake rope and near them the extra mule that was lucky to have
been following the wagon instead of being led behind it or alongside the team.

I lay there on my saddle blanket looking up at the twinkling
stars. About the only sounds were the occasional popping of a
red-hot mesquite ember in the ashes of the campfire and the snoring of the cowhand, who seemed to be swallowing his tongue.

Then a coyote began to yap close by, and almost immediately
another answered. In a few moments, it seemed as though we were
surrounded by the pesky varmints.

I threw some dry sagebrush on the fire, and it blazed up.
I could see its reflection in the eyes of two wolves standing near

the two lead mules. I threw a mesquite root at them, and they streaked over the top of the sand hill.

After a while, I heard a rustling in the sage grass on the farther side of the sleeping cowhand. Raising myself up on an elbow, I saw a striped skunk smelling around near him. I chunked a mesquite root at it, and judging from the odor which filled the atmosphere, I didn't miss.

During the early part of the evening, the sky was cloudless, but I could see flashes of heat lightning to the southeast. As the night advanced, a dark cloud formed in a half-circle to the northwest toward Fort Sumner, and lightning flashed above the top of the sand hills. It looked as if an electrical storm was moving our way.

Neither one of us had a watch to tell the time, but from standing guard around cattle on the bed ground night after night, I could tell by the position of the stars that I had been up about one-fourth of the night. I called Britches and told him to wake me at midnight.

He sat up, pinched off a small piece of chewing tobacco, and stuck it in his mouth. He sniffed the atmosphere and looked around. "Where's the polecat?" he asked.

I told him about our visitor and how I got rid of him.

He smelled both his sleeves, then pulled off his hat and smelled it. "It must have hit me," he said cheerfully.

He stood up and stretched his long legs and arms and shook his trouser legs down over his boots. "Shore looks like we're gonna have a cow-chip floater, don't it?" he said, looking toward the northwest.

Agreeing, I untied my slicker from behind my saddle and put it on to protect my body from the chill of the nighttime desert air. Laying my head on the seat of my saddle, I covered my face with my hat. I thought about the coyotes, and sat up to tell Britches about running them away and to ask him to watch and not let them get near the bodies of the mules. He promised to do so, and I settled down again.

It must have been nearly midnight when I was almost raised

from the ground by a clap of thunder. A gust of wind blew my hat off and took it up the sand hill. Britches recovered it and asked if we shouldn't get into the wagon before the rain started falling.

I agreed that we should. We pushed our saddles under the wagon and grabbed our saddle blankets to take with us. As we crawled into the wagon bed at its rear end, the rain started pouring down. Inside the wagon, the odor wasn't as bad as I had expected it to be. The wind was blowing in at the hole in the rear and carrying the scent away.

Britches was wondering if it was a cyclone, a possibility I had considered. As the cloud approached, I looked for a stem with a funnel-shaped top. Seeing none, I decided it wasn't a cyclone. I knew of only one twister in that part of the country. It had wrecked the adobe house at the T71 Ranch on Long Arroyo to the north of us, near Kenna.

As one bright flash of lightning after another lighted up the interior of the wagon, I caught glimpses of occupants sitting up ahead in the front seat. The strong wind blowing the wagon sheet caused the body leaning against it to move back and forth sidewise in a lifelike manner. It occurred to me that the body might become overbalanced and fall out onto the mules below.

Neither of us spoke for several minutes, then I heard Britches mumbling something about feeling safe in the wagon because he had heard that lightning never struck twice in the same place. I told him I hoped the storm wasn't a twister, because it might twist all four of us up in the wagon sheet together and carry us off.

Britches fidgeted, sighed, and after a while groaned. "Don't know what I'm gonna do," he said, "I took the last chaw of tobacco I had awhile ago, and setting here makes me crave one. If I don't get one, I'll go nuts. How much Bull Durham you got?"

I poured some out into the palm of his hand and told him that was all I could let him have. If I ran out of smoking tobacco, we would both go nuts.

The rain fell in torrents, and I could hear large hailstones striking the wooden bed of the wagon. One came through the wagon sheeet, and I had to move out of the drip. I feared our horses might break loose, run off, and leave us on foot. I raised the sheet on the side where the horses were staked, waited for a flash of lightning, and saw they were still there, with their heads down and tails to the storm.

Along toward morning, Britches was craving another chew of tobacco. "Maybe those fellows up there chewed tobacco when they were alive," I told him. "They might have some in their pockets."

He mumbled something about it would be robbing the dead. I told him if they had chewed tobacco like he did, they would understand his predicament and gladly give him a chew if they were alive.

He waited a few minutes, getting up courage. Then I heard his spurs rattling as he crawled toward the front of the wagon. I waited a while after he returned, then asked, "Did you do any good?"

He raised the wagon sheet, put two fingers to his lips, squirted a stream of tobacco juice between them over the wagon wheel, then told me he had found a plug of Drummond Natural Leaf in a vest pocket.

"How does it taste?" I asked.

"Let's not talk about that," he gagged. "I haven't had the nerve to taste since I put it in my mouth."

After a while, he growled in a threatening tone, "It won't be healthy for you if you tell anybody what I done."

The rain stopped falling, and the sky cleared before daylight. The wood was wet, but we found enough in the cowskin coosie stretched under the wagon bed to boil some coffee and fry some bacon, and with some crackers, had a good breakfast.

Even before the sun rose, we saw buzzards circling the area overhead, waiting to feast upon the mules. But we kept them shooed away, not allowing them to light nearby.

About noon, three men in a buckboard, leading a saddled horse beside the team, showed up. One was a justice of the peace, one was a mortician, and the other was a deputy sheriff from Roswell.

We helped them transfer the bodies from the wagon to the buckboard. They were able to identify the men, and the deputy asked us to take the live mule and keep it in our remuda until the owner called for it. He then mounted the saddled horse and headed for the Elida, New Mexico, area where the men had lived.

Britches and I watered our horses and the mule, saddled up, put a lead rope on the mule, and rode away to catch up with the roundup.

When we reached the top of the sand hill, we stopped and looked back at the pitiful scene below us. Britches, brushing his hands together, said, "I'm like the old fellow was when he whipped his old lady. I'm glad that job's over with."

As we came in sight of our chuck wagon, Britches warned me again: "Now don't you dare tell anybody where I got that chewing tobacco. If you do, I'll clean your dadgummed plow."

27.

Sutty's Wild Night in Roswell

IN the summer of 1906, I was with the LFD outfit rounding up and branding calves along Long Arroyo and the east side of the Pecos River near Roswell. Sutty was with the outfit that summer, too, and so was Britches, who had hired out that spring.

We were rounding up one day at the Bottomless Lakes, an area on the east side of the Pecos, about thirteen miles southeast of Roswell, that later became a state park.

On circle drive that morning, Sutty, Britches, and I were the first three men to be dropped off by the drive leader. We had come in early and were holding what cattle we found near the southern-most lake where the roundup would be worked, waiting for the other hands to come in.

From where we were sitting on our horses on the gyp hills that bordered the alkali flats along the river, we could see one of the lakes. Our chuck wagon was camped near the lake, and our remuda of cow ponies grazed around it.

It was Britches' first trip to that part of New Mexico, and he wondered aloud why those deep blue pools were called "bottomless lakes."

"Because they ain't got no bottom, you nut," Sutty said.

As Britches gently eased a tired leg across his bronc's withers in front of the saddle horn, he wanted to know how in the hell they could hold water without any bottom.

Sutty explained how lead lines had been let down in the lakes for several hundred feet without finding bottom, and told of deep-sea fish without eyes being caught in them. Then he changed the subject by pointing out to the newcomer some of the landmarks that were visible from where we were sitting. He indicated a grove of trees on South Spring River where John Chisum had located his Jingle-bob headquarters ranch when he moved from Bosque Grande, and had lived during the Lincoln County War. It was purchased by Governor Hagerman when the Jingle-bob outfit folded up. Then turning toward the northwest, he showed him trees marking the location of Roswell between the Hondo and North Spring rivers.

I butted in and showed the boy an old sun-dried adobe house near some cottonwoods on the near side of the Pecos River where Juan Chaves, the *viejo Mexicano* patriarch, lived. Chaves was said to have been born there 135 years before, when the Capitán Mountain to the west was a little bitty hill.

There at the Chaves place was the Juan Chaves Crossing, where the freight wagon road from Roswell to the Staked Plains crossed the Pecos River. The ford had quicksand and was dangerous. More than one freight wagon had sunk in that river bed.

Sutty looked over at me and wanted to know if I was going to Roswell with him that evening.

"I guess so," I said. "Someone will have to go to keep you out of trouble and lead your horse back to camp."

He invited Britches to go with us, but Britches refused the invitation for some reason.

After calf branding was finished that afternoon, Sutty and I rounded up the remuda and changed horses. We went to the chuck wagon and Sutty rolled out his bed and removed a .45-caliber pistol, which he tucked in his waistband inside his shirt.

I asked if he was going to take the gun with him. He said he always carried it when he went to town. I warned him that he might get into serious trouble, but he was as obstinate as a chuck wagon mule.

As we mounted our horses, the roundup boss yelled, "You scissorbills be sure and get back to camp in time to stand last guard."

We headed for Roswell across the alkali flats, forded the river at Juan Chaves' place, and were soon riding through apple orchards and farms irrigated with artesian wells. The head gates in some of the ditches were raised, and the green alfalfa was covered with water.

Giant cottonwoods lined the road for a long way through what was known as "Lover's Lane" where the branches overlapped to form a tunnel that shut the sun out completely. The lane ran long the south side of the LFD farm, where the remuda came in February of each year to graze in the green alfalfa fields.

As we rode through the shady lanes, Sutty pulled off his hat and told me it would be nice if we could punch cattle and flank calves in shade like this, instead of in the broiling sun and alkali dust on the east side of the Pecos. I wondered how there could be so much difference in the two sides of that river. Good water flowed from artesian wells on the west side, but on the east side one had to drink gyp water, holding his nose.

As we galloped along, Sutty asked me why I thought Britches refused to ride into town with us. I guessed maybe he was afraid he couldn't withstand the temptation of a monte or crap game in operation. There was something about the new cowhand that I couldn't understand. He acted like someone on the dodge.

Britches was shy when strangers were present. He was obviously an experienced cowhand, not a green cotton picker as we had believed when he came to the outfit wearing bib overalls. He had never mentioned his folks or where he was from, and I had seen some artillery and ammunition in his bedroll.

Riding into town, we put our horses up at a livery stable and went into Hoss Cummings' saloon to tell him hello and to buy a drink. Hoss gave us one on the house.

We ate a bait of ham-'n'-eggs in Big Jim's Chinese restaurant, went to Hub Williams' store for some new clothes, and moseyed down to the Grand Central barber shop for a bath, haircut, shave, and bootshine.

We then strolled into Josh Church's place, where Sutty began to play the roulette wheel. He lost a few bucks on red and black, and odd and even. He then laid two dollars straight up on single o in the pea green. The dealer spun the ball in the revolving wheel, and in a singsong voice, said:

> *Round and round the little ball goes.*
> *Where it will stop, nobody knows.*

The ball lost momentum, rolled down the incline, bounced around, and came to rest in a green-colored recess marked with an o. The dealer yelled, "Gents, it's single o in the green and the lucky player is paid thirty-five for one."

The cowhand raked his winnings into his hat and let the bartender put half of it in the safe with orders to not let him have it until he was ready to leave town, so he wouldn't blow it in.

We went into a rear room where a draw poker game was in operation. Big Jim was playing. There was one vacant seat. As Sutty sat down, he asked Jim if the seat was lucky.

"No," the old Chinaman replied. "A man just went bloke sitting there with full-house."

Sutty lost a few small pots, then won a couple of large ones. He evidently thought he was lucky and started plunging.

I stood behind Sutty's chair sweating the game. Big Jim opened a pot. Sutty peeped at his hand and saw he had a four-card straight flush open at both ends. He could make a straight, a flush, or a straight flush in the draw. He raised the Chinaman before the draw. The other players laid down, and Jim called.

Sutty was dealing. Jim asked for two cards, and Sutty drew

one. Without looking at his hand Jim checked the bet up to the one-card draw. It was table stakes, and the cowhand tried to make the Chinaman lay his hand down by moving in all his chips.

After studying the cowhand's countenance a few moments, the poker-faced old Oriental called. Sutty asked him what he had.

Spreading his cards out face up on the table, the Chinaman said, "Thlee ace-e."

"Take it, you slant-eyed heathen," the cowhand growled.

As Sutty slid his chair back to rise, the man running the game tossed him two poker chips and told us to get a drink at the bar. We did so. As we left through the swinging doors, my partner suggested that we go to Big Maud's parlor house and look the gals over.

The dance hall in the big woman's brothel was crowded. We danced several times and bought beer each time for our dancing partners. One of the girls was telling Sutty to put just one more quarter in her stocking for luck, and she would let him snap her garter. He declared it wasn't worth it, and claimed she was trying to two-bit and dollar him to death.

Suddenly, the front door of the dance hall swung open and a girl walked unsteadily through it with an empty beer bottle in each hand. "Whoopie-e-e!" she yelled. "I was born in a whorehouse and raised on a battlefield. I know how to do only two things, and one of them is fight!"

Suddenly, she hurled both bottles at Big Maud. "Duck, you bitch!" she yelled.

The madam ducked, all right, and the bottles crashed against the wall behind her.

Sutty allowed that business was picking up, and if we stuck around a while, maybe they would open a keg of nails and take a drive, or kill a chicken and churn.

The piano player started toward the girl, but Sutty stopped him. He told him it was a woman's fight and for him to stay out of it. If he wanted anything, he could take *him* on. The girls fell on the intruder and dragged her out and across the street to her own little crib.

One of the girls told me the madam had ejected the drunk girl from her place of business, and every time she got lit up, she came in and started a roughhouse.

Sutty was getting tipsy and mean. He was having an argument with the pianist, and I broke in and asked him what the trouble was.

"I asked that long drink of well water to play the 'St. Louis Tickle,' " he said indignantly, "and he played 'Rufus Rastus Johnson Brown' instead!"

He shoved me aside, and before I knew what was happening, he had grabbed the musician's necktie and tied it into several hard knots. He then mussed up the man's hair, which was parted in the middle, by running his fingers through it.

Sutty smiled and called the musician a sissy, making specific obscene allegations about his habits. The pianist thought the waddy was joking, but he didn't know Sutty as I did. I knew the angrier he became, the more he smiled. When he got that way, he often had a man whipped before the victim knew he was working up to a fight.

Still smiling, Sutty turned to the landlady and told her she wasn't running her joint to suit him. If things didn't change, he'd take charge, he promised, and run it to suit himself.

Afraid he might take a notion to use the gun concealed under his shirt, I dragged him off into a corner and tried to talk him into leaving with me. He promised me that he would leave after he danced one more time with "Miss Bobbed Hair."

Two men I thought might be bouncers entered the hall through a rear door. They picked out girls, and began to dance. Sutty grabbed the bobbed-hair girl in his arms and held her like a calf he was about to flank. He yelled at the piano player to play "St. Louis Tickle," and, believe me, the man played it.

One of the strangers bumped into Sutty on the dance floor. The cowhand turned and glared at him, but grudgingly decided that it was an accident. A few moments later, when the same man bumped into him again, Sutty knew it wasn't accidental, and that the man was trying to pick a fight in order to throw him out.

Releasing Miss Bobbed Hair, Sutty swung around with his back to a corner and his thumb hooked in the waistband of his trousers just above his belt buckle. He looked straight at the man who had bumped into him.

"I'm a rootin', tootin', fightin', shootin' hellcat from down on the Río Penasco," he snarled. "I'm a she-wolf. My tail drags the ground, and I dare any son-of-a-bitch to step on it. I ride a panther and curry it with a live centipede. Get high behind, you pimps and whoremongers!"

They "got," and so did the girls! The man who had bumped into the cowhand didn't wait to make his exit with the crowd through a door; he went out through the nearest window.

In seconds, the only ones left in the room were Big Maud, the pianist, Sutty, and me. The cowboy looked over at the musician. "You sissy looking hophead," he growled, "that means you travel too." He did.

Big Maud started toward the hallway.

"Where you going?" Sutty demanded.

"To call the law," she said with as much grit as she could muster.

He stepped in front of her. She plunged against him, knocking him to one side, and reached out to grab the doorknob. He fired, and the .45 bullet shattered the white porcelain knob into a hundred pieces. She jumped back, and, finding that her hand had not been hit, began to wring both her hands and beg us, with tears in her eyes, to leave.

Chiding her for turning her hired goons loose on him after he had spent his hard-earned cash in her brothel, he said he was leaving but might come back. If he did so, he said, and she sicked her bouncers on him again, her filthy bordello would be wrecked. We left, with him leading the way, and walked toward the main part of town.

As we walked, I tried to figure some way of getting Sutty out of Roswell before he got into serious trouble. He depended on me to look after him when we were out together, but I felt I wasn't having much luck with him on this trip. I knew he wouldn't leave town till he was good and ready, and that if he thought someone was trying to force him to go, he'd get bullheaded and refuse just to be ornery.

We entered the main street at the corner of the Green Front Saloon, a pretty tough place patronized mostly by Mexicans. I tried to steer Sutty past the door because I knew he was hunting trouble and there was no better place in Roswell to find it than in there.

"Come on, Sutty, let's go to camp," I pleaded as he stopped in front of the saloon. "You know we have to stand last guard."

He informed me that we hadn't yet been in the Green Front, and that we might miss something. He marched through the swinging doors, and I was right behind him. Inside, the scent of cheap whisky and beer filled the atmosphere. A bunch of Mexicans were lined up at the bar, drinking.

Sutty deliberately shouldered in beside a big *hombre* who looked drunk and quarrelsome. The man wore a large *sombrero* with the brim about even with the cowhand's mouth. He looked us over and said something to the other Mexicans. Sutty understood and spoke Spanish as fluently as he did English and knew what the man had said. "He thinks he's tough." Sutty said, turning to me. "I'm going to find out if he is."

The Mexican pulled a pack of brown cigarette papers and a bag of Duke's Mixture smoking tobacco from a shirt pocket. Sutty turned back around and watched the *hombre* lick his thumb, slip a cigarette paper out of the rubber band, dig the mouth of the bag open with a forefinger, and sprinkle some tobacco in the paper by tapping the bag with the same finger. Catching one string on the bag between his teeth and pulling on the other string, he closed the bag and left it suspended from his teeth while he carefully straightened out the tobacco in the paper.

With black eyes twinkling and a dangerous smile on his face, the waddy stepped in front of the Mexican, stooped over, drew in a deep breath, and blew the tobacco out of the paper. Then he caught the brim of the man's *sombrero* between his teeth, pulled it off his head, dropped it on the floor, and deliberately stepped on it, crowing like a rooster.

The room became deathly still. Every eye was on the two men in front of the bar. I expected the point of a knife in my back, the crash of a beer bottle against my skull, or the report of a gun. But nothing happened. The man took the insult.

Disappointed, but still smiling, the cowhand turned and calmly walked toward the rear of the saloon without glancing back. I followed him. The Mexicans watched us as we passed, and it was hard to resist the temptation to look back to see what they were doing.

Near the rear of the room, a gambler was dealing monte at a table surrounded by Mexicans and a few gringos. As Sutty approached, the dealer stopped the play and laid the cards on the table. He and the players got to their feet, but Sutty passed by without even looking at them.

My wayward protégé went to a table in one corner of the room where several Mexicans were sitting and drinking from a whisky bottle. My hellcat from the Penasco reached over, grabbed the bottle, emptied it with one long swig, then threw it at the Mexicans.

That did it! Something hit me and everything went black. I came to on my back and looked up just in time to see a boot heel aimed at my face. As I got to my feet, a man grabbed me, and I threw him clear over a monte table.

I looked around for Sutty and saw him knock a man down with his six-shooter. Then someone hit his arm with a chair, knocking him loose from his gun. The weapon fell to the floor and skidded across it, striking a spittoon in front of the bar. Sutty's hat was gone, his shirt was torn off, and I could see a stream of blood trickling down his back.

I dodged a chair that came flying through the air and reached Sutty just as the saloon lights went out. I guided him toward the rear door and shoved him through it. We climbed over a wall and raced up the alley to the livery barn where our horses were. Having reached the barn safely, we examined our wounds.

Both our hats were gone and Sutty was naked from the waist up. He was bleeding from a gash in his back where someone had slashed him with a knife. One of my eyes was closing fast from being trampled upon while I lay on the floor, and blood was running down into my shirt collar from a wound in the back of my head where I had been struck with a chair, bottle, gun butt, or brass knucks. While washing up at the horse trough, I asked my buddy if he was ready to go back to camp.

He allowed that he would be ready as soon as he went back to the Green Front Saloon and got his hat and gun.

I told the fool that the law was undoubtedly looking for us, and that he positively was not going back to the Green Front that night. "You are leaving town," I said grimly, "if I have to hog-tie you on your horse and lead it to camp."

"You and who else will tie me on my horse?" he sneered, still full of fight.

We yelled at each other some, and finally agreed to get something to eat at Big Jim's beanery before heading for camp. As we walked along the sidewalk to the restaurant, I told him I was ashamed to be seen on the street with a half-naked man. He told me that I didn't improve the scenery, bareheaded and with a black eye and a bloody head.

After eating, we got our horses, and Sutty insisted on going by Josh Church's saloon to get the money he had left with the bartender "and just one more drink." The saloon was deserted, except for a faro dealer and his lookout and several Chinese who were bucking the game. The bartender was polishing glasses, and a Mexican swamper was rolling up the mats, stacking chairs on top of pool tables, cleaning cuspidors, and mopping the floor.

With a broad grin on his face, the bartender looked us over. "Where was the cyclone?" he asked.

Sutty told him it was none of his dadgummed business.

"It's time all little peckerwoods like you two were in bed," the barkeep said as he handed the cowpoke his money. The good-natured man with a handle-bar mustache waxed to points and a diamond stud in his shirt bosom gave us a drink on the house, then told us, "Bye-bye."

Several times while riding to the chuck wagon, Sutty remembered losing his gun. Each time, he would turn his horse and start back, and I would have to head the animal in the other direction.

We reached camp, turned our horses loose and headed them toward the remuda, saddled our night horses staked nearby, and rolled out our bed. The only timepiece in the outfit was a clock in the chuck box that wouldn't run. A glance at the stars, however, told me it was almost time for us to go on last guard. I told Sutty there was no need for us to go to bed, because we would be called before we could go to sleep.

I put some cow chips on the smoldering campfire to heat the coffee and reached up to get my hat to fan them into a blaze before I remembered that I had left it in the Green Front Saloon. We dipped our tin cups into the coffeepot and sat down on the ground to wait for a man on third guard to ride in and call us.

Everyone except those standing guard around the cattle and remuda was sound asleep in tarpaulin-covered beds spread out around the chuck wagon. Some distance from camp, but visible in the bright moonlight, were the saddle horses, scattered out, some of them grazing and others standing asleep. On the opposite side of the wagon were the cattle on the bed ground. Most of them were lying down, although a few at the edge of the herd were grazing. Several big wild Mexican steers in the center of the herd were standing up, as they always were, ready to stampede.

I could see two men on guard sitting together on their horses on the far side of the herd. The other man was riding around the herd near camp. I could hear him faintly as he sung:

> *I had a piece of pie and I had a piece of puddin',*
> *I gave it all away to see Sally Goodin.*
> *I looked up the road and seen Sally comin',*
> *Good gosh a'mighty you oughta saw me runnin'.*

Sutty was sitting cross-legged with elbows on his knees, his head in both hands. I told him he looked like a picture from life's other side. "I feel like one," he murmured painfully.

When the men came after us to go on guard, they also called Britches. As we rode out to the herd, Sutty told him he should have been with us because we had a good time.

"I bet you did," Britches replied in a dry manner. "You look like two dogie calves that have been torn up by wildcats. I thought at first were two Injuns, with them bandannas tied around your heads.

"Where's your hat?" he asked Sutty.

"I left it in Roswell," the boy answered.

"Leave it there to be cleaned?"

"I guess it'll need cleaning!"

The cattle were quiet. We could see the whole herd in the bright moonlight. Britches and I rode together in one direction, and Sutty traveled the opposite way. We could hear him whistling and, at times, singing.

Britches told me to listen to the mockingbird and suggested that we dig it a worm. "Got a pretty voice, ain't he?" he asked.

I agreed, and told him Sutty could also play the French harp. I had seen people dance all night with no other music than Sutty's harp. He always had a crowd around him wherever he was, especially the gals, who seemed crazy about his black curly hair. When he was around, I felt like a stepchild.

Britches told me he knew a fellow like that one time. He was dark, tall, and slender, with black eyes and black curly hair, and was a lady's delight. "He took my best gal away from me and married her," he said.

That was the first time I ever heard him mention his past life.

Sutty had told us both about his girl friend who lived near the Texas–New Mexico line south of Bronco. He declared theirs had been love at first sight. He said the girl's pappy was a nester with a large family and a few milk cows, who tried to make a living on his 160-acre homestead by dry farming, but was having a tough time getting by. The boy said he had offered to help the old fellow out, but his offer had been scornfully rejected.

Sutty said his girl told him her pappy didn't like him and didn't want him to visit her because he considered him too wild. And maybe he was.

Sutty rode out to the chuck wagon, dismounted and "tied his horse loose" with the bridle reins dropped on the ground, got a tin cup from the chuck box, dipped it in the coffeepot hanging on the pot rack, and sat down on the ground cross-legged while he drank it.

After a while, he mounted his horse and, as he rode back to the herd, started singing again. His pleasant voice, floating across the sleeping herd on the bed ground, seemed to have a soothing effect upon them as they belched up their cuds and chewed them.

The song was one he told us his girl taught him to sing and act out. I had listened to him sing it so many times, I knew the words and tune, and I still remember them, although I never did know the composer.

> *Sitting in the parlor, nine o'clock at night,*
>   *spooning with the girl you love.*
> *Talk about the weather, then turn down the light,*
>   *everything is quiet up above.*
> *Keep on moving closer, till at last you find,*
>   *there's room for both inside the rocking chair.*
> *Heads are close together, girlie doesn't mind,*
>   *rocking back and forth without a single care.*
>
> *H-o-l-d-i-n-g h-a-n-d-s, h-o-l-d-i-n-g h-a-n-d-s.*
> *You and she both sigh as you sit side by side.*
> *The moon looks on and then it tries to hide.*
> *H-o-l-d-i-n-g h-a-n-d-s.*
> *The clock is striking twelve out in the hall.*
> *All the time you sit there, holding hands,*
>   *you don't say nothing at all.*
>
> *Go to work next morning feeling mighty blue,*
>   *all you do is mope and sigh.*
> *Think about your sweetheart, don't know what to do,*
>   *wishing for the time to hurry by.*

Sutty's Wild Night in Roswell

Call again that evening, meet her at the door,
   walk into the parlor just the same.
Both sit in the rocker, as you did before,
   then commence to play the same old game.

The next day we rounded up at Riverside, about sixteen miles northeast of Roswell. Britches and I were working between the roundup and the cow-and-calf cut when I saw a man on horseback coming from the direction of Roswell. He looked familiar, and as he approached, I recognized him. "That's Sheriff Fred Higgins from Roswell," I told Britches.

A few minutes later, Britches rode to the chuck wagon, threw his bed off, unrolled it, removed something, rolled it back up, and put it back on the wagon. He rode away toward the river, and that was the last time I saw him that day.

The sheriff rode up to roundup boss Charlie Walker. A few minutes later, they both went to Sutty. Then all three came to me, and we shook hands. The sheriff said he had come for Sutty to take him to court at Roswell. He wanted me to go along as a witness. Looking at Sutty, the sheriff added slyly, "Judge Pope wants to see you—something about a doorknob."

The boss invited the sheriff to stay for dinner. He told Sutty and me to have the wrangler round up the remuda so that we could change horses. As we rode to the remuda, I bawled Sutty out for being too bullheaded to leave his gun in his bed the evening before. He completely ignored my tirade.

While eating dinner, the sheriff told Sutty and me to eat a good meal because the Higgins Hotel at Roswell fed their guests nothing except bread and water.

"I didn't know Higgins ran a hotel," Sutty said in a low voice.

"He means the hoosegow, you simpleton!" I muttered.

Higgins warned us that Judge Pope was in a bad humor. Two hands from the Block outfit rode their horses into a saloon at Roswell, ordered drinks for the crowd, shot up the bar fixtures, then rode out of town shooting at everything that moved. Higgins rounded them up and herded them back to town, and the judge gave them each a fifty dollar fine and sixty days in jail.

Sutty said he could pay the sixty days in jail, but would hate to give up fifty bucks in addition to losing his hat, shirt, and gun.

The sheriff searched us to see if either of us had a gun. Then we mounted our horses and headed for Roswell. I had borrowed an old hat the boss had in his war bag, but Sutty was still wearing a bandanna, with its four corners tied in knots, for a cap.

When troubles and worry upset Sutty's tranquility, he showed his feelings by absent-mindedly humming little ditties. He now hummed a few lines of the song that figured in his escapade the evening before—"The St. Louis Tickle":

> *I thought I heard somebody say,*
> *The St. Louis Tickle, oh take it away.*

I followed him with a parody I'd made up that might fit the results of the court hearing the next day:

> *I thought I heard old Judge Pope say,*
> *"Fifty dollars and sixty days, put him away."*

The cowhand gave me a vicious look but didn't say anything. The lawman smiled and looked off toward the Capitán Mountain.

When Sutty got in a good humor with me, I told him—in a low voice the sheriff couldn't hear—how Britches had behaved that morning. He said Britches might have thought the officer was looking for him.

When we reached the courthouse at Roswell, Higgins told Sutty it was too late to see the judge, and he guessed he'd have to put him in jail overnight to keep him from high-tailing it out of town.

Swearing with upraised hand that he wouldn't leave town, Sutty begged the sheriff not to lock him up.

"Well, all right," the lawman said, "but remember, if you ain't here in the morning, I'll catch and pistol-whup you."

While we ate supper at the Grand Central Hotel, I asked Sutty what we would do that night.

He declared that he was gentle enough to be curried below his knees and was going to bed and get some sleep so he would be in shape to face the judge the next day.

After eating, I suggested that we both buy new hats so we would look decent when we entered the courthouse. In addition to hats, we also purchased new shirts. The collar of the one I was wearing was caked with dried blood.

The next morning when court convened, the judge examined his docket and called Sutty's case without a jury. He asked the prisoner if he wished to be represented by an attorney, telling him that he was charged with carrying a concealed weapon and destroying property. The defendant told His Honor that he would plead his own case.

The judge asked the complaining witness to take the stand. The bawdyhouse madam was sworn in and displayed several pieces of broken porcelain she claimed had been a knob on a door in her house before it was broken by a bullet from the defendant's gun. She swore that the defendant's language and actions had caused all her customers to leave and had ruined the reputation of her place of business. The judge asked the defense if it wished to cross-examine the witness. The answer was, "No questions."

The musician took the stand and told how the defendant had embarrassed him by mussing up his hair before an audience, tying his necktie in knots, forcing him with threats to play certain tunes, calling him indecent names, and forcing him to leave his place of employment against his will. There was no cross-examination of this witness either.

The state rested its case. I was called as a defense witness. Judge Pope asked me to relate what I knew about the affair.

I told him the defendant, who had been out in cow camps for several months, had come to town to have a good time. He merely wanted to dance a little and enjoy himself. He was free-hearted and a good sport and had bought several rounds of beer from the madam at a dollar a bottle. He had also complied with several of the girls' requests to put quarters in their stockings—for luck.

I told the judge that the musician probably didn't know that it was customary in such places for the pianist to play certain dance tunes when requested to do so by cash customers. The defendant had made such a request, but it had been ignored by the piano player.

223

The defendant gently mussed up the man's carefully groomed hair that was parted in the middle, I said, and jokingly tied his necktie in hard knots such as those tied in bridle reins.

I described how the two men had come into the hall, started dancing, and rudely bumped into the defendant and his partner. He had seemed to regard their actions as accidental the first time, but when the bumping continued, he had seemed to realize they were trying to pick a fight.

I related that the defendant had suddenly stopped dancing and told the two men just who he was, where he came from, and some of his past history. He then requested that everyone leave the room, and they complied, all except the madam and the pianist. The defendant went over and told the musician that request also included him, whereupon he exited. I supposed that my friend wished to have a private talk with the madam. When the woman said she was going to call the law and started toward a door, the defendant playfully shot the doorknob off so she couldn't open it to use a telephone in the hall. He then quietly left the house.

The judge asked the defendant if he wished to be sworn, take the witness stand, and say anything in his own defense.

The waddy took the oath to tell the truth and seated himself in the witness chair. He told the judge he reckoned he was as peaceable as he could be till them guys tried to pick a fight so they could bounce him. He declared there was no rubber in him and he couldn't be bounced. He guessed he flew off the handle and asked them to leave the dance hall. In conclusion, he told the judge, anything he did couldn't possibly ruin the reputation of that dump nohow.

The judge reprimanded the cowboy for not behaving himself and leaving town after the affair in the brothel. "Instead," His Honor declared sternly, "you entered and wrecked the Green Front Saloon."

"We didn't wreck the saloon," the boy answered. "It wrecked us."

The Court ordered him to pay a fine of fifty dollars for carrying a concealed weapon, and to serve sixty days in jail for wantonly destroying property with a firearm. The judge also admonished the cowhand to leave his gun in camp when he came to town thereafter.

After allowing the cowpuncher a few moments time to digest the verdict, the judge told him he would suspend the jail sentence provided he didn't appear in his court for another law violation during the next sixty days. If he did, the jail sentence would have to be served.

By pooling our resources, we found that we had enough cash to pay the fine. Before leaving, Sutty asked His Honor if we could go to the Green Front Saloon and get our belongings. He told us to stay away from that place and let the sheriff get our missing items.

We got our horses, and, as we were leaving town, I saw Old Negro Ad in front of the Grand Central Hotel. He was sitting on Sunflower, the most powerful roping horse in the LFD remuda. I asked him if he was going to ride to camp with us. He said he would be with us soon as Mister Tom White gave him a letter to take to the roundup boss.

While sitting on our horses waiting for Ad, we heard a commotion and, looking down the street, saw a runaway team pulling a milk wagon toward us at breakneck speed with lines flying and no driver.

Ad reached down and pulled the latigo strap on his cinch one hole tighter. He jerked down his rope, double-half-hitched one end of it to his saddle horn and built a big loop in the other end. As the team passed by, he jumped Sunflower alongside it and dropped a big "blocker" around both horses' necks. He threw the slack in his rope over the wagon, dropped his weight over in his left stirrup and turned off as if he was "fairgrounding" a big steer. Sunflower stacked the whole shebang in the middle of the street. Both horses went down, the wagon toppled on its side with the tongue broken, and milk and broken bottles scattered over a wide area.

The driver came and removed Ad's rope from the horses' necks, and the old Negro cowpuncher came riding back coiling up his rope. "Them hosses sure would've tore things up if I hadn't caught them," he remarked slyly.

When we reached camp that evening, I asked Britches where he had been when we left for town with the sheriff the day before. He said he saw a cow and a calf down by the river that had been missed in circle drive, and brought them to the cow-and-calf cut.

28.

Holdup at Fort Sumner

WORKING on up the Pecos River through the Bar V range, we camped one night near Bosque Grande, that "Large Grove" of cottonwoods on the Pecos where John Chisum, in 1867, established his first headquarters camp in New Mexico.

The old camp house was about two miles north of where Salt Creek joins the Pecos River on its west side. The old adobe shack with one door and one Mexican-type window with panes broken out and the openings covered with cowhide was about 150 yards from the river bank and was surrounded by a growth of salt cedars. The cottonwoods that gave the camp its name were on the east side of the river.

Salt Creek, south of the camp, was so boggy it couldn't be crossed. When an animal walked into that quagmire, it bogged down. The more it tried to free itself, the deeper it sank, and none ever got out without the assistance of a bog rider with his horse and rope. When going from Roswell to the camp, one had to ford the Pecos River twice—below the Salt Creek junction, then back above the junction.

As we sat around the campfire the evening we camped there, an old waddy who had worked for the Jingle-bob outfit and had seen life in the raw along the Pecos got strung out telling some of the history of the famous place. He had come there with the Jingle-bob and had been with the outfit till Chisum's death in the mid-1880's. He had known many of the participants in the Lincoln County War: McSween, Tunstall, Murphy, Brady, the Seven Rivers gang, Pat Garret, Kip McKinney, John Poe, Billy the Kid, and others.

He told of necktie parties in that grove of cottonwoods where so many horse thieves and cattle rustlers were hanged the trees just died off, and the place became ha'nted. All kinds of noises could be heard there at night—gruff voices, cries, groans, chains rattling, and the wheezing of someone being choked. Night horses staked out would get to snorting, break loose, and run off. Even old chuck wagon mules would skedaddle.

The old fellow's mind seemed to be going back over the years, and we waited for him to continue. He absent-mindedly raked some ashes out of the fire, smoothed them down, and with a twig, drew an outline of a cow's ears with the jinglebob earmark for which the outfit was named. To one side, he traced Chisum's Long Rail brand.

Finally, picking up the thread of his narrative, he told of seeing strange things happen at those necktie parties, such as a man who had stolen hundreds of cows pulling on a rope—the other end of which was around a poor bastard's neck who had been caught stealing his first calf.

There used to be some graves around the bosque, but the Pecos River occasionally got on a rampage, cut a new channel, and deposited a lot of sand and silt over the countryside. The graves had either been washed out or covered with sand so that they were no longer visible.

Britches, sitting beside the old man, was an attentive listener and seemed disappointed when he ceased his historical narration of the Old West. Squirming around, the *viejo vaquero* managed to stand erect on his rheumatic legs and hobble to his bed a short distance from the fire. Pulling off his boots and laying them on the brim of his hat, he crawled under a Navaho blanket and pulled the tarp up over his head, boots, and hat.

A few days later, we rounded up near the historic frontier town of Fort Sumner. After calf branding that afternoon, all except those on day herd or first guard went into town.

Sutty, Britches, and I went into a saloon and gambling house in an old adobe building. A Mexican bartender was on duty. The games in progress were craps, monte, faro, stud and draw poker, and blackjack. Sutty and I played draw poker while Britches stood behind us sweating the game. The only sounds were the rattle of poker chips, clink of coins, low voices of the players, and jingle of spurs as the men shifted in their chairs around the tables.

Suddenly, a gruff voice commanded: "Reach for the ceiling!"

I reached. I was sitting with my back to the front door and couldn't tell who had spoken without turning around, which I didn't want to do. Everyone must have reached quickly except the bartender, who apparently had reached too slow or made some move the speaker did not like. A gun roared, and from the corner of my eye I saw the bartender fall. The body rolled out from behind the bar with a stream of blood spurting from a hole in the forehead.

"Stand up, everybody," the voice growled, "and don't make no crooked moves."

Chairs scraped on the bare floor and spurs rattled as the men got on their feet.

"Line up along that wall," the man ordered.

When I turned around, I saw a tall white man standing just inside the front entrance with a gun in each hand and a bandanna pulled over the lower part of his face. Wisps of smoke were still oozing from the barrel of one gun. Under the hat brim pulled down low over his forehead, were eyes that took in everything in the room.

"*Bueno!*" the man hissed, and I heard someone mumble, "Gosh, there's two of them."

For the first time, I saw another man standing just inside the rear doorway with a gun in each hand and a bandanna over his nose. He was wearing a large *sombrero* and a sash wrapped around his waist Mexican-style.

When the first man spoke, the Mexican slipped his pistols into holsters at his hips, pulled a cloth sack from under his sash and walked around to the gaming tables. He picked up the gold and currency, from both tables and cash drawers, dropping the money into the sack. He was careful to keep from getting between the other bandit and the men lined up against the wall.

Sutty was standing just ahead of me, and something shiny caught my eye. Glancing up, I saw that he still held the cards he had been looking at when the command to reach was given by the holdup man. My arms were aching and my thoughts went back to boyhood school days in Odessa, when the teacher would punish me for playing pranks by making me stand in a corner facing the class with my arms in that position.

Looking at the gunman, I noticed that the hands holding the two guns weren't as steady as they had been at first, evidently because it was hard to hold the heavy guns in one position so long. The black holes in the gun barrels were wavering. The bandit was holding the hammers back with his thumbs, and I wondered if the triggers had been removed, as they sometimes were, to eliminate the necessity of having to pull them. My gaze finally came to rest upon a round Bull Durham tobacco tag dangling from a vest pocket just above one of the gun barrels.

The only sounds in the room were the deep breathing of the men lined up against the wall, the creaking of loose floor boards as someone shifted his weight from one foot to the other, and the clinking noise the Mexican made as he gathered and dropped coins into the bag. Somewhere out in town, a dog barked. Someone on horseback rode past the front of the saloon, and I wondered what would happen if he dismounted and entered the door behind the outlaw.

When the Mexican finished with the gaming tables, he calmly stepped over the body lying on the floor and emptied the cash drawer behind the bar. As he stepped back over the remains of the bartender, he reached down and removed a purse from the dead man's hip pocket and dropped it into the sack. Then, looking at the other man, he pointed to us. His partner shook his head, saying *"No más."* Pulling a gun with one hand and carrying the bag in the other, the Mexican slowly backed out through the rear door.

The other man stepped back toward the partly closed door and turned his head to glance back as he stepped over the threshold. A deafening blast almost burst my eardrum, and I felt the side of my face burn as gunsmoke hid the door from view. I whirled around and saw Britches holding a derringer pistol in his hand.

"Guess I missed," he said. "Reckon he must've been expecting it and jumped behind the adobe wall."

While the boy was speaking, I heard hoofbeats of horses leaving in a dead run.

Sutty claimed he didn't know Britches packed a gun, and wanted to know where he carried it. Britches pulled open his shirt and dropped the derringer into a shoulder holster under his left armpit.

We asked Sutty why he hadn't laid his cards on the table before he reached. He complained that he didn't have time, and, furthermore, he had drawn to a straight flush and made it for the first time in his life. He was going to wrap the hand in oilcloth and store it in his war bag as a souvenir of old Fort Sumner. Britches declared that four six-shooters, like those we had looked at that night, beat a straight flush anyhow.

We made a few more roundups as we swung around to the Staked Plains at the T71 Ranch near Kenna. There, the day herd was rounded up and worked. Outside men who had worked through with us cut the cattle out belonging to the outfits they represented, put their bedrolls on pack horses, cut their mounts out of the remuda, and, driving the cattle and saddle horses, headed toward their home ranges.

Our outfit then moved on south across the sands to the LFD

headquarters ranch at Four Lakes. There, "Cat Head" Smith met us to pay off the lints who would be laid off till the next roundup started. The remuda was then taken to the horse camp at Mescalero Spring.

Britches was one of those laid off. When the bookkeeper gave him his check, he also handed him a letter. After reading the letter, Britches called Sutty and me to one side and told us his secret.

In a Central Texas town where he and his folks lived, his teen-age sister had been buying shoes in a department store one day when the salesman fitting the shoes made improper advances and insulted the girl. She told her folks what the man had said and done.

Britches went to the store to talk with the man, but found that he had resigned. He finally found the culprit, and during a violent altercation, shot him. Thinking he had killed the man, Britches left for parts unknown.

Using an assumed name, he hired out to the LFD outfit and notified his folks of his whereabouts. The letter he received that day was more than a month old. It was from his folks, and it informed him that the salesman hadn't died, but had fully recovered.

He told us he was tired of being on the dodge and was going home to stand trial. When he mounted his horse to leave, we both shook his hand and wished him the best of luck.

29.

Abandoned by Lady Luck in Kansas City

DURING the fall roundup in 1907 the LFD outfit gathered their fat stock to ship to market at Kansas City. Tom White, LFD manager, gave me permission to gather some of my cows I had bought with my savings from the nesters along the Texas line who were abandoning their 160-acre government homesteads and were heading back to the tenant cotton farms of Central Texas. As I bought the cows, I branded them and turned them loose on the LFD range, where grass, water, and looking after them cost me nothing.

When the roundup was finished at the Four Lakes headquarters ranch, the trail herd was formed, including ten head of my cows, and we headed north up the trail for the shipping pens at Bovina, Texas.

The trail herd was a mixture of range cattle. There were barren and dry fat cows and a large remnant of big Mexican steers that would go to slaughterhouses for beef. Many were old bulls and cull cows for the canneries, and a large number were two- and three-year-old steers that feeders in western Kansas and Nebraska would buy. It had been a wet year with plenty of grass, and the cattle were nice and fat.

The steers, especially the Mexican longhorns, were wild and easily scared, but we had no trouble with them till one night when we camped in the Muleshoe range and an electrical storm came up out of the northwest.

Everyone except the cook and the man standing guard around the remuda were riding around the herd expecting a stampede. The heavens were filled with jagged and chain lightning, and the thunder was one continuous roar. Static electricity caused ghostly balls of fire to dance on everything that had a point, such as steers' horns and horses' ears.

The herd got to milling, and we could see them only when the lightning flashed. Finally, there was a sudden clap of thunder and a blinding flash, and we could not hold them any longer. The steers broke away, and the only cattle we had on the bed ground when daylight came were four lying in a pile. They had been killed by lightning.

We lost a day making the circle drive to round up the others, cut out the strays, and count our herds to see if any were missing. The next day, the trail boss rode on in to Bovina to see whether the railroad had any cattle cars ready for us to load. We knew there were several herds in that area waiting for cars. If no cars were available, the boss wanted to hold the herd out some distance from town where grass was plentiful till cars would be ready. He returned with the news that he had cars for one trainload.

We rounded up the herd and strung them out between riders stationed on each side, and the boss counted out the number required to fill the first train. We then watered them and drove them into the loading pens, which had three chutes for loading three cars at one time.

Some of the men rode into the large corral and worked the steers into the loading pens in carload lots. The floor of the chutes that led up the incline to the car door had cleats nailed on it to give the animals a foothold so that they wouldn't slip down.

The string of cars backed up on the siding and were stopped

so that a car door was even with the gates of the chutes. The floors of the cars had been covered with a thick coat of dry sand to keep the animals from slipping and falling on a slick floor. The car doors slid back, the gates of the chutes opened out against the cars, and a platform was placed in position between the chute and the car door. Then the loading got under way.

The steers were worked into the chutes, and a man on each side with prod poles drove them up the incline into the cars. When a car was filled, its door was securely fastened. Then the loading pens were again filled. At times, a steer with horns so long they wouldn't go through the chute came up, and it was necessary for two men to grab the horns and turn the animal's head sidewise in order to get it into the car. The horns on several with an extra-wide spread were cut off with a saw.

Quite often, the last steer in the pen couldn't be made to see the gate to the chute and would get on the "prod" and defy anyone to get in the pen with it. Two men would rope it and run their ropes around posts on each side of the chute. Then a man on horseback would wrap the steer's tail around his saddle horn, and all three men would manage to pull it into the chute.

Inspectors for the Texas–Southwestern Cattle Raisers' Association checked brands on the cattle as they were loaded. If any strays were found, they were either cut back or allowed to go on to market (in which case a note was made so that the owner would get proper credit for the sale).

The loading went along nicely until we got to the cars at the rear end of the train. Then the train crew had trouble in spotting the car doors even with the chute gates. The slack in the draw-heads would allow the cars to stop first on one side of the chute, then on the opposite side.

The brakeman gave the engineer a "go-ahead" signal, then a "back-up" signal, then another of each kind, and finally blew his top. Looking toward the front end of the train where he could see the "hog head's" head sticking out of the cab window, he yelled, "They let a man fire an engine till he bakes what little brains he has, then they give him an engine to run. BACK UP!

You s—— of a b——!" Of course the hog head was too far away to hear what the brakey was saying, but from experience, he knew what it was. He moved the train again, the brakey gave a "washout" signal, the engineer "big-holed" his automatic brake valve, and the cars were spotted.

Sutty, who went up the trail with us, was working the cows into the car on one side of the chute, with me on the other side. When the cars were finally spotted, Sutty yelled, "That brakey must have read the hog head's mail and knows something about his ancestors, judging from the names he's calling him."

Two of the LFD hands went with the first trainload to look after the cattle en route. We moved the herd back away from the shipping point where they could grass, and camped to await another string of cars.

After coming from off day herd at noon the next day, Sutty and I saddled fresh horses and rode eleven miles to the little town of Texico, on the Texas–New Mexico line southwest of Bovina, with orders to get back in time to stand last guard. I didn't care about going, but knew someone would have to bring Sutty back. Texico was a wide-open little town in those days. Sutty and I visited several places, and he got to feeling pretty good. I told him to watch his step or I'd have to head him back to the chuck wagon.

"Oh yeah!" he sneered. "I ain't like you, just smell of a cork in a bottle and go bye-bye. It takes a lot of that stuff to make me put my head under my wing. I only want to drink enough to bring the bright side full in view and make one dollar look like two."

I told him he'd missed his calling and should have been a poet. He said he knew a lot of poetry, and if I didn't believe him, he'd show me.

We entered a saloon, and he walked up to the bar, pounded on it with his fist, then made his anouncement: "Boys, I'm an orator from the South Plains, and I'm longing to give you an oration. If you'll furnish the drinks, I'll orate that beautiful old poem *The Face on the Bar-room Floor* as you never heard it orated before."

"Uh-oh!" I muttered to myself. "I know now I'll have to lead his horse back to camp."

When he reached certain places in the poem, he had to take a drink to emphasize his point. I knew from experience that it took seven drinks for him to recite the poem properly.

Since no one in the crowd offered him any encouragement, he said, "I'll speak the first two verses free of charge just for a teaser, then maybe you'll offer to spend your spondulics to hear the rest of the poem." he pulled off his Stetson, made a sweeping bow to his audience, and started off with the first verse:

> *'Twas a balmy summer evening, and a goodly crowd was there,*
> *Which well-nigh filled Joe's bar-room, on the corner of the square;*
> *And as songs and witty stories came through the open door,*
> *A vagabond crept slowly in and posed upon the floor.*
> *"Where did it come from?" someone asked. "The wind has*
>   *blown it in."*
> *"What does it want?" another cried. "Some whiskey, rum or gin?"*

At that part in the poem, he was supposed to get his first drink. He looked around, his face wreathed in smiles, but no one offered to buy one. One man winked, jerked his head sidewise toward the speaker, and tapped his forehead with a finger. I could tell that the cowhand was getting hot under the collar and decided to try to get him out before trouble started.

"Sutty, let's go across the street to that other saloon," I said, "and maybe you can speak your piece in there."

"Okay," he said, and as we passed through the swinging doors, he threw the following remark back over his shoulder: "You birds ain't got enough brains to appreciate good entertainment nohow." And as we crossed the street, he added, "Think I'll go back and clean out that dump 'fore I leave town."

We entered the other saloon and found it crowded. "Wonder what's goin' on," said Sutty. Then, giggling with glee, he said, "Oh, I know. They're going to have a *badger fight!*"

One man was holding a fierce-looking bulldog. Another had hold of a rope stretched out across the floor that went under a box in which there was supposed to be a badger full of fight. Bets were being placed right and left.

Sutty became so interested, he forgot all about speaking his poem, and, waving a ten-dollar bill, bet me the badger would whip the dog. The betting was furious, the bartender holding the stakes.

When the betting stopped, the crowd started searching for some disinterested person, who hadn't placed a bet on either animal, who would be qualified to pull the badger from under the box. The only person in the crowd with those qualifications was a steer buyer from Kansas City. After considerable coaxing, he consented to do the job.

They gave him the rope and told him that when the signal was given, he should jerk the badger right out in front of the dog, but show no partiality between the animals.

Everything was all set. Some of the crowd were standing on chairs and tables. Then a voice yelled, "*Jerk*" and the steer buyer yanked on the rope with all his might. But instead of a vicious animal full of fight coming out from under the box, a vessel with a handle on it that was usually seen under the bed or in the bottom compartment of washstands in hotels in frontier towns came rolling across the floor and stopped right in front of the angry bulldog.

Of course, the victim of the prank knew the drinks for the crowd were on him. They lined up at the bar. But the steer buyer wasn't the inexperienced greenhorn they judged him to be. With the aid of the bartender, he was fixed to turn the tables on them. Instead of the usual drinks they thought they would get, the bartender gave each one a big hunk of Limburger cheese with crackers, and a bottle of soda pop to wash it down.

Sutty smelled his hunk of cheese, tasted it, and said, "*Wow!* Where'd they dig this stuff up. It smells and tastes worse'n that gyp and alkali water we drink along the east side of the Pecos River."

As he nibbled his cheese and sipped his soda pop, he examined the Limburger and wondered aloud how they got the taste and stink into the stuff. An old XIT cowhand standing beside him who also was nibbling his cheese winked at me and told him he didn't know for sure how they did it, since he had never seen any of that kind of cheese made; but someone had told him they take it out to the barnyard and bury it in manure till it is seasoned and ripe enough to be easily digested.

"It smells like it has already been digested once," Sutty grunted.

Since it was almost time for us to go on guard, we mounted our horses that were tied to a hitching rack patiently waiting for us and headed for camp.

Two days later the railroad gave us another string of cars. While we were loading them, I asked the boss to let me go with that train because my cows were in one of the cars. He consented and told an Oklahoma boy we called "Okie" to go with me. I put my spurs in my bedroll and pulled my slicker off my saddle to take with me. The train crew furnished us with lanterns and prod poles. When the conductor gave the hog head a highball signal, we climbed onto the rear steps of the caboose and waved bye-bye.

It was our duty to look after the cows in transit. We were supposed to walk along each side of the train every time it stopped, looking for any that were down on the car floor, and prod them with the sharp points on the poles till they got back on their feet.

If allowed to remain lying on the floor any length of time, with others trampling on it, an animal could become so badly injured that it could never stand up. Such an injury would make an animal a total loss. Several cows were jerked down in a car near the engine by what the brakemen said was rough handling of the train by the engineer, who applied the air brakes improperly. We managed to get them all on their feet just as the train started moving again.

We climbed the ladders on the side of the car with our prod poles and lanterns, and started back to the caboose along the narrow walkway on top the cars. The train quickly picked up speed and hot cinders in the black smoke being belched from the smokestack showered us. We would run to the end of a car expecting to jump across to the next one, but stop dead in our tracks and look down between the cars at the grinding drawheads, then gingerly step across.

The cars got to rocking sidewise so badly we could hardly stay on our feet. The car we stood on would be leaning in one direction and the next one in the opposite direction, and they would change positions before we could step across. I sat down and told Okie I was going to sit there till the wiggling snake stopped.

After one stop, we were caught near the locomotive when the train started moving again, so we climbed the steps of the gangway into the cab of the engine and rode there till the train stopped again.

Okie persuaded the fireman to let him shovel some coal into the firebox. The waddy filled his shovel and finally got the fire-door open. When he started to throw the coal into the furnace, the engine hit a low spot in the rail on one side. The coal missed the door completely, scattering over the apron and cab floor, and Okie nearly went out the gangway headfirst.

The fireman neatly spread several scoops of coal over the glowing mass in the furnace, then dipped a small hand scoop of sand from a box in the gangway and held it at a hole in the fire door. The draft in the boiler pulled the sand into the firebox. The cowpuncher asked why he was burning sand.

"I ain't burning it," the fireman replied. "I'm only sanding her out to clean the soot out of the flues so she'll steam better."

"Why do you call the engine a she and a her?" the cowpoke wanted to know.

"For several reasons," he said. "One is because she has a petticoat up there above her exhaust nozzle. Another one is, she has an apron which you are standing on between her and the tender." Then proudly throwing out his chest, he declared, "It takes a man to run her."

We were traveling at a fast clip when the engineer blew

several short blasts on the whistle. The fireman looked out the cab window and yelled, "Look out, we're going to hit a bull!"

The waddy grabbed the handrails on each side of the gangway, leaned way out, and looked ahead just as the locomotive cowcatcher hit the animal. The bull burst, and the cowpoke's face was covered with a layer of undigested prairie grass.

"You durn fool," the fireman giggled, "I didn't tell you to look out at the gangway."

"The hell you didn't," the puncher growled, wiping his face with a wad of wet cotton waste the fireboy gave him.

"I've stepped in a lot of this stuff," the cowboy said, "been thrown from horses into piles of it, and wore out my John B. Stetson hat fanning it to make it burn, but this is the first time I ever washed my face with it."

While we were crossing the Indian Territory, Okie told me he wanted to start back from Kansas City as soon as we arrived because he wanted to stop off and visit his mother, who was living on a homestead in the Cherokee Strip near Alva. His father had won the property in the "Run" when the strip opened for settlement. He said this was the first chance he had had to visit her in several years, and he didn't want to miss the opportunity.

The railroad company unloaded, fed, and watered our stock at a small town in Kansas—Wellington, I believe. When we pulled into the railroad yards at Kansas City where our train of cars would be switched to the stockyards, the Oklahoma boy lost no time in getting his drover's ticket from the commission firm to whom the cattle had been shipped, and caught the first southbound passenger train to visit his mother.

After unloading at the stockyards in Kansas City, I got my check from the commission firm, registered at the old St. Louis Hotel across the street from the stockyards, and caught a cable car uptown. I got off around Twelfth and Main streets and put my cash in a bank, holding out a few dollars to see the sights.

I returned to the hotel and went around the corner to a clothing store to buy a new outfit, except for hat and boots. One of the hashers at the hotel volunteered to show me the town, and she did just that!

We went to a theater, the Majestic or the Century, and it sure put on a hot show. I wanted to throw out my chest and put on a little "dog," so I bought box seats right up against the stage where I could put my boots on the railing and be comfortable.

In one of the acts, a buxom brunette with more curves than a no-hit baseball pitcher in a World Series ball game, came out wearing a picture hat and not much else. She seated herself in a swing. A spotlight was turned on her, and with a small mirror, she deflected the light upon faces in the front row as she sang a song. At certain points in the song, she pulled off some part of her wearing apparel and tossed it to the gent upon whom she was holding the light. She had stripped down to practically nothing but tights when I saw her glance at me, and, believe me, I longed for the wide-open spaces.

She turned the light on my face, which I could feel turning the color of the Painted Desert in a rosy Arizona sunset. The yelling audience could see the "cow country" written all over me as I slipped down in my seat on about three joints of backbone, trying in vain to hide.

I watched in numb embarrassment as she removed the only remaining dainty little garment from over her tights and tossed it to me as she sang, "Oh you kid, you're my affinity! Here's my card, I'll be in from one till three!" She then went into her swinging, tightrope walking, and trapeze act. She and her act, were both something *wonderful* to see!

The hasher and I went on and did the town up right. I never knew when or how I got back to my hotel room, but I woke up the following morning slapping at a fly that kept lighting on my nose. I lay there looking up at the ceiling, wondering where I was and why I was there.

I had a dark-brown taste in my mouth, and my temples felt as if a couple of chuck wagon mules were kicking away inside my skull. I eased up out of bed, holding my head as level as possible, and moseyed over to the washstand, poured a glass of water from the pitcher, and gulped it down. I caught a glimpse of my face in the mirror. My eyes looked as if I had been facing a West Texas sandstorm. I shook my head, the room started to spin, and I went into orbit.

I made a break for the bed, which seemed to be moving in a circle around the room. The floor started tilting up, first on one side, then on the other. Finally it flew up and hit me square in the face. I lay still for a while until things slowed down and stopped in their right place. Then I got up, dressed, and frisked my pockets. All I found was a thin dime.

I went down to the dining room, and the hasher who had showed me the town the night before came over to wait on me. She looked as if she'd had a bad night too. Her black eyes in her sallow face resembled two buckshot in a bowl of clabber. I gulped down two cups of coffee, then went out and caught a streetcar uptown to the bank to draw a few more bucks out, spending my last dime for carfare.

When I got to the bank, I saw a long line of people in front strung out like a row of ants going to the sugar barrel. I asked the man at the tail end of the line what was going on. He looked at me bug-eyed and croaked, "They're makin' a run on the bank!"

I fell into line, and when I reached the window, the man in the cage said, "We're not paying out anything, and don't know when we will." Well sir! That was about like getting hit in the seat of the pants by an old mossy horn steer on the prod.

Those were the days when Teddy Roosevelt was twirling the Big Stick. Some of the men standing around the bank said there was a "money panic on." I knew they were telling the truth, because I started having a money panic of my own right there.

There I was in a strange town where I didn't know a soul, flat broke with not even a dime to pay my streetcar fare back to my hotel. Of course I had my drover's ticket that would allow me to ride the cushions of a passenger train back to the Staked Plains, but I didn't have any money to eat on while traveling. Of more immediate urgency was the fact that I couldn't pay my hotel bill.

As I stood leaning against a lamppost studying the situation

243

over, I remembered reading a notice tacked on the wall in my hotel room telling in no uncertain terms what would happen to any jasper who might jump his board bill or room rent.

Just to show how Lady Luck had completely abandoned me after leaving me without carfare or breakfast, an old fellow dressed in rags and wearing a battered derby hat shuffled up near where I was standing, reached down, and picked up a four-bit piece from the sidewalk almost under my foot!

I tried to convince the old codger that it was my coin, but he glared at me and snarled, "Listen, Sonny! You do your snipe-hunting on the other side of the street. I'm shooting them along this gutter."

High-heel boots are not made to walk in, and mine rubbed big blisters on my feet during the long walk to the hotel. I hunted up the hotel manager. "How about me working for you to pay up my bill?" I asked him.

"What's the matter, cowboy?" he inquired. "Big town take you to the cleaners?"

"The bank I put my money in has gone busted, and I'm flat broke," I replied. "I'd like to work for you till I can pay you what I owe you so I can leave town."

"Just what can you do around a hotel?" He smiled as he glanced from the crown of my Stetson hat down to the toes of my Hyers boots.

"Hell, I ain't particular what I do so long as I can pay my bill, and have a few bucks to eat on while going home," I pleaded. "I'll chambermaid, peel spuds, and help the cook. Or I'll go back there in the kitchen and pearl dive."

"What do you mean, *'pearl dive'*?" he asked, staring at me like a Kentucky thoroughbred might stare at a little old mangy mustang pony.

"Man, you run a hotel and don't know what pearl diving means? That means washing dishes."

"Have you ever washed dishes?" he asked, eyeing me sort of skeptical-like.

"Yeah, lots of them," I assured him. "Washed dishes all my

life around ranches and cow camps, and helping Mother when I was a kid."

He went to the register, figured up my bill, and found I owed him six dollars. "Tell you what I'll do," he said. "I'll pay you a dollar a day to wash dishes. You can sleep on a cot in the hall. And for your grub, you can eat the comebacks from the dining room."

I shook hands with him real quick before he could back out of the offer. He took me back to the kitchen sink filled with breakfast dishes and handed me a towel, and I started to work.

I didn't think it would be a hard job. About the worst things to remove from the tin plates I'd been used to washing was sorghum lick, frijole bean juice, and gravy. But they didn't have eggs in cow camps, and I soon found out what I was up against.

Those dad-blamed hotel dishes looked as if everyone who had used them had eaten eggs for breakfast! Thick layers of yolk were smeared over them, yolk that had dried hard and had to be scraped off with a knife. Many small dishes and glasses had been used to serve soft- or medium-boiled hen fruit, and these were in the same sorry condition.

After washing and drying them, I stacked them where the old hard-boiled Simon Legree–type cook could reach them. He handed many dishes back to me with a growl to "Git the yeller off 'em!" The hashers even brought dishes back from the dining room with yellow streaks on them the cook had overlooked.

Man, it was rough! I stayed with it for ten days, squared myself with the hotel manager, and had four bucks to eat on while riding the cushions back to the Staked Plains.

Ever after, when I ate soft or medium-boiled eggs or "two with their eyes turned toward heaven," I took a piece of bread and carefully mopped the yellow off the dish while it was still soft, so the pearl diver back in the kitchen would get a break. In my book, he is one of life's unsung heroes.

30.

The Cowboy Takes a Bride

AS civilization crept westward across the Llano Estacado, the state of Texas placed its school land on the market. The limit was four sections per person, with one section designated the "home section," which had to be improved.

Sealed envelopes containing the price per acre offered by the bidders were opened on a certain date at the Land Office in Austin, and the land was sold to those who made the highest bid. The lucky bidders—usually small ranchers—drilled wells, erected windmills, built a dugout or other living quarters, fenced their land, and moved small herds of cattle in.

The border counties, adjacent to the New Mexico–Texas state line, were organized and county seats established. Gaines County, with Seminole as county seat, was organized in 1905; Yoakum County, with Plains as county seat, in 1907; and Andrews County, with Andrews as county seat, in 1910.

Many people from central and eastern Texas—called "nesters" by the large cattle owners and their cowhands—came across the Texas–New Mexico line into what was then Chaves and Eddy counties New Mexico, and filed on 160-acre U. S. government homesteads. Many drove teams of mares with sucking colts trotting alongside their working mothers. All the worldly possessions of the homesteaders were in their covered wagons, and often a son followed behind the wagon, riding an old mare bareback with a blind bridle driving the milk cows.

They "squatted" on their homesteads, dug wells, erected tents or built dugouts, and plowed under the sod and cow trails to start "dry farming." They put in crops of corn, milo maize, sorghum, kafir corn, black-eyed peas, and watermelons.

The coming of the nesters was a serious threat to the cattle barons, who had been running their herds on the open ranges for many years. As the settlers kept moving farther west, homesteading on the watering places, and cluttering up the open ranges with wire fences, the ranchers saw that they were doomed and started cutting down on the size of their herds or moving them to other ranges.

As the country was settled, many small communities sprang up and get-togethers began to be held such as picnics, barbecues, all-night dances, horse races, and roping and riding contests. The most lavish activities usually took place on the Fourth of July and at Christmas time. Cowhands thought nothing of riding forty miles to a dance, dancing all night, and riding back to their camps the next day.

When I was young, an elderly couple who were totally blind furnished the music for many of those dances. They had a beautiful daughter about eighteen years old who drove her parents from place to place and looked after them. The old fellow played the fiddle, and his wife accompanied him on a small organ which they hauled around in a small spring wagon. The cowhands thought a lot of the old couple and were generous when the hat was passed, so that the old folks earned enough to be independent.

By then, some of the cowpokes had been to the "big" cities— such as Kansas City, St. Joseph, Chicago, and Fort Worth—with trainloads of cattle and had learned the art of "round dancing," which was coming into style on the Staked Plains. They had no trouble getting partners when the "caller" yelled, "Ladies choice. Get yore podners for a waltz."

All the girls wanted to learn the waltz and two-step, and broke for a waddy who could teach them. At some dances, every other set would be a waltz, waltz-quadrille, or two-step. The nester boys resented being wallflowers, as they watched some wild cowboy with his arm around a clodbuster's best girl dancing cheek-to-cheek in a dreamy waltz to "Over the Waves" or the "Home Sweet Home" waltz, always the last dance before we said, "Good-bye till we meet again," and the dance was over.

"Arizona" Bowen, a windmill oiler for the LFD outfit, stayed alone at the old Keenam Ranch near where Tatum, New Mexico, is today and was host for many of those dances at his old "stag camp."

He would set the date for the affair, then spread the news among the small ranchers and nesters along the Texas line as far south as Lovington, sending word to the cowhands on the range and in the widely scattered cow camps. He would ask old Professor Griffith, or some other old-time fiddler, to furnish the music.

It was at one of Arizona's shindigs that I met the girl of my dreams. I invited the pretty miss with red hair braided down her back to dance "Cotton-eye Joe" with me, and asked her also to be my partner for the "Home Sweet Home" waltz.

She was wearing a white gingham dress, black slippers, and a bright ribbon tied in a bow to the braid that hung down to her waist. I really took to her as I looked into her sparkling brown eyes and at her cheeks and the Cupid's bow lips set just right for kissing, with color in them that didn't come from a mail-order house. She was lively and happy, and her voice bubbled with laughter.

She was smooth and graceful, whether she was dancing a waltz, two-step, "Put Your Little Foot Right There," or square dance to the tune of "Sally Goodin."

During an intermission, we went outside to the windmill to get a drink of water. It was a beautiful moonlit night, and we sat on the Bermuda grass on the tank bank with several other couples.

She told me that her name was Zelma Beal and that her father was a rancher near Bronco, Texas.

Sutty, with whom I had come to the dance, sat down near us and tried to start a conversation with her. She wasn't very talkative. He asked her for the next dance, and she replied that she had already promised that set. He asked her for the "Home Sweet Home" waltz, and she told him she was booked for that one, too.

Sutty was always bragging about being more handsome than I, and saying that he could take my best gal away from me any time he wanted to. I was determined that this was one girl he wasn't going to get, so I leaned over close to his ear and muttered, "Two's company and three's just too big a crowd. So mosey on down the line and take some other guy's gal away from him, but let my gal alone."

He growled something as he walked off, and I wondered what the consequences would be when he got me alone.

While dancing the final waltz that night, I asked my pretty partner if I might pay her a visit at her home. "Sure," she said. "Anyone is welcome at our ranch."

About a month after the dance, we had a roundup at Ranger Lake, near Bronco; and after we finished branding calves in the afternoon, I saddled a fresh horse and headed for the ranch where she lived, about ten miles away.

We visited a while, until I said it was time for me to start to where the chuck wagon would camp that night, since I would have to catch my night horse and stand guard around the day herd. I had started out to the front gate where my horse was tied when a disconcerting thing happened. My girl's pappy fell in behind me with a shovel and began to pick up my tracks and throw them over the gate after me. I took it as a hint that he didn't approve of a wild cowboy visiting his fifteen-year-old daughter.

But when youth is bitten by the love bug, the virus from the bite addles the brain and makes one immune to such things as hints, warnings, and threats.

A list of Zelma Beal's close relatives resembled a roster of the leading ranchers of Central and West Texas and eastern New

249

Mexico at the dawn of this century. Her close friends called her "Bob," and since she was an expert horsewoman, she was occasionally referred to as "Lucille Mulhall." She was the youngest daughter of A. A. (Turk) Beal and his wife, the former Molly White, a member of a pioneer ranching family of South Central Texas.

Zelma's oldest brother was Roy Beal, widely known over the range as "Cotton-belt." He owned the old Sarat Ranch just east of the Texas–New Mexico line in Yoakum County. He and another brother, Joe Beal, both married daughters of the Long family, who operated the first hotel in Plains, Texas. Pete Beal, the youngest brother, stole and eloped with the daughter of Lum Hudson, the first sheriff of Yoakum County. They were married in Portales, New Mexico.

When Zelma's sister Bernice married Bert Jackson, they became the first couple to obtain a marriage license at Plains after Yoakum County was organized.

Another sister, Pearl, married Raleigh Conley, who was ranch foreman at the old McElroy J Cross Ranch on Sulphur Draw, southeast of Plains.

Some of Miss Beal's rancher uncles were Guff Beal and Fount Oxher of Fort Worth and Southwest Texas; Tyra Sneed of Georgetown, Texas; the Whites of South Central Texas; Nick Beal of Lubbock and Post City, Texas; and "Massa" John Beal, who managed the old Jumbo Ranch belonging to the St. Louis Cattle Company, located on the Double Mountain Fork of the Brazos River, southeast of Lubbock, and who later established a ranch a few miles east of Ranger Lake.

The seven sons of "Massa" John Beal—Sid, Boss, Tyra, George, Ellwood, Sam, and Charlie Beal—and their two sisters—Mary and Anna Beal—were Zelma's cousins. So were Tom Bess and his wife (who was called "Cousin" Georgia) and their three sons, Lawson, Russ, and Marion (who was known as "Sweetie") and three daughters, Inez, Jewel, and Thelma. Other cousins were Dink Logan, Henry (Wrang) White, and his brother Walter (all of whom lived on the South Plains), Beal Sneed of North Central Texas, and Joe Sneed of Amarillo.

The two Beal families in New Mexico, with ten sons, several cousins, and "in-laws" were able to operate their own roundup and trail outfits, filling all the positions, including wagon boss, cook, horse wrangler, and cowhands, without hiring any additional help.

In the latter part of June, 1908, I was staying at the LFD headquarters ranch at Four Lakes, breaking some broncs. "Massa" John Beal came by on his way to Roswell, stopped overnight, and told us that "Uncle" Ed Tyson, his daughter, Anna, and her husband, Sid Beal, were planning a celebration to be held at the OHO Ranch on July 3, 4, and 5, with horse racing and roping and riding contests each afternoon, dancing every night, and plenty of barbecue with all the trimmings.

I borrowed LFD manager Tom White's team and big ranch buggy and saddled my "ropin' hoss," Puddin, to lead alongside the team. I drove to Uncle John Causey's ranch under the west breaks of the Plains and picked up my cousin Dot Causey, and we headed for Turk Beal's ranch, where we spent the night.

Tyra Beal was there to take Dot to the blowout. After supper, I cornered "Pap" Beal and his wife, and asked them in a stammering way if I could take their daughter to the "shindig." They glared at me as if I was a sheep-killing coyote, but said I could, since they also were going.

The next morning we loaded into the buggy and drove to the OHO. Nesters and small ranchers and their families from a wide area on both sides of the Texas–New Mexico line came in buggies, buckboards, and spring wagons, with chairs in them for seats. Many cowhands came on horseback, some leading outlaw horses for the riding contests. They brought in some steers off the range and corralled them to use in the roping contests. Several cowboys were leading horses they would enter in the quarter-mile races.

Two old and experienced chuck wagon cooks were already roasting and basting the beeves, furnished by the host and hostess, over the barbecue pits. Mesquite roots were scarce in that part of the plains, but someone had found enough of them to make the coals in the pits. Coffeepots hanging from pot racks were simmering over cow-chip fires.

Herschel Robert ("Gravy") Fields, who operated the little store at Bronco, and some of the merchants at Plains sent or brought coffee, pickles, onions, and lemons and sugar for the lemonade, but of course there was no ice. Many of the women brought baskets of homemade lightbread, biscuits, cakes, pies, and cookies.

Some fast nags ran in the matched races, and their owners backed them with their money, marbles, and chalk, but mostly with IOU's, several of which changed hands. I know, because I was one of the stakeholders.

I didn't gather any honors in the riding and roping contests. I drew a steer in the roping contest almost as large as my horse, and it threw my mount down. "Tie the horse!" the crowd yelled. In the bucking horse contest, I rode a notorious outlaw from the LFD remuda named Black AXL for its color and the brand on its left shoulder. I knew the horse better than anyone else, because it had thrown me several times. I lost out here when the judges spied me "clawin' leather," and I was disqualified.

After the outdoor activities were over, dancing started, with Professor Griffith and a "git-tar picker" furnishing the music. The Professor was not only one of the best of the old-time fiddlers on the plains who ever "sawed the cat-gut," but he also was editor of the first newspaper to be published in Yoakum County.

Along about daylight on the morning of July 4, after dancing all night, Zelma and I decided we would elope. We suggested to Dot Causey and Tyra Beal that they go with us and make it a "four-in-hand hitch-up," but they didn't want to take such a drastic step. Zelma's sister, Bernice, and her husband, Bert Jackson, agreed to go along with us.

We camouflaged our true intention by putting out the story that we were going to Bronco after the mail and some Bull Durham smoking tobacco for me. Then the four of us loaded into the buggy and headed hell-bent for the Texas line.

We waved at Postmaster "Gravy" Fields as we passed Bronco, and drove on to Plains, fifteen miles away, the nearest county seat where we could get a license. A cloud of dust fogged up behind the buggy.

Since it was a holiday, we found the courthouse at Plains closed, so we drove north across Sulphur Draw to the home of Less Boyd, the first county clerk of Yoakum County, and told him our troubles.

He grinned as he glanced at my fiancee and said, "Miss, I'm sorry I can't accommodate you, but your pappy has given me strict orders not to issue license for you to marry anyone." He then added that the injunction had come to him over the telephone line from Bronco a few minutes before we drove up.

I was unaware at that time of the existence of a telephone line between Bronco and Plains. The line was a new fangled, makeshift affair that utilized the top strand in barbed-wire fences most of the way to make the circuit. Had I known this, the order probably wouldn't have reached Plains ahead of us.

Boyd obligingly called the county clerk of Terry County at Brownfield, Texas, thirty-two miles farther east, and was told he had the same orders. Then he called the county clerk of Gaines County at Seminole, thirty-five miles southeast of Plains, and was told he had no such orders, so we started in that direction over the deep sandy road between the two towns.

As we drove south from Plains, I could imagine Pap Beal trying to call Seminole. What a predicament we would be in, if he was successful in doing so!

Knowing that most ranchers carried a pair of wire-cutters in their vehicles with which to make repairs to wire gates or for other emergencies, I thought maybe Tom White had a pair of cutters in his buggy. I stopped, looked under the seat, and sure enough, found them.

The high telephone line between Plains and Seminole, paralleled the wagon road. I pulled the team over alongside a telephone post, climbed up on a buggy wheel, looked up and down the road both ways, and scanned the horizon in every direction to see if anyone was in sight. When I was sure no one was around, I snipped the line of communication between the two towns, praying that I had beaten Pappy to the draw.

We had watered the team at Plains, and we watered them again at Sligo. While the horses were resting, we bought some crackers and sardines and ate lunch. The hot July weather near 100 degrees—the sandy road, and four people in the big buggy made it a grueling trip for the horses. They were covered with lather and had a bad case of "thumps" when we stopped in front of the courthouse in Seminole.

Before getting out of the buggy, my fiancee asked me for a piece of paper and pencil. I gave her a stub pencil about an inch long I had in my pocket, but couldn't find any paper, so I gave her the round tag from a Bull Durham tobacco sack, upon which she wrote the figure "18." Then, pulling off her slipper, she put the paper inside it. Later when the clerk asked her age, with a heart as pure as gold, she truthfully answered, "I am over 18."

J. W. Miller, the deputy county clerk for H. C. Whitfield, was in his office, and he issued the license. Then he went out to round up a parson.

Seminole was having a Fourth of July celebration of its own that day, and the town was crowded with people, many of whom we knew. The clerk spread the news about what was happening at the courthouse while he was out hunting a preacher. When the Reverend G. C. Berryman showed up to make the hitch, the clerk's office was jammed with cowhands and women to witness the show. Several waddies I knew gathered around us, and a friend of mine named Jay Heard steadied me on my feet while the knot was tied. (Jay later became a U. S. Customs officer and was killed on the Mexican border.)

One cowboy yelled, "The Fourth of July may be Independence Day for some people, but it won't be for you!" "No," another yelled, "but we will be celebrating his wedding anniversary every year!"

After the ceremony, we turned our team over to the livery stable and went to the little frame hotel to register. There was no vacancy. A bachelor rancher we knew loaned us his room.

After supper, we went to a dance where they were expecting us. When we entered the hall, the music and dancing stopped and the fiddler began the old tune "Cheyenne."

An early-day crooner accompanied the fiddler with a parody he made up for the occasion, substituting "Seminole" for "Cheyenne," and "buggy" for "pony" in the lyrics:

> *Seminole, Seminole, hop in my buggy.*
> *There's room here for two, dear,*
> *And after the ceremony,*
> *We'll both ride back home, dear, as one*
> *In my buggy from Sem-i-nole.*

The song fit the occasion quite well, and we both made elaborate bows to the crowd. They watched us closely, but sometime after midnight, we slipped out and went to the hotel to our room on the second floor.

I blew out the light in the coal-oil lamp, but before I could get into bed, a big cowbell that some ornery cowhand had tied to the bed springs clanged out. I found and snipped the cord tied to the bell, which ran through the window to the ground. Then a great hubbub started up below the window. Our "friends" were beating on washtubs and dishpans. I told my bride that they were shivareeing us, and we would have to go down before they would stop. We took the crowd to a temporary cold-drink stand and treated them to soda pop and lemonade before we were allowed to return to our room.

We stayed in Seminole for a couple of days to let the team rest, then headed back toward home. Although I wouldn't admit it to my bride, I was worried and a little leery about how her parents would take to their new son-in-law. My apprehension grew when we met my wife's brother, Joe Beal, in Plains, and he told us, "Pap saddled his horse when you didn't come back from Bronco. He stuck a .30–30 rifle in the scabbard under his stirrup leather and headed out after you."

He said his dad had tried to call Seminole from Plains, but found the toll line dead. Less Boyd, he said, finally quieted him down and told him to let nature take its course. Beal told Boyd he had only one objection to the wedding, and that was, "I don't think that cowboy should have robbed our cradle of our baby girl, the only child Molly and I had left who wasn't married. Now we'll be all alone."

After Joe congratulated us and cheerfully extended the wish that all our troubles would be "little ones," we drove to the home of my brother-in-law, Roy Beal, to spend the night before going on to the New Mexico ranch.

We had no idea Pap Beal would be there, but when we stopped at the front gate, the door of the house opened and the man I sorely dreaded to see stepped out onto the gallery.

Bert Jackson nudged me with an elbow and whispered, "Boy, you'd better say your prayers, because here comes Pap."

I lived through a lifetime as the old fellow moseyed out to the gate. I thought I could detect a smile flickering over his face, and my heart quit ticking so fast.

He walked up and squirted a stream of Star Navy tobacco juice to one side. "Now, you all have sure played hell, haven't you?" he growled, but not unkindly.

After spending a short honeymoon in Roswell, we returned to Pap Beal's ranch and were greeted with open arms by Zelma's parents. They insisted that she continue living with them, especially while I was away from home working on the range for a month at a time. They said they didn't want her to live in some lonely cow camp while I was away.

During calf-branding roundup that summer, ten cattlemen with whom I worked each placed my brand on one of their best heifer calves as a wedding present. I greatly appreciated this, because it showed they had confidence in my integrity.

When roundup work was over that fall, I quit my job and bid on three sections of school land in Yoakum County. I drilled a well and erected a windmill, built a small house, and moved my small bunch of cattle from the open range in New Mexico.

Later on, I sold my dogies and traded the land for the telephone exchange at Plains, which had caused us so much worry during our elopement. A short time after the birth of our only child, we left the Llano Estacado for the Pacific Coast, and many years passed before I saw my boyhood home again.

PART FOUR
Llano Estacado Revisited

31.

Llano Estacado Revisited

FOR many years, I had wanted to revisit southeastern New Mexico to see if I could find that old rock house where I spent my childhood, where my mind was as free of troubles as the Staked Plains were of trees, where I could sleep all night without dreaming that the old job was shot from under me and I was told I was too old to get another one.

The opportunity came in 1963 when the Downtown Lions Club of Hobbs, Lea County, New Mexico, invited me to be guest of honor at their annual High Lonesome Estampeda three-day rodeo celebration on May 23, 24, and 25. They had decided to add a new feature to the program by inviting an early settler of that region as their special guest, and since I was one of the earliest settlers of what is now Lea County, I was selected to be that year's guest.

My grandson, Beal Whitlock, Jr., drove me down there, and we were accompanied by great-grandson Beal III, who went along for the ride and to see the rodeo. We mounted a freeway in the San Fernando Valley, Los Angeles County, and the first traffic light that stopped us was in Phoenix, Arizona.

We tied up east of Globe, Arizona, for some shut-eye and ate breakfast in Safford, Arizona, where my Uncle Bob Causey is buried and where his daughter still resides. We were traveling through a part of the country that is rich in history of the Old West, through the homeland of Apache Chief Geronimo, across the trail traveled by Coronado in 1540, and along the Butterfield Trail through Lordsburg and Deming to Las Cruces.

Las Cruces, New Mexico, is said to have been given its name, "The Crosses," because the routes traveled by the Spanish explorers Espejo and Oñate crossed the route of Cabeza de Vaca at that point. Las Cruces and Mesilla, two miles to the south, are famous in western history for several reasons. A historical marker beside the highway bears the following inscription:

> The historic plaza in the village of Mesilla was the scene on November 15, 1854, of a flag-raising which confirmed the Gadsden Purchase, establishing the present U. S. boundaries. Mesilla was, in 1860–61, the capital of Arizona Territory, during the Confederate occupation.

It was also there that William Bonney, alias Billy the Kid, was tried, convicted, and sentenced to hang.

Going east from Las Cruces, while climbing the west side of the Organ Mountains, we passed the spot where the famous former sheriff of Lincoln County, Pat Garrett, was waylaid and killed.

From San Augustin Pass, we dropped down into the Tularosa Valley where the highway passed through part of the White Sands Missile Range. We skirted the east side of the White Sands and passed near the place where the world's first atomic blast was touched off.

That mass of white gypsum which is always shifting with the wind seems sinister. Several people who were last seen in that vicinity have mysteriously disappeared, never to be seen or heard from again. Two of these were District Attorney A. J. Fountain and his small son. The only sign ever found of them was one of the boy's shoes.

We passed on through Alamogorda and Tularosa into the Mescalero Apache Indian Reservation, then down into the Río

Ruidoso valley, in what is known as "Billy the Kid country," made famous by the Lincoln County War.

We followed the Rio Hondo into the old cattle town of Roswell, which had become famous more than sixty years ago, with its fields of lush alfalfa and orchards of splendid apples, irrigated with artesian wells.

While at Roswell, we paid a short visit at the home of Mrs. Herman Burkstaller, the former Dorthy Causey, oldest daughter of my Uncle John Causey. We also visited the grave of my uncle, who was buried there in 1903.

East out of Roswell, the highway crossed the Pecos River by a bridge several miles north of where the freight wagons used to ford the quicksand bed of the river at the Juan Chaves Crossing, a short distance west of the Bottomless Lakes where we used to round up when working up the east side of the river.

We headed on east from the Pecos River, across the alkali flats and gyp hills, then dropped down into Long Arroyo. My Uncle John Causey had established a ranch a few miles south of the highway back in the nineties.

A short distance north of the highway, are two rows of black volcanic rocks, uniform in width, parallel, and equidistant. These are visible from many points between the breaks of the plains and the Pecos River. The cowhands used to call them "The Devil's Race Track." They are called on current highway maps El Camino del Diablo.

As we approached the Mescalero Sands, the highway seemed to follow the route of the first automobile road between Roswell and the Llano Estacado. The road was built around 1905 or 1906 when LFD Tom White bought a two-cylinder Buick automobile and introduced modern transportation to the Staked Plains.

He had his ranch hands clear, level, and drag a road from the old wagon road on Long Arroyo, which meandered through the sand hills across some "hard spots," then climbed the breaks a few miles west of the old Hedgecoax Ranch in the vicinity of Cap Rock, then went on to Four Lakes. The freight-wagon road climbed to the plains a few miles to the south at the Gap.

As we drove over a paved modern highway through those sand hills, where one could let his conscience be his guide about speed, my thoughts went back to July, 1909, when I, along with seven others, almost died from thirst when a Pope-Toledo automobile broke down there and we had to walk about twenty miles to water.

We entered Lea County, at Cap Rock, and from there on east, we drove through the heart of the old LFD spread where Littlefield and the White brothers grazed their vast herds of cattle upon the free range for many years, with only the expense of providing water places and living quarters at their headquarters ranch and at several camps.

At Tatum, we turned south to Lovington, which became the county seat when the eastern portions of Chaves and Eddy counties were cut off and Lea County was formed. From there we drove on southeast to our destination—Hobbs. We reached Hobbs just ahead of the kind of hard rain and severe hailstorm that had always been welcome to the early ranchers because it filled the surface lakes.

The first night, we were house guests of Raymond F. Waters, Sunday editor of the Hobbs *Daily Sun-News*. The following day, we were settled in the Lamp Lighter Motel and given meal tickets for the Drake Restaurant.

Since Lea County is in the area of Pecos City, Texas, where the American rodeo was born, the people of Hobbs are "rodeo-minded" and enjoy "going western" once each year during their High Lonesome Estampeda to commemorate the Old West and relive the lives of their immediate ancestors. The Lions Club sponsors the annual event. At the Lions Club luncheon in a packed dining room at the Drake, I was introduced to the members and their guests.

After telling them how I appreciated the honor of being chosen as their special guest, I said, "It is very unusual for an old buckaroo to be able to return to his old stomping grounds and be met by the citizens with open arms, instead of by the sheriff." That remark prompted High Sheriff J. C. (Jake) Fort of Lea County to present me with a deputy sheriff's commission, of which I am very proud.

The 1963 Souvenir Program contained my photograph and a 150-word biography. It had been easy to get the photograph, but I found it rather difficult to corral seventy-seven years of life in the West with only 150 words to round them up. The programs were handed out during the luncheon by a man wearing a badge displaying the words "Tail Twister." It was said that he was a "lion tamer," and he wouldn't hesitate to twist the tail of any lion who might become unruly and refuse to obey orders.

Miss Joyce Shelley of Silver City, New Mexico—the 1963 Miss Rodeo America—was also introduced at the luncheon, along with the 1962 Estampeda Queen and ten contestants for the 1963 title. Miss Shelley was Miss Rodeo New Mexico in 1962, and won her title as Miss Rodeo America over eighteen contestants from seventeen other states and Canada at Las Vegas, Nevada, in November, 1962.

I rode in the parade in an open-top sports car, with my grandson driving and my great-grandson sitting on the back of the seat between us. Placards on both car doors displayed in large letters, OLD WADDY. In the parade just ahead of us was Miss Barbara Parker, queen of the 1962 Estampeda; and riding alongside her on a fine horse was Miss Rodeo America, a beautiful girl and an expert horsewoman, well qualified for the title she carried.

The parade was a success, but shortly after it was over, rain started falling and the evening performance was cancelled, announcement being made that there would be two performances on the final day.

At the rodeo on the following evening, I was introduced over the public address system by the famous rodeo announcer, Clem McSpadden, state senator from Nowata, Oklahoma, a nephew of Paula (McSpadden) Love, curator of the Will Rogers Memorial Commission in Claremore, Oklahoma. I stood up and waved my Stetson to about six thousand rodeo fans.

There was plenty of action in the arena, but I believe the highlight of the performance occurred during an exhibition of highly trained horses and expert horsemanship, when a Roman-style rider stood on the backs of two horses and made them jump into the body of a moving truck.

One afternoon, Mr. and Mrs. Waters held "open house" for us, inviting many of the early settlers of that area. The guests registered in a leather-bound Guest Book, which was given me as a souvenir of the occasion.

We saw only two of the old waddies I had known and had worked with fifty-five to sixty years before. They drove down to the open house from their homes in Tatum. One was Dick Miller, the LFD windmill man, in his nineties, who repaired the windmills at the LFD watering places over the range for many years. The other was Harve Harris, with whom I punched cattle for the LFD. He was well up in his eighties.

We had quite a bull session, reminiscing of days on the open range. I learned that all ten sons of the two Beal families who ranched in New Mexico and Texas had "cashed in their chips."

Miller told us he was with the Jones Ranch in northern Lea County. "I'm too old to climb windmills now," he said, "but I can still tell others what to do to keep them running. I've been thinking for several years about retiring, but can't make up my mind to do so."

Harris talked about fine cattle and sheep, irrigated farms, and oil (with which Lea County is saturated). "You remember when we used to have our own mount of cow ponies in the remuda when we worked the range?" he asked. "Well, nowadays we punch cattle on foot or in pickup trucks. There's no more real cow-hands."

Waters and Walter Linam, a long-time resident of Lea County, took us for a drive to see some old landmarks we wished to revisit. We saw what was left of the ghost town of Knowles, a few miles north of Hobbs. There had been no city of Hobbs when we left there in 1908. We saw the place where the old LFD drift fence used to be, and visited the old High Lonesome Ranch (from which the Estampeda got its name), one of the most famous old watering places on the South Plains. I had played around that ranch more than seventy years before with Mr. and Mrs. Dave Earnest's two children, Pool and Edith, when it was the Mallet Ranch and Dave Earnest was manager there. They had been our nearest neighbors, and my mother and Mrs. Earnest had visited each other quite often.

Different reasons have been given by early-day ranchers for the name "High Lonesome."

Uncle Bob Causey, who worked for the Mallet outfit in 1889–90, claimed the "High" part of the name described the ranch site, a high rise of the plain that enabled the eastern owners of the ranch to find it when they came out on a visit and drove up from the railroad at Midland.

He said the "Lonesome" part was given it by the Mallet waddies who heard the easterners complain that it was the most lonesome place they had ever been. No other ranches, trees, or landmarks were in sight to break the monotony. All the owners saw when gazing across the prairie were shadows of thunderhead clouds moving across the plain, whirlwinds, and heat waves dancing along the horizon; and at night they were lulled to sleep by the serenades of coyotes, the lonesome howls of lobo wolves, and the mooing of cattle around the water troughs.

Allen Heard bought the ranch after the Mallets left, along with water rights and windmills at two other watering places. He and his brothers, Lee, Top, Jack, and Jay Heard, and their partner, "T Bar T" Tom White, moved their cattle from the Midland area to the High Lonesome. The Heards and White gazed their herds on the free range till the nesters moved in and crowded them out with their plows and barbed wire.

The old ranch house was still in very good condition, much as I remembered it, and the two windmill towers were still standing, minus their tails and wheels. The dirt dump of the original tank for water storage was still visible but was dry and unusable. I suggested to my companions, Linam and Waters, that the ranch be made a state monument and Lea County Museum.

Leaving the High Lonesome, we headed for the old Causey Ranch about twelve miles away.

I had always felt that if I ever returned to that old ranch, all I would find where the rock house had stood would be a large pile of rocks. It didn't seem possible that such a house could stand the elements for so many years.

When we stopped in front of the old house, I saw that it was a story-and-a-half and built of rocks, but the exterior looked unfamiliar. I found out later that some additions had changed its appearance.

We met the present owner of the ranch, Mason Graham, who said that it was indeed the old Causey place, that he had been living there since his birth in 1903. When we entered the large living room, everything was as I remembered it. There was the large fireplace where I used to hang my stockings on Christmas Eve, and in one corner of the room was the steep stairway I used to climb to go to bed under the bare rafters. I went into the lean-to kitchen where we used to sit on long benches around a long, rough table and eat with the cowhands.

The large surface-water tank, walled inside with rocks, looked just the same as it had when I used to lie there on the Bermuda grass and watch longhorns, wild mares, burros, and the two old buffalo bulls come in to water.

The rock corrals where I used to sit and watch the bronc twisters ride the young geldings had become a pile of rocks. There was no sign of the small, shed-type bunkhouse and the small store building which used to be there, or of two mulberry trees which used to stand in the front yard.

There was so sign of a small grave on a little knoll out in the horse pasture of the corrals, where a baby belonging to a family of homeseekers was buried over seventy years ago.

Many small but prosperous cattle, horse, and sheep ranches with windmills and modern improvements dotted the region. Some dry farming was still practiced, but many of the farms were now irrigated with pumps and underground water. The main crops were grain sorghums, corn, alfalfa, and cotton.

The people there were still friendly, the way they used to be, thinking the word "neighbor" meant something more than the family next door. If we ran out of Bull Durham smoking to-bacco in the old days, we would ride over to our neighbor's ranch and borrow a few bags; and if their supply of Arbuckle's coffee became exhausted, they would send one of their hands over for enough to last till their freight wagons went to town.

As we drove away, we could see the deep ruts of the old wagon road crossing the paved road that had been traveled by those freight wagons. The old ruts went under wire fences and meandered across the prairie and into ground that had since been plowed under.

Wildcatting for oil had reached the Llano Estacado a few years after 1901, the year that the famous Lucas Gusher near Beaumont, Texas, blew in, marking the beginning of the Petro-leum Era. In 1963 some of the most important oil fields in the country were there on the Staked Plains. Looking across the level prairie where we used to see cattle, horses, and bunches of ante-lopes, we now saw little walking beams attached to pumping units nodding up and down, bringing oil from deep in the earth and forcing it into pipelines. Wherever residents congregated, the topic of conversation was dry holes, barrels per day, prora-tion, and the price of oil per barrel, instead of range conditions, calf crops, and the price of fat stock at the Fort Worth market, as in days gone by. People whose parents used to ride in wagons, buggies, and buckboards rode in sleek automobiles, diesel-pow-ered buses and trucks, and jet airplanes.

If Coronado were to visit the Llano Estacado today, would he recognize it?

Index

271

Odessa, Texas: 111, 112, 114, 118, 120, 121, 230
OHO Ranch: 19, 134, 251
Oklahoma: 44, 50–51, 119, 169; *see also* Indian Territory
Old Mobeetie (Sweetwater), Texas: 7, 14
Old Negro Ad (cowhand): 61–62, 66, 67, 68, 69, 70, 136–37, 173, 174, 175, 186, 225–26
06 brand: 145
Outlaws: 4, 15–16, 29, 86–89, 90, 91, 176–77, 229–31; *see also* rustlers
Oxher, Fount: 250

Palo Duro Canyon: 13, 78, 146
Parker, Barbara: 265
Pecos City (Pecos), Texas: 88, 120, 164, 184, 264
Pecos River: 8, 14, 19, 42, 77, 78, 79, 83, 84, 86, 123, 133, 134, 135, 141, 148, 149, 161, 164, 178, 179, 182, 184, 192, 196, 197, 208, 209, 227, 228, 263
Pecos River Valley: 11, 138, 180
Pecos Valley and North Eastern Railroad: 138, 184, 188
Plains, Texas: 246, 250, 252, 253, 254, 255, 257
Poe, John: 148–49, 228
Polk County, Texas: 144
Pope (judge at Roswell, New Mexico): 221, 223–24
Portales, N. Mex.: 189, 250
Pot Hook brand: 145
Practical jokes: 116, 158–59, 160–61, 163
Prairie Cattle Company: 134, 146
Pridemore, Tom: 172
Professor Griffith (fiddler): 248, 252

Rabies: 85, 105–106
Railroad Mountain: 135, 161
"Rain-in-the-Face" (LFD cowhand): 136
Ranger Lake, N. Mex.: 10, 12, 18, 19, 134, 249, 250
RAT brand: 145
Rathburn, "Pop": 114
Rattlesnakes: 60–61, 85, 103, 104, 126, 188–89
Red River: 7, 50, 77
Reynolds (rancher with Lee): 145

Rifles: 5, 7, 9, 24, 71
Río Hondo: 40, 78, 209, 263
Río Penasco: 78, 80, 121, 123, 181, 214, 216
Riverside, N. Mex.: 221
Roberts, Cub: 112
Roberts family: 115
Robertson (rancher with Scott): 145
Robertson, "Old Man" Harry: 136, 183
Rock Island Railroad: 119, 120
Rodeo Cowboy's Association: 168
Rodeos: 164–71, 265–66
Rogers, Will: 168
Roosevelt, Theodore: 243
Rope making: 126
Roping: 165, 168, 225–26, 251
Roswell, N. Mex.: 40, 79, 108, 112, 130, 133, 138, 139, 155, 161, 172, 173, 176, 177, 180, 181, 182, 184, 186, 189, 200, 202, 206, 208, 209, 210, 214, 219, 221, 222, 251, 256, 263
Round-top open A brand: 20, 145
Roundups: 26–27, 71, 129, 139–40, 153, 155–56, 161, 179, 192, 199, 200, 201, 207, 208, 229, 231–32, 233, 249
Russell, Charles: 186
Rustlers: 77–78, 80, 123, 146, 147–49

Safford, Ariz.: 113, 262
St. Louis Hotel: 241, 244–45
Saloons: 121–23, 192, 194, 229–31, 236–39
Sanborn, H. B.: 145, 150, 151
San Fernando Valley: 261
San Juan Mesa: 135, 177
Sarat Ranch: 250
Schools: 90–91, 114–18, 119, 121
Schoonover, Sol: 112, 196, 198–99
Scott (rancher with Robertson): 145
Sears, "Doc": 136, 157
Seminole, Texas: 16, 246, 253, 254–55
7HR Ranch: 137, 173
Seven Rivers, N. Mex.: 78, 80, 123
Seven Rivers gang: 228
Shafter Lake: 84, 95
Sheepherders: 189–90
Shelley, Joyce: 265
Shipman, Daniel: 145
Shorty (old line rider): 75–83
Skunks: 85, 93, 105, 106, 204
Slaughter (rancher): 145